CATHOLIC EVANGELIZATION TODAY

A New Pentecost for the United States

KENNETH BOYACK, C.S.P.,
editor

With a Preface by Joseph Cardinal Bernardin

D1167622

PAULIST PRESS
New York / Mahwah

Library of Congress Cataloging-in-Publication Data

Catholic evangelization today.

Includes bibliographies.

1. Catholic Church—United States—History—20th century. 2. Evangelistic work—United States. 3. United States—Church history—20th century. I. Boyack, Kenneth.
BX1406.2.C36   1986   269' .08822   86-21196
ISBN   0-8091-2846-2   (pbk.)

Published by Paulist Press
997 Macarthur Boulevard
Mahwah, New Jersey 07430

Printed and bound in the
United States of America

CONTENTS

Section II
THE BROAD HORIZON OF CATHOLIC EVANGELIZATION

CATHOLIC EVANGELIZATION TODAY
A New Pentecost for the United States

is published under the auspices of
The National Council for Catholic Evangelization

and dedicated to the memory of
Carl E. Koch
1903 – 1985
May he rest in God's eternal peace.

PREFACE

Joseph Cardinal Bernardin, Archbishop of Chicago

This is truly an exciting time to be a Catholic. There are many signs of ecclesial life and growth all around us. One of the most encouraging is the growing Catholic consciousness about evangelization, an awareness predating the 1974 Synod of Bishops on the topic and Pope Paul VI's *Evangelii Nuntiandi*. The preparation for and experience of the Second Vatican Council refocused the Catholic Church on its mission to proclaim the good news to the whole world. The very term "evangelization" speaks of movement, doing something.

Perhaps that is why some Catholics have trouble appropriating the word for their own sense of mission. The word "evangelization" challenges us to break out of the stagnation or complacency into which we all can easily fall as disciples of the Lord. As we reclaim evangelization as our central mission, as Pope Paul VI encouraged us to do, we must be involved in two simultaneous processes: the ongoing evangelization and conversion of ourselves as a Church and the movement into the world to share the good news.

Pope Paul VI explained why both are necessary: "The Church . . . begins by being evangelized herself by constant conversion and renewal, in order to evangelize the world with credibility" (*Evangelii Nuntiandi*, § 15). He continued, "Evangelizing means bringing the good news into all strata of humanity, and through its influence transforming humanity from within and making it new" (§ 18).

Pope John Paul II has re-echoed Pope Paul's emphasis on evangelization in his statement on catechesis, *Catechesi Tradendae* (1979), identifying it as one aspect of the Church's total mission to evangelize. He also expressed a concern that those engaged in religious education—namely, children, youth, and families—may not be fully benefiting from catechesis because they have not yet heard an effective proclamation of Jesus and the good news. Without such a basic encounter with the Gospel, the impact of catechesis remains limited.

As I noted above, the term "evangelization" connotes movement or dynamism. Our evangelizing Church is indeed countercultural, continuing the work of the Old Testament prophets and the saving mission of Jesus. Israel

1

gradually came to see itself as God's chosen people and a "light for the nations." Moreover, Jesus has sent his Church into the world. We who are the Church must not allow ourselves to be paralyzed by a kind of spiritual narcissism that focuses too much on individual, private salvation. We must remember Pope Paul's challenging understanding of evangelization: the transformation of humanity and the whole world from within.

To engage in this noble mission, we must continually remind each other that ". . . by divine mandate . . . the duty of going out into the whole world and preaching the Gospel to every creature rests upon the whole Church. The work of evangelization is a basic duty of the people of God" (*Evangelii Nuntiandi,* § 59). Perhaps one of our greatest challenges is to convince all believers that they are evangelists, sacraments of God's presence and love to the rest of the world. Catholic Christianity is not a collection of religious information that we can "bank" for our own comfort, pleasure, or security. Rather, the essence of discipleship is to be so responsible for the world around us that we want to bring the light and truth of Jesus into all its dimensions. We need to rescue the Church from the undertow created by those who merely attend Church services without actively participating in its mission and ministry.

Let me hasten to add that such "active non-participants" are not the only undertow about which we need to be concerned. Bishops, priests, deacons, religious, and lay ministers—those who have both professional credentials and careers in ministry—need to watch out for what Pope Paul VI described as a real obstacle to evangelization: "Lack of fervor . . . manifested in fatigue, disenchantment, compromise, lack of interest, and, above all, lack of joy and hope" (*Evangelii Nuntiandi,* § 80).

We who have been called to leadership in the body of Christ must not allow our vocation to become a series of empty tasks. In such situations, the lack of quality or depth in our lives, or our own obvious distance from God, sends a message louder than the words we may speak. Without a constant focus on our own journey in faith and a willingness to surrender more deeply into the mystery of God, we cannot be the leaders that God's people need for evangelical renewal.

Pope Paul VI reminded us that evangelization is essentially a work of *love.* That love consists in our continually giving our hearts to the Lord and, in turn, giving our hearts and experience of Jesus to one another.

To evangelize is to become instrumental in facilitating and continuing God's self-revelation to our world. We believe that Jesus is the summit, the fullness of God's self-disclosure. In evangelizing, we proclaim the Word of God, Jesus, to the modern world. To partake in this ministry of revelation is to do much more than hand on doctrine, tradition, memorized passages from Scripture, or transitory religious peak experiences.

Rather, to evangelize is to touch someone's heart, mind, and imagination with the risen Lord. That encounter becomes so significant that the person begins to reinterpret and redirect his or her whole life around Jesus. To evangelize is to help another person pay attention to, celebrate, and live in terms of the living God, revealed fully by Jesus, and present in our human experiences.

As we embrace this exciting concept of evangelization; as we allow God's powerful word to energize us; as we assess the height, breadth, and depth of the evangelical mission; as we shake off any paralyzing complacency; as we realize that evangelization continues God's self-revelation—let us not be naive about the unique challenges that lie ahead for the Catholic Church in the United States.

The National Conference of Diocesan Directors of Religious Education and the Chief Administrators of Catholic Education of the National Catholic Education Association articulated five national concerns in their 1985 report:

1. *Changes in Contemporary Family Life.* The family, one of the building blocks of the Church, continues to undergo many changes. The future will be characterized by fewer children, more senior citizens, more single parent families, a continuing high divorce rate, and a rise in blended or reconstituted families. We need to rethink how to evangelize the contemporary and future American family.

2. *Changes in Ethnicity of U.S. Population.* The United States has been undergoing rapid changes in ethnicity. The parishes of our sprawling urban centers are largely the result of the faith and personal investment of Eastern and Western European immigrants to this country. Now, the largest number of immigrants come from Latin America and Asia. In addition, in many urban centers, blacks have largely replaced the Caucasians who used to populate such areas.

These emerging racial and ethnic groups are being evangelized militantly by a variety of churches. The U.S. black bishops' pastoral letter *What We Have Seen and Heard* and the U.S. bishops' pastoral letter *The Hispanic Presence: Challenge and Commitment* are attempts to highlight the need for extra effort and creativity in evangelizing a racially, ethnically changing nation.

3. *Economic Issues.* Economic issues—such as the widening gap between rich and poor, the expanding underclass, the growing feminization of poverty, the lingering problems of the unemployed, and the American farmer—are impacting people's religious understanding, questioning, and experiences. We cannot hope to evangelize effectively without addressing these concrete conditions.

4. *Impact of Technology.* Technology is greatly challenging our capacity to evangelize. It is estimated that today approximately one-third of all the television-owning households in the U.S. have video recorders. Technology offers us exciting new tools for the work of evangelization. The audio and video cassette and recorder, the expanding world of cable and satellite station TV, religious radio and television stations, and the compact disc player are all leading both the entertainment industry and evangelizers into a new world.

5. *Global Interdependence and Peace and Justice Concerns.* The media, especially the immediacy of news on television and radio, have helped make the world smaller. We can see and hear ever more clearly how close, interdependent, and mutually vulnerable the nations of the world are. As the possibilities for peace and the dangers of war become ever more obvious to us, we must also evangelize toward global peace and justice. Pope Paul VI noted that evangelization is incomplete if it is not wedded to such concerns as authentic liberation and development (cf. *Evangelii Nuntiandi,* § 29).

Sensing the movement toward a renewal of Catholic evangelization, aware also of the "undertows" that can undermine such efforts, and, finally, recognizing the changing U.S. and global scene which gives shape to evangelization today, I welcome this compendium of theory and praxis, *Catholic Evangelization Today: A New Pentecost for the United States.* May it be but the beginning of serious theological reflection about and pastoral planning for a truly new Pentecost for Catholic evangelization in our country.

INTRODUCTION
Kenneth Boyack, C.S.P.

This collection speaks a word about Catholic evangelization in the United States. It is not the final word, but a current statement which addresses the crucial question raised by Pope Paul VI in his Apostolic Exhortation *Evangelii Nuntiandi:* "... does the Church or does she not find herself better equipped to proclaim the Gospel and to put it into people's hearts with conviction, freedom of spirit and effectiveness?" (no. 4). This question is addressed to any baptized Catholic, including lay persons, priests, sisters, members of parish evangelization committees, scholars—all who share in Christ's mission to proclaim the good news of God's kingdom.

Catholic Evangelization Today presents a contemporary meditation on evangelization in the United States, similar to the way in which Pope Paul VI in *Evangelii Nuntiandi* presents a contemporary meditation on evangelization in the modern world. The authors probe broad questions specifically within an American context: What is Jesus' evangelizing mission? What is the history of Catholic evangelization in the United States since Vatican II? What is the nature and content of Catholic evangelization? Who are the beneficiaries? Who are the workers? What are the methods? The first six essays in Section I form an American commentary on *Evangelii Nuntiandi*—the first of its kind.

The articles for Section I were written as part of the conference sponsored by the National Council for Catholic Evangelization (NCCE) to celebrate the tenth anniversary of the issuing of *Evangelii Nuntiandi* by Pope Paul VI. Held at the Capital Hilton, Washington, D.C., November 9–10, 1985, the conference was titled, *"Evangelii Nuntiandi* Ten Years Later: An American Meditation." The attendees responding to the NCCE invitations comprised an important group of Church leadership: the pre-registration count of 281 included 59 bishops, 31 major superiors of men (or their delegates), 99 major superiors of women (or their delegates) and 92 NCCE members or other leaders in evangelization. The conference was the first occasion during which Church leadership specifically meditated upon the implications of *Evangelii Nuntiandi* for the United States.

Why the need for this type of conference and this book? Unfortunately for many Catholics, the word "evangelization" evokes images of television evangelists and door-to-door canvassing to invite people to make a personal

5

decision for Jesus Christ. Contrary to these limited views, *Catholic Evangelization Today* paints a more rich and complex picture of Roman Catholic evangelization. Pope Paul VI speaks of this broader horizon when he writes:

> Any partial and fragmentary definition which attempts to render the reality of evangelization in all its richness, complexity and dynamism does so only at the risk of impoverishing it and even of distorting it. It is impossible to grasp the concept of evangelization unless one tries to keep in view all its essential elements (no. 17).

This book pursues the task of creating renewed images of evangelization for American Catholics. In addition to the six articles in Section I, the nine specially commissioned and original articles in Section II deal with many areas within the broad horizon of Catholic evangelization. The authors in Section II explore such topics as conversion, the RCIA, and social justice—and relate them to evangelization. Other authors explore a shared praxis method and findings in sociology which make for effective evangelization. Taken together, Sections I and II reveal the dynamic horizon of Catholic evangelization: from interior conversion to the Church's role in evangelizing the American culture, from one-to-one witnessing to presenting a strategy for the evangelization of the south. The fifteen articles offer an exposition of the length and width, the height and depth of Catholic evangelization today.

New images and understandings do not come easily—they emerge slowly for most people and develop only with time and struggle. Pope Paul VI recognizes this difficult challenge and lays out in *Evangelii Nuntiandi* a twenty-five year vision for the emergence of a new evangelizing consciousness. He roots his reflections in Vatican Council II and in the Third General Assembly of the Synod of Bishops which was devoted to evangelization. It was Paul VI's hope and prayer that the impetus created through the 1974 Synod and the 1975 Holy Year would continue through ". . . a program of pastoral action with evangelization as its basic feature, for these years which mark the eve of a new century, the eve also of the third millennium of Christianity" (EN, no. 81). Pope Paul VI considers the period of 1975 to 2000 crucial in implementing a renewed Catholic vision of evangelization on a worldwide scale.

The articles in *Catholic Evangelization Today* present a composite of ideas and images ten years into this twenty-five year plan. Fr. Cyprian Davis notes in his article on the history of evangelization in the United States that we have made significant progress. But what of the next fifteen years? What is needed for the Catholic Church in the United States to ". . . find herself better equipped to proclaim the Gospel and to put it into people's hearts with conviction, freedom of spirit and effectiveness?" (no. 4). The articles in this book help the reader to deal with that challenge.

Fundamentally, however, the most significant challenge for the American Church today is to develop within the heart of each Catholic, and within parishes and dioceses, an evangelizing consciousness—what Pope Paul VI refers to as the "interior attitudes" of the evangelizer (EN, no. 74). If a new era of evangelization, a new Pentecost, is to have a profound effect on Catholics in the United States, the first step requires a continuing conversion of mind and heart, a conversion based on a spiritual awakening that each baptized Catholic Christian is a responsible, co-missionary with Christ. An evangelizing consciousness includes an awareness of the power of the Holy Spirit working everywhere as well as the need for a more explicit sharing of the Gospel (EN, no. 22). The articles in this collection assist the reader to develop this evangelizing consciousness. The sections at the end of each chapter entitled "Discussion Questions" and "For Further Reading" are available for the person or group wanting to explore further the topic of that chapter.

This introduction would be incomplete without an explicit recognition, in faith, of the action and power of the Holy Spirit. Pope Paul VI writes powerfully of the presence of this third person of the Blessed Trinity:

> We live in the Church at a privileged moment of the Spirit. . . . It must be said that the Holy Spirit is the principal agent of evangelization; it is he who impels each individual to proclaim the Gospel, and it is he who in the depths of consciences causes the word of salvation to be accepted and understood. But it can equally be said that he is the goal of evangelization: he alone stirs up the new creation, the new humanity of which evangelization is to be the result, with that unity and variety which evangelization wishes to achieve within the Christian community. Through the Holy Spirit the Gospel penetrates the heart of the world, for it is he who causes people to discern the signs of the times—signs willed by God—which evangelization reveals and puts to use within history (EN, no. 75).

The traditional Catholic prayer is most appropriate as the reader begins *Catholic Evangelization Today: A New Pentecost for the United States:* "Come, Holy Spirit, fill the hearts of your faithful and enkindle in them the fire of your love."

I am especially grateful to Rev. Alvin A. Illig, C.S.P., the Director of the Paulist National Catholic Evangelization Association, for his undaunted support for this project, as well as to each of the contributors for their inspiring commitment to the cause of Catholic evangelization. I also wish to thank Rev. Mr. Michael Kerrigan, C.S.P., for his professional editorial assistance and Mrs. Monica Theis Huber for her skillful editing, proofreading and preparing of the manuscript.

Section I

A Meditation on *Evangelii Nuntiandi* within the
United States Context

A SCRIPTURAL MEDITATION ON EVANGELII NUNTIANDI

Eugene LaVerdiere, S.S.S.

Ten years after its issuance, *Evangelii Nuntiandi* is widely recognized as the greatest and most far-reaching Church document issued since Vatican II. Taken seriously, together with the Rite of Christian Initiation of Adults, it can bring about the transformation of the Church inaugurated by the council.

Evangelii Nuntiandi is an apostolic exhortation. With it, Paul VI wanted to confirm the brethren. He had heard Jesus' word to Peter and taken it to heart: "But I have prayed for you that your faith may never fail. You in turn must strengthen your brothers and sisters" (Lk 22:32). With *Evangelii Nuntiandi,* Paul VI fulfilled his personal mission by confirming the brethren "in their mission of evangelizers" (#1). He did this on the tenth anniversary of the closing of Vatican II (December 8, 1965), whose objectives he summarized as wanting "to make the Church of the twentieth century ever better fitted for proclaiming the Gospel to the people of the twentieth century" (#2).

Paul VI saw *Evangelii Nuntiandi* as "a meditation on evangelization" in which he shared the wealth of the Third General Assembly of the Synod of Bishops (1974), which was devoted to evangelization. He hoped that this meditation would give a fresh impulse to everyone, but especially to those dedicated to preaching and teaching. For this to come about, however, the entire Church would have to make the same meditation. *Evangelii Nuntiandi* is thus both a meditation and an invitation to meditation (#5).

Today we have accepted that invitation. Like the disciples in the company of the Lord at prayer, may we be drawn into the spirit of *Evangelii Nuntiandi:* Lord, teach us to pray; teach us to meditate on evangelization in America today, and may our meditation also be an invitation for others to join in the same meditation.

Our meditation is a scriptural one. It consequently focuses especially on Chapters I and VII of *Evangelii Nuntiandi,* which are profoundly biblical in inspiration and contain the vast majority of the scriptural references found in the exhortation. All of these references are from the New Testament.

Chapter I is entitled, "From Christ the Evangelizer to the Evangelizing Church" (#6–16). It reflects on the witness and mission of Jesus and on how these now belong to the Church. The first part of our meditation also reflects on the witness and mission of Jesus, but instead of reflecting on the Church in general, it bears on the witness and mission of the Church in our own country.

Chapter VII of *Evangelii Nuntiandi* is entitled, "The Spirit of Evangelization" (#74–80). It reflects on the interior attitudes and fundamental conditions necessary for fruitful evangelization. The second part of our meditation will follow its path by reflecting on the action of the Holy Spirit, the need for both personal and corporate authenticity, reverence for the truth of the Gospel, a spirit of love, and willingness to overcome the obstacles to evangelization.

FROM CHRIST THE EVANGELIZER
TO OUR EVANGELIZING CHURCH

Paul VI used many New Testament texts in describing the witness and mission of Jesus. To present Jesus as the first and greatest evangelizer, he turned to the title of Mark's Gospel: "Here begins the gospel of Jesus Christ, the Son of God" (Mk 1:1), and to the opening verses of Paul's Letter to the Romans where Jesus is described as "the good news of God" (Rom 1:1–3). To outline Jesus' evangelical message, he referred to the five great discourses of Jesus in Matthew's Gospel (Mt 5–7; 10; 13; 18; 24–25). Two texts, however, were given greater prominence than all the others. Both are from Luke's Gospel.

The first text is Luke 4:43: "To other towns I must announce the good news of the reign of God, because that is why I was sent." This text is first cited in the opening lines of the exhortation's first chapter where it sets the tone for the entire meditation. It is again quoted in a paragraph on Jesus' evangelical signs (#12), and again later on to show the relationship of the witness and mission of the Church to that of Jesus (#14). In the first chapter, Jesus' proclamation that he must announce the good news of the reign of God is thus a significant leitmotiv and a unifying thread. We are in the presence of a well-woven tapestry.

The second text is Luke 4:18. It too appears in the introductory paragraph (#6), where it is presented as necessary background for understanding Lk 4:43:

> The spirit of the Lord is upon me;
>   therefore he has anointed me.
> He has sent me to bring glad tidings to the poor,
>   to proclaim liberty to captives,
> Recovery of sight to the blind
>   and release to prisoners.

Paul VI's citation of Jesus' reading in the Nazareth synagogue, a quotation from Isaiah 61:1, actually stops at "glad tidings to the poor," but the rest of 4:18 is evoked by the verse's introductory challenge. Nor can the next verse, "To announce a year of favor from the Lord" (Lk 4:19; see Is 61:2), which refers to a Year of Jubilee, have been lost on Paul VI, who noted that his exhortation was being written at the end of a Holy Year (#2).

Luke 4:18 also lies close to the surface when the Holy Father presents the evangelization of the poor as the most important of Jesus' evangelical signs: "Among all these signs there is the one to which he attaches great importance; the humble and the poor are evangelized, become his disciples and gather together 'in his name' in the great community of those who believe in him" (#12). It is in this context that, in the chapter's second quotation of Luke 4:43, Jesus is described as the one who declared, "I must preach the good news of the kingdom of God."

Shortly before this, the exhortation had quoted Luke 4:22 to show the impact of Jesus' message and the authority with which he spoke: "And he won the approval of all, and they were astonished by the gracious words that came from his lips" (#11). In Luke's Gospel, this is the narrator's description of the synagogue's reaction to Jesus' reading from Isaiah 61.

At Simon's Home in Capernaum (Lk 4:31–44)

Jesus had spent part of the previous day and the night at Capernaum in the home of Simon, the same who would later be called Peter, his first and chief disciple (Lk 5:1–11). There he had cured Simon's mother-in-law from a severe fever, and this allowed her to take up her service of hospitality, her *diakonia,* to Jesus and the others. Crowds later gathered, bringing the sick to him, and he cured them. He also expelled demons from many.

Before all this, he had come from a synagogue where he had been teaching on the sabbath. When he successfully expelled an unclean spirit from someone, the narrator notes the reaction of the demonic powers who see that he had come to destroy them as well as the reaction of those who had gathered in the synagogue. They were filled with wonderment over his authority and power.

The following day, when Jesus left Capernaum for the open country, the crowds who had benefited from his ministry and the many who heard about it went after him to prevent him from leaving. It is to these people, who sought to keep Jesus' extraordinary ministry for themselves, that Jesus announced: "To other towns I must announce the good news of the reign of God, because that is why I was sent."

Jesus' response to the crowd reveals both urgency and a sense of purpose. He says that he *must* announce the good news. The Greek word employed to say "must" is *dei* (it is necessary), an important term in Luke's Gospel, where it expresses prophetic necessity—the promises must be fulfilled—and is used only in contexts referring to Jesus' life mission and ultimate destiny. We find it, for example, in Jesus' answer to Mary after his parents found him in the temple after passover on the third day: "Did you not know I had (*dei*) to be in my Father's house?" Jesus' words are meant to evoke his ascension which climaxed the events of the third day in Jerusalem (Lk 24:1–53).

We find the same necessity and the same term in the risen Lord's Easter catechesis to the Emmaus disciples: "Did not the Messiah have to (*edei*) undergo all this (*pathein*) so as to enter into his glory?" (Lk 24:26). Jesus' entire mission is governed by the same prophetic necessity. He cannot be restrained, even by those who appreciate what he does for them and welcome his word. His mission is to defeat the powers of evil, and he must go forth to preach the Gospel of God's reign wherever it has not been heard.

At the Synagogue in Nazareth (Lk 4:16–30)

The events at Capernaum are closely related to those which immediately preceded them at Nazareth. However, whereas the Gospel stressed the deeds of Jesus at Capernaum, at Nazareth it had stressed his words. Both episodes evoked wonder and raised questions about his true identity. At Capernaum, the cures Jesus performed so pleased the crowds that they tried to prevent him from leaving. At Nazareth, his words so angered those in the synagogue that they did all they could to destroy him. The two reactions complement one another; each tried to prevent Jesus from fulfilling his mission of evangelization.

Nazareth is the place where Jesus had been brought up. People knew him there, and he felt a oneness with them, as they themselves felt with him, both in the town and in the synagogue where Jesus was accustomed to hearing the Scriptures. Nazareth was Jesus' place and its people were his people. They had certain expectations with regard to him and he with regard to them. Humanly and religiously, Jesus and the people of Nazareth were bonded to one another in solidarity.

It is in this place and cultural context that Luke situates the beginnings of Jesus' ministry. When Jesus read the Scriptures and interpreted them in the Nazareth synagogue, his Spirit-filled presence, the biblical words he quickened with new life, and his interpretation had serious implications no one could escape. If the Spirit was upon Jesus, this meant the Spirit also had to be upon all those who were with him in religious solidarity. Jesus' message, a summary of his life and activities, was an invitation to join him in his mission. If he was one of them and they were one with him, they would have to join him in bringing glad tidings to the poor. In this way they would stand in the tradition of Elijah and Elisha, who reached beyond the boundaries of Israel to bring healing and nourishment to Gentiles, to men and women who did not share in Israel's special covenant with the Lord. With Jesus the synagogue was asked to fulfill the mission of Israel, a people set apart not for its own sake but for the sake of others.

The people of Nazareth, however, those who marveled at the appealing discourse spoken by Jesus in whom they saw only Joseph's son, would have none of it. They were unable to recognize that while they themselves may have been needy and poor, the need and poverty of others was even greater. Blind to the identity of Jesus, they could not join him in opening the eyes of the blind. Captive to their self-absorption, they could not proclaim liberty to captives and release to prisoners.

Reacting to Jesus' challenge with violence, the people in the Nazareth synagogue brought him to the brow of the hill and tried to hurl him over the edge. He had to be expelled from the synagogue and banished not only from the town in which he had been brought up but from the human existence and history he shared with the entire human race. As a result, they assured that he would die to all social and cultural limitations and rise to be Lord of all. Rising he made his way straight through their midst, and ascending he went away. Unwittingly, in prophetic anticipation, the people of Nazareth had released the energies which would bring the good news of salvation to all of God's poor.

In the Homes and Churches of Our Land

From Simon's house in Capernaum and the synagogue at Nazareth we move on to our own homes and churches. As Paul VI wrote in his exhortation, "Those who have received the Good News and who have been gathered by it into the community of salvation can and must communicate and spread it" (#13). He saw that the Savior's word, "I must proclaim the good news of the kingdom of God," applies in all truth to the Church. "Evangelizing is in fact the grace and vocation proper of the Church, her deepest identity" (#14). What Paul VI wrote of the Church as a whole applies to every local church, every diocese, every parish, and every family and individual person in the Church. What does it mean for the Church in our country today?

For us as for others, as in fact it has been from the very beginning, the danger is to become so preoccupied with our own internal needs and concerns that we lose track of our essential mission of evangelization and the most basic ministry of the word. The danger is especially great in view of the huge influx of new immigrants who daily are transforming our culture and invigorating our society. We could easily become like the early Church of Jerusalem as presented in Acts (6:1–7).

As the Christian community grew in number and became linguistically and culturally diversified, including newer Greek-speaking members alongside of the older Aramaic-speaking members, the needs of the poor, especially among those who had recently joined the community, went unattended. The situation in our Church is far more complex, as our communities welcome new populations from all over the world. Indeed we must attend to the internal problems which accompany this fresh growth and rich diversity. But it must not lead us to echo the attitude of those who had gathered with Jesus in the Nazareth synagogue or of the crowds who witnessed his cures in Capernaum. Rather we must be able to join him in announcing the good news of God to every town and place, indeed to all who have not yet heard the good news of salvation in Christ Jesus. As Paul VI wrote, "The Christian community is never closed in upon itself" (#15).

The reaction of the apostles in the Jerusalem community suggests a course of action for today. Rather than merely intensify their own efforts to meet the needs of the poor, they found a way to diversify the ministries of the Church. Others would provide the service (*diakonia*) they had provided until now. And this would allow them to pursue their essential mission of evangelization and to give themselves to prayer, an essential condition for effective evangelization.

Taking our lead from the apostolic community, we too are diversifying our ministries and seeing to the needs and to the leadership of the Church in new ways. May we always remember that the basic purpose of this reshaping of sectors of Church life is to enable us to become a more evangelical community. Through those of us who already have heard the Gospel of Jesus, the risen Lord continues

> to bring glad tidings to the poor,
>   to proclaim liberty to captives,
> recovery of sight to the blind
>   and release to prisoners.

And he continues to invite all those who hear to join him in reaching out to still others, until the Gospel has been proclaimed to the ends of the earth.

THE SPIRIT OF EVANGELIZATION

"What is the state of the Church ten years after the Council?" (#77). This question, first raised at the beginning of Paul VI's meditation, dominates the entire chapter on "The Spirit of Evangelization" (#74–80). Not that the Holy Father intended to answer the question. He simply wanted to raise it in relation to the basic conditions and criteria for fruitful evangelization. Accordingly he inquired into the Church's openness to the Holy Spirit, the personal authenticity of Christians, the Church's own corporate authenticity, our dedication to the salvific truth of the Gospel, our love for those we are called to evangelize, our willingness to overcome all obstacles. Paul VI's meditation is thus transformed into an ecclesial examination of conscience and an invitation to join him in the same self-examination.

The Scripture texts used to articulate and challenge the Church's life in these many areas come from Paul's letters, the Gospels of Matthew, Luke and John, and the Book of Acts. Again the most important texts are from the work of Luke (4:14, 18, 21) but with much greater emphasis on Acts (2:17; 4:8; 6:5, 10; 7:55; 9:17, 31; 10:44; 20:28).

Openness to the Holy Spirit

The chapter begins with a call for openness to the Holy Spirit. It does this by reviewing many of the great moments in the life of Jesus and the early Church where the New Testament focuses on new beginnings, infusions of new life, unforeseen and dramatic changes, and departures from what has been. The Holy Spirit is the creative Spirit of God. It is the source and energy of Jesus' mission to preach good news to the poor. The Holy Spirit is also the empowering Spirit of the risen Lord. It is the source and energy of the Church's own evangelizing mission.

The Spirit which is at the source of Jesus' very life (Lk 1:26–38) is the Spirit of Pentecost (Acts 2:1–11). Just as Mary was not able to conceive the life of God by herself or through any human relationship, the Church was unable to embark on the universal mission and to speak the word of God through her own efforts. Both required the intervention of God's creative Spirit. The image that comes to mind is that of lifeless and formless chaos in the beginning when God created the heavens and the earth. There was darkness over the deep, but the spirit of God hovered over the waters, ready to join God's word in the work of creation. This creative Spirit was necessary for Jesus' conception, for the incarnation of the good news of God. It was also necessary for the rebirth of Jesus' disciples into a Church equipped to continue Jesus' work of evangelization. At Pentecost the Spirit moved over the chaos of Babel and gathered all of humanity in one word, the Word of God, and one faith. That same Holy Spirit is needed by the Church in America, with its Babel of languages and cultures. Only the Holy Spirit will enable us to speak the Gospel in a voice that can be heard by all and a word that is grasped as good news in each one's language.

The Spirit which quickens and empowers the Church is also the Spirit of the risen Lord (Jn 20:19–23). The image that comes to mind this time, as Jesus breathes the Holy Spirit on the Christian community, is that of God, the divine potter, at the potter's wheel of the universe, fashioning the earth, molding Adam, the child of earth, from clay, and breathing his own life-breath into the soft, moist clay before it could dry. The Spirit Jesus breathed into the community was the Spirit of peace: "Peace be with you," he said to a frightened Church which had hidden behind locked doors for fear of persecution. So strengthened and filled with new life, they were to go and bring the peace they had received to others. Their message was the Gospel of peace. We need to hear that Gospel in America today, and the Church needs to speak it. Only the Holy Spirit, which we await with the openness of prayer, will enable us to do so.

Authenticity, Personal and Corporate

Second, the Holy Father invites us to examine ourselves on the authenticity of our presentation of the Gospel, a quality which meets one of the great human thirsts of the twentieth century. Two kinds of authenticity are needed, personal authenticity, which is grounded in holiness of life and nourished by prayer and the Eucharist, and corporate authenticity, which springs from the unity of the Church.

We need that authenticity which was so evident in Jesus' proclamation of the Gospel. All who heard him were amazed. Unlike the scribes, he spoke with authority. His word was clearly perceived as the word of God, and that word so resonated with his entire life that his personal presence was welcomed by all who were children of God as the word of God made flesh.

We also need the authenticity which was so characteristic of the primitive Christian community at Jerusalem, at least in the way Luke presents that community in Acts. If they performed signs and wonders and if their tongue was afire with the Spirit and the word spread in so extraordinary a fashion, it was because they were of one mind and heart. Their unity was expressed in communal sharing to the extent that there were no poor and needy among them. In our search for unity, both among churches and within the Church, success has been limited. To give authenticity to our Gospel word, however, it is critical that we keep searching, both sincerely and honestly. Like the early Church, whatever measure of unity we have arrived at should be reflected in the way we share with one another to eliminate discrimination and poverty. To the extent that we do not share, our authenticity is impaired.

In Truth and with Love

Third, Paul VI speaks to us of service to the truth and genuine love for those we are evangelizing. Both qualities are intimately connected with personal and corporate authenticity. The truth in question is liberating or salvific truth as we find it presented in the council's Constitution on Divine Revelation. Ultimately, that truth is God himself and his self-communication in the person of Jesus. Jesus was the Word of God; he was also the truth. The truth of which Paul VI spoke was consequently not so much the abstract expression of truth but the truth inherent in personal knowledge of faith.

This message is addressed to all members of the Church, each according to his or her role and responsibility. I quote Paul VI's message to Christian scholars:

> Men of learning—whether you be theologians, exegetes or historians—the work of evangelization needs your tireless work of research, and also care and tact in transmitting the truth to which your studies lead you but which is always greater than the heart of men, being the very truth of God (#78).

The love we must have for those we evangelize is described as more than the love of a teacher. It is the love of a father as well as of a mother. Reference is made to 1 Thessalonians 2:7–11, which bears reading since it presents Paul as relating to others with a mother's love as well as with a father's love. Here is Paul at his androgynous best.

> While we were among you we were as gentle as any nursing mother fondling her little ones. So well disposed were we to you, in fact, that we wanted to share with you not only God's tidings but our very selves, so dear had you become to us. . . . You are witnesses, as is God himself, of how upright, just, and irreproachable our conduct was toward you who are believers. You likewise know how we exhorted every one of you, as a father does his children.

The love of which the Holy Father speaks requires respect for the religious and spiritual situation of those being evangelized. Jesus did not coerce, he invited. Our attitude can be simply expressed. As we look out to those who have gathered to hear us, we must say: "Come as far as you can, and stay as long as you can." Love is also concerned to share only the truth. It does not wound. It does not bewilder or scandalize. Paul VI has given us a new hymn to love, one for our time, just as St. Paul had given the Corinthians a hymn for their time (1 Cor 13).

Overcoming the Obstacles

Finally, Paul VI calls attention to various obstacles to evangelization, and he appeals for nothing less than the fervor of the saints in meeting them. All the obstacles can be summarized under one heading, lack of fervor, which is all the more serious because it comes from within. It is manifested in fatigue, disenchantment, compromise, lack of interest and above all lack of joy and hope. We exhort all those who have the task of evangelizing, by whatever title and at whatever level, always to nourish spiritual fervor (#80).

In response, with Paul VI, we raise our eyes above the horizon to Mary, whom he named the Star of evangelization. On the morning of Pentecost, she was with the apostolic community at prayer, watching over the beginning of evangelization with the gift of the Holy Spirit. As we look to the Star, may she watch over us and our efforts as well.

DISCUSSION QUESTIONS

1. How did Paul VI describe *Evangelii Nuntiandi,* and what did he hope to achieve in writing it?

2. How did Paul VI use Luke 4:43 and 4:18 in *Evangelii Nuntiandi,* and how are these texts related to one another, taking into consideration their context in 4:31–44 and 4:16–30?

3. Why did those present in the synagogue at Nazareth become violent and try to destroy Jesus (Lk 4:16–30)?

4. What are the implications of Acts 6:1–7 for the life of the Church, its ministries, and especially for evangelization?

5. What is the nature of Chapter VII of *Evangelii Nuntiandi,* and what are the important issues raised by Paul VI?

6. What is the role of the Holy Spirit and prayer in evangelization? Which texts in the New Testament are especially important for understanding this role? How do these texts relate to the Old Testament stories of creation?

7. What does Paul VI mean by the love we must have for those we want to evangelize? Discuss 1 Thessalonians 2:7–11 with regard to this.

FOR FURTHER READING

Joseph A. Fitzmyer, *The Gospel according to Luke I–IX, X–XXIV (The Anchor Bible, Vol. 28, 28a).* Garden City: Doubleday & Company, Inc., 1981, 1985.
    An excellent, comprehensive, and up-to-date commentary bound to become a classic in its genre. A foundational source for anyone who wants to explore Luke and its relevance for today.

Eugene A. LaVerdiere, *The New Testament in the Life of the Church.* Notre

Dame: Ave Maria Press, 1980.

A study of the use of the New Testament in various areas of Church ministry. The first of four chapters is devoted to the use of the New Testament in evangelization.

———. *Luke (The New Testament Message,* Vol. 5). Wilmington: Michael Glazier, Inc., 1980.

Focuses on Luke's message to the early churches he addressed. The approach is literary and rhetorical rather than historical-critical.

Amos N. Wilder. *Theopoetic: Theology and the Religious Imagination.* Philadelphia: Fortress Press, 1976.

A work which explores the relationship between the churches' use of the New Testament and the original Gospel inspiration. Important for anyone who wants to penetrate the various expressions of New Testament teaching to the spirit from which they spring.

EVANGELIZATION IN THE UNITED STATES SINCE VATICAN COUNCIL II

Cyprian Davis, O.S.B.

Words not only sometimes have gender; they can have religious affiliation. Twenty years ago "evangelization" was not a Catholic word. It was Protestant and had a faintly fundamentalist allure. It could not be found as a subject entry in the *Guide to Catholic Periodical Literature*. Its first appearance in the American Catholic context came about fifteen years ago, and at first it would be included under the more comprehensive title of "convert-making."

THE TIMES

Thomas Carlyle once wrote, "Happy the people whose annals are blank in history books!" Historians a half century or more from now, when a critical appraisal will be truly possible, will find the pages for this half century densely packed with events, for it has been a time of rapid change, shifting currents, collapsing structures, and—to be sure—silent growth.

The Second World War changed the course of world history and contemporary civilization. The Second Vatican Council was part of the chain reaction. Pope Pius XII brought to an end an ecclesiastical style dating from the early nineteenth century; Pope John XXIII began another. Questions raised in the harsh climate of war and total destruction demanded new answers as a new society was formed across three worlds.

THE NATION

In the United States, 1965 marked not only the end of Vatican II but the coming of age of a generation conceived and born during the Second World War. This generation conceived in upheaval unleashed across America a flood-tide of change that was at once chaotic and creative as well as vital and violent. In the United States, 1965 marked the climax of the civil rights movement that just fell short of a full-fledged revolution as Martin Luther King, Jr. led the march from Selma to Montgomery. The civil rights movement profoundly altered society in the United States. On a national scale public demonstrations

22

succeeded in changing laws and effecting legislation. Civil disobedience became a mark of Gospel obedience.[1] The evangelistic fervor of the black preacher became the rallying cry to which black and white, Protestant and Catholic, priest and sister responded. The call to change that rang out from county courthouse steps to Lincoln Memorial steps was delivered in the cadences of black evangelical preaching that challenged a nation's conscience and proclaimed a national conversion call.

In the United States in 1965, the Catholic Church found itself involved in the civil rights movement in a way in which it had never been involved in a national movement before: direct involvement by both clergy and religious and demonstrations in religious habit and Roman collar. The Church which had rejected the abolitionists and their cause in the nineteenth century began a commitment to social change and social concern in the twentieth century that would set a direction to the end of the century.

In the United States, 1965 marked an escalation in violence in a violent society. Malcolm X was assassinated. Watts and other ghettoes burst into flames. The escalating Vietnam War brought protesters to the streets and bloodshed to college campuses. Anti-war evangelistic fervor marked both Catholics and Protestants as priests and nuns again joined liberal churches and pacifist groups against the war. The quiet witness of Dorothy Day[2] and her Catholic Worker movement bore its fruit in this time of youthful outcry and public outrage. By the end of the decade the assassination of Robert Kennedy and Martin Luther King would end a dream and awake an era of disillusion. Black consciousness would bring calls for black power; distrust of the political process would unleash the rioting that marred the Democratic national convention in Chicago; Woodstock became the symbol of a new cultural renaissance and a new "lost generation."

In the United States we moved to the end of the 1960's and the beginning of the 1970's aware of four new politico-cultural social movements, all of which took inspiration from the civil rights and peace movements: the "conscientization" among all groups of Hispanics, the awakening consciousness of women, the growing determination of Indians to preserve their culture and define themselves as native Americans in their ancestral land, and last of all a recognition among those who loved the land that we who were part of a complacently wasteful society lived in a world that had limited resources and in a universe where pollution could undo the marvels of creation.

THE UNITED STATES CHURCH

Prior to the 1830's the Catholic Church was a colonial Church, the Church of the settlers and their slaves, Church of the Conquistadors and the intrepid missionaries. From the third decade of the nineteenth century to the Second

World War, the American Church was the Church of immigrants, the Church of brick and mortar and close attachment to the Roman See. After 1965 the Church in the United States became a Church with fissures and cracks, a building rocked by a mighty earthquake.[3]

None of the movements mentioned in the previous section bypassed the Church in our country. In a sense the American Church was forced to bear the brunt of turmoil and change not so much because it was the object of hostile forces from without but because, being truly Catholic, it was moved by its members from within. The Church could not be the detached observer from Olympian heights, for it was by its very nature called to be a pilgrim walking amidst pilgrims through the valleys and the plains.

James Hennesey, in his book *American Catholics. A History of the Roman Catholic Community in the United States,* describes this period in this way:

> American Catholics had now to cope with the staggering reality of dissent, change, and diversity at the highest levels of the church they had grown up believing was "the same all over the world," the one institution impervious to history. Dissent, change, and diversity quickly filtered down. Many American Catholics were also coping with their own unaccustomed prosperity and the new way of life, business, and leisure that came with it.[4]

The American Church, thanks to the bishops, took decisive steps to comply with the new legislation regarding civil rights. It acted against segregation both in pastoral letters and in diocesan directives. Despite this, the turmoil within the nation was mirrored within the Church as many white communities met rage with fear and determination with resistance. A new ethnic consciousness came to birth; a new mentality and pride was produced. Statements evoked response; response evoked counter-response; determination evoked self-determination; definition created new terms and finally even forced a change in language. Black priests formed a Black Catholic Clergy Caucus a month after the violent death of King. Black sisters and seminarians were organizing themselves within the year. The National Office of Black Catholics came into existence in 1970. Hispanic priests formed PADRES in 1969 and Hispanic sisters created *Las Hermas* in 1971. A year later the Mexican-American Cultural Center was created in San Antonio. In Wisconsin the Menominee Indians seized the Alexian Brothers' abandoned buildings in 1975. Many missionary groups turned over their mission stations to newly self-determined Indian organizations. In 1979 the Tekakwitha Conference, then renewed and reorganized, became a "faith-proclaiming" event for native Americans within the Church every summer.

Social unrest and social movements have always affected ecclesiastical recruitment and religious vocations—sometimes strangely enough in inverse proportion. The last two decades may be a showcase for later historians for such a phenomenon. In the past two decades some eight to ten thousand priests and more than twenty thousand religious departed from active service in the United States. The number of seminarians decreased by seventy-five percent.[5]

Historically, female religious underwent sharp modifications at precise turning points in Church history. In the United States the post-Vatican II period will perhaps mark such a classic turning point as did the Crusades and urbanism for the Beguines in the fourteenth century. The change in ministries and the change in habit heralded a much more profound change in constitutions and concepts of community living. Catholic women religious within the last decade have been more profoundly affected by the cultural and social development of women today than any other women's group. From this perspective has come a call for women's ordination and a deeply committed concern for women's rights. Perhaps no other socio-cultural movement has so jolted the Catholic Church in the United States within the last two decades as has this one.

All of these forces that have shaped American Catholicism since the end of the Second Vatican Council have left a mark on the development of the liturgy during the last twenty years. Music, gesture, style, language, preaching, and art along with vesture and furnishings—in a word all that goes into the unfolding action of the Church's praise in the United States—all of this bears the mark of recent cultural forms. There has been adaptation, at times innovation, sometimes renovation and even cross-fertilization, more rarely restoration; but certainly a gradually constructed blend of celebration that reflects more or less tradition and a sensitivity to pluralism has emerged.

EVANGELIZATION IN THE UNITED STATES: POST-VATICAN II BEGINNINGS

The word "evangelization" has been a word in Catholic usage for only a little more than a decade. The cultural climate of the Post-Vatican II era only solidified what had begun in the wake of the Second World War, that is, a movement toward dialogue between Catholics and Protestants and a greater respect for the religious values of non-Christian religious traditions. The aggressive stance of triumphant Catholicism had already begun to be attenuated in the American atmosphere of official tolerance. The diminution of anti-Catholic bias raised among us a desire for greater tolerance. In the American Church Pope John XXIII's call for renewal was met with more enthusiasm than indifference, more compliance than overt obstruction. The context of renewal within the United States Church was marked out by pastoral letters and pastoral statements dealing with all aspects of Christian life, such as "To Teach as

Jesus Did" in 1972, "Brothers and Sisters to Us" in 1979, "The Challenge of Peace: God's Promise and Our Response" in 1983, and "The Hispanic Presence. Challenge and Commitment" in 1983.[6] The spread of the permanent diaconate, the increase of lay ministries, and the development of the parish councils are all a part of most local ecclesial structures.

The United States Church between 1965 and 1985 became more spirit-centered and spiritually alive through the charismatic renewal begun at Duquesne University in 1967 and through the new interest in prayer—especially contemplative prayer—with the resulting search for competent spiritual direction and directed retreats. It also resulted in the widespread practice of the Cursillo on the parish level and Marriage Encounter on the diocesan level. By the end of the 1960's, Hispanic communities had begun to share an experience created in Latin America known as "base communities." It is in these movements that American Catholics began to experience the meaning of evangelization on the grass-roots level. Within the last five years various forms of the "Renew" program on the parish level have appeared and borne fruit in a more fully alert laity open to the challenge of *Evangelii Nuntiandi*.

THE MORAL, CULTURAL, AND RELIGIOUS CLIMATE
FOR EVANGELIZATION IN UNITED STATES SOCIETY

Evangelization both as a promise and a program made its appearance in an American society where forty percent of the population claims no religious affiliation.[7] It is a society where there has been a dramatic shift in moral consciousness since the Second World War. Despite the outcry against it, Americans seem more or less comfortable with abortion under certain conditions. It is, moreover, a society where pre-marital and extra-marital sexual relationships are more widely condoned than a generation ago.

Ours is a society where traditional family structures have been greatly weakened. The single most notable characteristic is the increase of single-parent families, for the most part headed by women. Divorce and remarriage are now half as common as first marriages. Extended families have acquired a new meaning as children from multiple marriages move between respective households.

A shift in cultural values over the past forty years is partly the result of a technological revolution which will continue to affect us all culturally for the remainder of this century. The media has produced a generation of screen watchers in place of book readers. The universal spread of television has made it and not the newspaper or the periodical the main source for news and information on the popular level. On the other hand, TV soaps and docu-dramas have become for many not only the measure of historical reality but its justification and a source for ethical principles. Video-cassettes make not only retrieval of information painless and non-discriminating, but with the explosion of computer software and programs in the home, Americans have a new way to store information and locate it again. The TV screen has now made rock stars instant folk heroes and within two decades our values and our culture have been tailored by rock balladeers from Bob Dylan and the Beatles to Prince and Bruce Springsteen. Our notions of religion on the most basic level have perhaps been best expressed in terms of *The Exorcist*. Our cultural expression of the incarnation has perhaps been best expressed in the dramatizations of *Godspell* and *Jesus Christ Superstar*. Finally, the tragic side of a morally ambivalent culture is the consumption of drugs that distort and destroy the affluent and the abjectly poor in a sensation-hungry generation.

American society in the past twenty years has become a split-level society with the Catholic Church caught between. For the first time United States Catholics are a large part of the white middle class. Catholics are also now a large part of the young, upwardly mobile generation. They are part of the post-labor union generation. They live in the suburbs; they purchase their condominiums. Still, for many the climb to the top can be slippery and the perch precarious.

The gap, moreover, is widening in our split-level society. Many slide back and many more have little hope of escaping the level designated as "poverty" in our society today. Poverty is a badge of shame and a source of blame in today's USA. It means blocked escape hatches and no-exit signs. It means inner-cities and brown and black minorities, many of whom are Catholic and too many of whom are disaffected from all religion.

Within the last two decades we have begun to talk of a permanent underclass of drop-outs, shut-outs, and slide-outs. No church may seem able to reach them except the store-front Spiritualist churches or the Pentecostal denominations. Some may be Moslems; others may be the individuals that even pollsters and interviewers will not reach. They are part of the unchurched for whom our evangelization is not yet well prepared. Yet even in this inner-city of urban decay and human waste, welfare recipients, one-parent families, abused children, and battered women the Catholic Church has been and has remained the institution of good news with churches, schools, and hospitals. The parish plant that was perhaps two generations ago the signal raised aloft to let America know that those who came on clipper ships and steamers had now finally arrived, today signals the reality of an American dream yet unfulfilled.

If the computer is the symbol of the revolution in communication in the last score of years, then our prisons with their increasing population and our extensive prison network must signal a more somber side of this generation: namely, violence and fear as a constant shadow in our daily living. The invention of microchips was a tremendous breakthrough with all sorts of possibilities for human achievement, and yet nothing has changed when a society can only reproduce criminals and not rehabilitate them. Rich in technology, we remain poor in human resources. Yet, surprisingly in the last twenty years evangelization has begun for many in prison. Here both the Black Muslims and the Protestant fundamentalists have reached farther and with better understanding than has our own program of evangelization.

In the mid-1980's American society has continued its slow movement to the right of the political spectrum. For the Church in this next to the last decade of the century, this will create a period of crucial decision and a new type of anguish. This may affect the way in which the Gospel will be proclaimed. In another generation the answer may be completely different when we ask: Who are the unchurched?

A SIGNIFICANT DECADE OF EVANGELIZATION IN THE UNITED STATES: 1975–1985

In 1974 the Bishops' Synod in Rome discussed evangelization. Later that year, the Paulist Fathers, founded by convert-priest Isaac Hecker in 1858 to evangelize the United States according to the cultural ethos of nineteenth-century America, decided to hold a symposium on the question of evangelization today in America. Two other religious congregations, equally dedicated to evangelizing, served as co-sponsors, namely the Josephites, an American congregation with origins in England called to evangelize the black population of America, and the Glenmary Fathers, established to evangelize the people in the rural south. The third sponsor was the United States Catholic Mission Council, established in 1970, and representing at that time the bishops, religious, and laity in fostering the worldwide missionary efforts of the Church.[8] The symposium was held in November 1975 at Marriottsville, Maryland. The title defined the scope and the goal of American evangelization: "Exploratory Consultation on Evangelizing the Eighty Million Unchurched Americans."[9]

Rev. Alvin A. Illig, C.S.P., coordinator and convenor, had been the originator of a program to reach the unchurched and the church-alienated in Mississippi. Working in thirty parishes in the diocese of Natchez-Jackson, a program of door-to-door visitation was initiated, special events held in the local churches were well publicized in the media, invitations were warmly extended, welcome committees were formed, and follow-up procedures were implemented. As a result, a well-orchestrated process of individual contact had been gradually developed which involved for the most part lay persons reaching to lay persons. These would be the same components in the evangelization techniques which were utilized in the following decade.[10]

In fact, Father Illig would use the same process in the "We Care/We Share" Evangelization project for reaching the unchurched in Washington,

D.C. from 1975–1977. As coordinator for the project for the next two years, Fr. Illig convinced four parishes to introduce the program.

In 1977, the National Conference of Catholic Bishops established an *ad hoc* committee on evangelization with Francis Hurley, the archbishop of Anchorage in Alaska, as episcopal chairman. Father Illig became the executive director and funding was supplied by the American Board of Catholic Missions. The purpose was to provide a resource office for purposes of consultation only and not for implementation, for inspiration but not concrete production, and for over-all education rather than for specific short-term goals on the local level. The committee resulted from twelve regional consultations on evangelization carried out by the National Council of Catholic Bishops earlier that year.[11]

On the diocesan level evangelization centers of diverse kinds opened up. Some were the result of diocesan-wide planning such as in Cincinnati in 1977. Others were centered in a given region such as the Catholic Evangelization Center in the Worcester Diocese in Blackstone, Massachusetts, established in 1981. Perhaps even more significant was the response to the minority members of our nation. The Juan Diego Missionary Society in Texas reaches out family to family in the Mexican-American community. Most important is the fact that in many instances there has been the effort to provide training along with incentive and background or content along with enthusiasm. As a result, there is the program of leadership training for evangelization in base communities in the Santa Fe archdiocese, the RCIA Training Institute begun at St. Mary's Seminary in Baltimore and now located in Washington, D.C. at CARA, and finally, the LAMP Ministries, who as groups of lay ministers organize for evangelization among the poor, with their headquarters in New York City.

A nationwide evangelization center was established in Washington, D.C. at St. Paul's College in 1977, the same year as the establishment of the *ad hoc* committee on evangelization. Fr. Alvin Illig was also chosen to be the director of the Paulist Catholic Evangelization Center as it was named. This center has been and continues to be an action-oriented and program-producing agency, working to coordinate a multitude of events and disseminating a variety of information related to evangelization.

Among these events the most significant has been the National Catholic Lay Celebrations of Evangelization. The first and second were held in Washington, D.C. in 1979 and 1980 with over fifteen hundred participants each time. The conventions included celebration, workshops, testimonials, and shared insight. Their purpose was and still is to heighten awareness and strengthen support for evangelization among the unchurched as both a task and an opportunity for the laity. Perhaps most of all it is a reminder that the Church first evangelizes the Church; in other words, evangelists must first evangelize the evangelizers. In 1981 the evangelization celebrations became regional. The last several from 1983 to 1985 were hosted by New Orleans, Omaha, Buffalo, and in 1985 Chicago and Atlanta.

Publications from the Paulist Evangelization Center include the newsletter *Evangelization and Initiation.* Begun in 1980 as the *Goodnewsletter,* it serves today as a clearing-house on information regarding evangelization. *Share the Word,* begun in 1980, became in time a very important tool for the training and education of evangelizers on the parish level as it supplied background on Scripture in the context of the weekly liturgy. *Share the Word,* produced on video-cassettes in 1984, is regularly broadcast on cable television network for parish groups. It is an example of carrying out evangelization using the techniques and the tools of contemporary mass media.

In 1982 the National Conference of Catholic Bishops decided to withdraw support from the *ad hoc* committee on evangelization and the committee became inactive. This action can be interpreted in a variety of ways. In terms of evangelization efforts throughout the country, it resulted in the creation of the "National Association of Catholic Evangelization Directors," an organization bringing together all those responsible for evangelization in the various American dioceses as well as religious coordinators for the respective religious congregations and other organizations. By 1983, the organization had become known as the "National Council for Catholic Evangelization," which in 1985 numbered some nine hundred members with four hundred and eighty representatives from forty-eight dioceses and archdioceses along with representatives from seventeen religious orders, ten national organizations, and forty-seven parishes.

Of utmost importance is the responsibility for evangelization that both Hispanics and blacks have assumed within the last decade. In 1982 the Hispanic bishops of the United States wrote a pastoral letter addressed to the Virgin of Guadalupe for the sake of the rapidly increasing Hispanic membership in the American Church. This letter was to encourage and to exhort the Hispanic communities. As early as 1977, the Hispanic bishops had addressed the Hispanic communities in terms regarding evangelization that have great significance for us all:

> Every Christian has the right to be evangelized and the duty to evangelize in the context of his or her own culture. We urgently ask the Church to take fully into account the Hispanic culture and the living reality of our people in evangelization.[12]

Or to put it more succinctly—if the Church is evangelical by its very nature, then it is Catholic in its very essence. In 1983 the American bishops issued a pastoral letter on Hispanic ministry.

In 1984 the black bishops of the United States reminded the American

Church and their fellow black Catholic sisters and brothers in their pastoral letter, *What We Have Seen and Heard,* that to be gifted was to be called to share one's gifts, for evangelization includes the giving, the giver, and the gift. Black bishops reminded the black Catholic community that maturity in the faith means responsibility for evangelization.

CHRONOLOGY OF EVENTS IN CATHOLIC EVANGELIZATION: 1972–1985

1972.   Promulgation of the Rite of Christian Initiation of Adults.

1974.   Rome. Synod of Bishops on Evangelization.

1975.   November. Marriottsville, MD. Symposium on evangelizing the unchurched.

    December. Rome. *Evangelii Nuntiandi* promulgated by Pope Paul VI.

1976.   NCCB gave priority to evangelization.

1977.   NCCB established an *ad hoc* committee on evangelization.

    Establishment of the Paulist National Catholic Evangelization Center in Washington, D.C.

1979.   August. First National Catholic Lay Celebration in Washington, D.C.

    October. Pope John Paul II's visit to the U.S. and a call to evangelization.

1980.   *Share the Word* publication begun.

1981.   Juan Diego Missionary Society to train lay evangelists started.

1982.   LAMP Ministries, lay evangelization group for the poor begun.

    RCIA Training Institute established at St. Mary's Seminary in Baltimore.

    National Association of Catholic Evangelization Directors begun as a planning committee.

1983.   *Goodnewsletter* became *Evangelization and Initiation.*

    The Catholic Evangelist published.

CHRONOLOGY OF EVENTS IN CATHOLIC EVANGELIZATION:
1972–1985 *(Continued)*

1983	Formation of Catholic Evangelization Association of America from the National Association of Catholic Evangelization Directors. Then became the National Council for Catholic Evangelization.
	Establishment of *Another Look* program for inactive Catholics.
1984.	*Share the Word* made available on video cassettes.
	Formation of National Music Ministry for Young Catholics.
	Publication of *Invitation,* a Catholic learning guide for adults.
1985.	November. Conference *"Evangelii Nuntiandi* Ten Years Later: An American Meditation."* Washington, D.C.

FUTURE CONCERNS

Within the last ten years evangelization has become, if not a household word in all Catholic homes, certainly a part of rectory and workshop vocabulary. It brushes even the most casual of Catholic churchgoers with a sense of responsibility. If all are not yet ready "to witness" or "to testify," we are all accustomed to someone else being ready to do so. The faith one possesses is now no longer a private matter; it has become a public accountability. For good social graces and good breeding no longer mean reticence about one's religious convictions.

There are concerns, however, for the future. An historian betrays his or her profession who only casts a critical eye on the past without a look of appraisal to the future. In my opinion there are three areas that evangelizers must be prepared for in the remaining decade and a half in this century.

The first concern is the phenomenon of "civil religion." Religious sociologists like Robert Bellah have pointed out that the United States is a religious country in a public sense because common religious elements provide a "religious dimension for the whole fabric of American life, including the political sphere."[12a] In the past two decades those concerned with the analysis of American culture have pointed out how several religious themes have shaped the American spirit—some of them being contradictory. Themes have emerged such as the providential role of the United States in the world, the United States as a "chosen people," the notion that every individual can advance as far as one wishes with hard work and physical energy, that success and prosperity prove the existence of God's blessing, and the value of rugged individualism and fierce competition.[13]

This civil religion which is a pervasive element in United States history is neither particularly Christian nor a systematic structure of beliefs. It is nondenominational, latitudinarian, and very American in its worldview. It has, however, provided a religious consciousness to Americans and a religious language to American statesmen, especially in presidential addresses from George Washington to Ronald Reagan.

In what sense are the ninety million unchurched in our country followers of the American civil religion? In what sense does our civil religion provide some sort of transcendence to our increasingly secular modes of thought and system of values? Even more to what extent are Catholics, especially the upwardly mobile, moderately successful, highly educated young Catholics finding their value system in the American civil religion and the secular creed of personal success? To what extent has our American Catholicism been shaped by the values of the American civil religion?[14]

The second concern emerges from the first, namely the relation between Catholicism, civic responsibility, and public policy. A very perceptive and intriguing study appeared in 1985 entitled *Habits of the Heart. Individualism and Commitment in American Life*. The team of collaborators explore the two poles of the American cultural ideal: public duty and responsibility based on a set of common traditions and private individual pursuits based on a tradition of personal freedoms and enlightened self-interest. The rise of privatism has coincided with the decline of mainline Protestant denominations, but the authors have this to say about the Catholic Church:

> . . . just when the mainline Protestant hold on American culture seemed decisively weakened, the Roman Catholic church after Vatican II entered a much more active phase of national participation. Though never without influence in American society, the Catholic church had long been more concerned with the welfare of its own members, many of them immigrants, than with moulding the national society. The period 1930–60 was a kind of culmination of a long process of institution building and self-help. . . . The unprecedented ecumenical cooperation that brought Catholics together with Protestants and Jews in a number of joint endeavors from the period of the Civil Rights movement to the present has created a new atmosphere in American religious life. With the American Catholic bishops' pastoral letter of May 3, 1983, on nuclear warfare, the promise of Vatican II began to be fulfilled. The Catholic church

moved toward the center of American public life, invigorating the major Protestant denominations as it did so.[15]

Catholicism in America has emerged as a moral force in American public life. It is a "political factor," not in the "wardheeler" sense but in the area of public policy and national concerns. As Catholics we speak to issues of the nuclear age, to issues of global and national economy, to issues of human life and human rights from ovulation to old age. At the same time we do this in the context of a pluralistic society. Where does personal belief intersect with national policy? How can one implement public laws that contradict personal religious views? Even more serious, how can a "public" Church like Catholicism permit issues of life, death and personhood to be reduced from publicly held values to the private sector of personal morality? This tension between public and private morality will not lessen as medical technology increases. It will not go away as more and more Catholics assume positions in the public sector. It will more and more test the position of individual Catholics as they try to place themselves in a society where a common tradition of values has given way to a secular concept of utility and private preference. Evangelization may become more than the transmission of faith but also the acceptance of the cross, not what do you believe but also what is the price of belief?

On the other hand, the rise of fundamentalism within Protestantism, the resurgence of evangelicalism, the appeal of more conservative charismatic communities with their stress on instant grace and personal assurance of God's will is of increasing appeal to many Catholics in a highly complicated world.[16]

The third concern, further complicating matters, is the changing face of evangelization and evangelizers. In the next two decades we will have an American Church that will be more Hispanic and that will have a large community of Asians and Haitians.[17] We are a Church that is neither North European nor South European. It is a Church that in numbers is now one of the largest Afro-American religious bodies, a Church that is a significant portion of the Asian community. Evangelized within a Church that is not a static force but a dynamic organism pulsating with the increase of new peoples, new accents, new gifts, and new cultures, we will tell the good news in a new language and we will sing of it in a new song, we will dance like new Davids before the ark, and we will prophesy with a new spirit in a new valley of dry bones, and we will shout from the housetops the new melody to the ancient psalm:

Sing to the Lord a new song:
Sing to the Lord, all you lands.

Sing to the Lord; bless his name;
announce his salvation, day after day.

(Psalm 96:1–2)

NOTES

1. It is not an exaggeration to point to the evangelical preaching style of many black preachers such as Martin Luther King, Jr. and the impact such writings as his *Letter from Birmingham City Jail* had on the national audience. See Robert N. Bellah, Richard Madsen, William M. Sullivan, Ann Swidler, and Steven M. Tipton, *Habits of the Heart. Individualism and Commitment in American Life*. Berkeley, Univ. of California Press, 1985, p. 249.

2. Dorothy Day (1897–1980), a convert to Catholicism and founder of the Catholic Worker Movement for the poor and downtrodden, was profoundly Catholic. She brought Gospel values to bear on social issues long before it was fashionable for many to do so in the Catholic context. See William D. Miller, *Dorothy Day. A Biography*. San Francisco, Harper and Row, 1982.

3. See James Hennesey, S.J., *American Catholics. A History of the Roman Catholic Community in the United States*. New York, Oxford University Press, 1981, pp. 5–7.

4. *Ibid.*, p. 314.

5. Exact statistics are not yet available. These are conservative estimates received informally from the office of the Priestly Life and Ministry Committee in the U.S.C.C. Estimates for seminarians were taken from the back issues of *The Catholic Almanac* and Adrian Fuerst, O.S.B., *CARA Seminary Directory, 1985. U.S. Catholic Institutions for the Training of Candidates for the Priesthood*. Washington, D.C., CARA, 1985, p. vi.

6. See Hugh J. Nolan, *ed., Pastoral Letters of the United States Catholic Bishops*, Vol. III. 1962–1974. pp. 306–338, and Vol. IV, 1975–1983, pp. 342–355 and 493–581. Washington, D.C., National Conference of Catholic Bishops/United States Catholic Conference, 1983, 1984. For the last Pastoral Letter on Hispanic Ministry, see *Origins,* 13 (1984) 529–541.

7. See *The Unchurched American* (Princeton, N.J.: The Princeton Religion Research Center and The Gallup Organization, 1978), pp. 2–3. "For the purpose of this study, the working definition of the 'unchurched' is a person who is not a member of a church or synagogue or who has not attended church or synagogue in the last six months, apart from weddings, funerals, or special holidays such as Christmas, Easter, or Yom Kippur. . . . Using the above definition, 41 percent of all adults in the current study can be classified as 'unchurched' while 59 percent can be classified as 'churched' (that is, have attended church or synagogue other than a holiday and are members of a church)."

8. Reorganized in 1981 as the United States Mission Association.

9. The significance of the Marriottsville symposium cannot be overestimated. Present were 152 bishops, priests, and laypersons. Following the symposium, a core group met with the late Bishop James Rausch, at the time general secretary of the NCCB, and Archbishop Thomas Kelly, O.P., at the

time associate general secretary. A draft resolution on evangelization was submitted to the bishops at their meeting in November 1976. At this meeting the *ad hoc* committee on evangelization was created. (See undated memorandum in the files of the Paulist National Catholic Evangelization Association in Washington, D.C.).

10. See above mentioned files in the Paulist Evangelization office. One of those who gave both financial support and moral encouragement was Mr. Carl E. Koch, who died May 30, 1985. Mr. Koch desired to aid the missionary effort in the United States. Beginning with an initial donation to Father Illig during the evangelization program in Natchez-Jackson, Mr. Koch continued his enormous support throughout the last decade.

11. Information regarding the committee was supplied in a personal interview with Father Alvin Illig, C.S.P. by the author.

12. "Segundo Encuentro Nacional de Pastoral," *Origins*. 7 (1977) 355.

12a. Robert Bellah, "Civil Religion in America," *Daedalus* 96 (1967) 1–21. See pp. 3–4.

13. See Dick Anthony and Thomas Robbins, "Spiritual Innovation and the Crisis of American Civil Religion," *Daedalus* 3 (1982) 215–234. The earliest treatment of the American civil religion is found in the article by Robert Bellah, "Civil Religion in America," *Daedalus* 96 (1967) 1–21.

14. See Robert Bellah, "American Civil Religion in the 1970's," *Anglican Theological Review. Supplementary Series* 1 (1973) 8–20. See also the book by the same author, *The Broken Covenant. American Civil Religion in Time of Trial*. New York, Seabury Press, 1975.

15. Robert Bellah *et al., Habits of the Heart*, p. 238.

16. See Dick Anthony and Thomas Robbins, "Spiritual Innovation and the Crisis of American Civil Religion," in note 13. The authors write on p. 219: ". . . it can be argued that the Catholic Church and the "liberal" Protestant denominations are caught between the spread of "permissive" countercultural morality on the one hand and the strident moralistic evangelical revival on the other. If the churches opt for evangelical absolutism, they will continue to lose members among the well educated and affluent; but if they embrace the 'new morality,' they are, in effect, embracing a modern 'secular' ethos hostile to theism."

17. For the significant increase in the black Catholic population because of the influx of Haitians, see John Harfmann, S.S.J., *Statistical Profile of Black Catholics, 1984*. Washington, D.C., Josephite Pastoral Center, 1985, p. 3.

DISCUSSION QUESTIONS

1. In what way did the Second World War and the Second Vatican Council affect your diocese and your parish neighborhood?

2. In what ways have your family and friends been affected by the social changes during the past twenty years?

3. Which of the following issues has had the most effect on the attitudes of your friends and relatives?

   a. The bishops' teaching on racism.
   b. The bishops' teaching on nuclear weapons.
   c. The Church's teaching on contraception.
   d. The Church's stand on abortion.
   e. The Church's attitude toward present-day sexual morality.

      Has this effect been positive or negative?

4. What person, Catholic or Protestant, exemplified best in your opinion the ideals of evangelization during the last twenty years?

5. How do you feel about American civil religion?

FOR FURTHER READING

David Bohr, *Evangelization in America. Proclamation, Way of Life and The Catholic Church in the United States*. New York, Paulist Press, 1977.
    A seminal work, giving a theological analysis of evangelization and placing it in the context of the United States experience. All serious study of evangelization must begin with this work.

Dean Hoge, *Converts, Dropouts. Returnees. A Study of Religious Change Among Catholics*. New York, The Pilgrim Press, 1981.
    A study of the phenomenon of religious change among Catholics and former Catholics in the United States, using the research techniques of the social sciences. The book is based on a series of interviews. The author presents his conclusions regarding evangelization and the people involved.

Glenn C. Smith, ed., *Evangelizing Adults*. Washington, D.C., Paulist National Catholic Evangelization Association, 1985.
    A collection of short writings concerning evangelization from all points of view, both Protestant and Catholic, and in all sorts of evangelization styles. The purpose is to give insights from the perspective of personal accounts.

Evangelization. Portrait of the Month.
    A periodical published by the Paulist National Catholic Evangelization Association. It comes in two editions: Anglo/Black and Hispanic (in both Spanish and English). Each issue is a case study presenting evangelization methods and operations in a given diocese or parish.

BECOMING AND SHARING THE GOOD NEWS: THE NATURE AND CONTENT OF EVANGELIZATION

Msgr. David Bohr

This chapter focuses on two key aspects of evangelization: its *nature* and *content*. It intends to be primarily a theological reflection upon Chapters 2 and 3 of *Evangelii Nuntiandi*.

THE NATURE OF EVANGELIZATION

Allow me to introduce this part with a story:

> God, as we all know, created the heavens and the earth. He created everything through the use of words, for words, of course, are power. "Let it be done," God proclaimed, and it was done. And everything he made was good.
>
> Well, God was especially proud and loving of the man and woman he had made because he had breathed into them a part of himself, his spirit.
>
> But the devil, not surprisingly, was jealous and angry. He sauntered up one day as God was enjoying the man and the woman in the garden. He asked what he liked so much about these creatures. And when God opened his mouth to speak, the devil craftily bound his tongue. God could not talk.
>
> The devil, then, laughed at God and quite had his way with the man and the woman. As eons went by, the devil came back to mock God—he couldn't resist, such is his nature. He scoffed at the silent deity, and God responded by holding up one finger.
>
> "One?" asked the devil. "Are you trying to tell me you just want to say one word?"
>
> Yes, God nodded, pleading with his soft eyes. The confident devil thought to himself. "Not even God could do very much harm with one word." So the devil removed the bond from God's tongue.

And God spoke his one word, in a whisper. He spoke it for the man and the woman and it brought great joy. It was a word that gathered up all the love and forgiveness and creativity God had been storing in his heart during the time of his silence.

The word he spoke was Jesus![1]

The Necessity of Proclamation

God created everything through the use of words, as our story tells us, "for words, of course are power." In *Evangelii Nuntiandi* Pope Paul VI first recognizes the initial importance of what he calls "the wordless witness of a genuine Christian life" (EN #21). But immediately he adds, "even the finest witness will prove ineffective in the long run if it is not explained, justified. . . . There is no true evangelization if the name, the teaching, the life, the promises, the kingdom and the mystery of Jesus of Nazareth, the Son of God are not proclaimed" (EN #22). Evangelization is the proclamation of the good news of Jesus of Nazareth, the Son of God. The word God spoke was Jesus!

In light of the Second Vatican Council's affirmation of the universality of grace,[2] some Church members today question the very need of explicitly proclaiming the Gospel. Some theologians maintain that while Jesus of Nazareth was certainly the Christ, other peoples and cultures have their own christs. "Why, then, send forth missionaries?" others are asking. On the home front, too, some Catholic educators feel that the Catholic school's primary task is to offer quality education, not to evangelize. Proclaiming the good news of Jesus Christ, they maintain, is a direct infringement upon the freedom and personal conscience of the non-believer.

When we look, however, at the manner of divine revelation itself and at our traditional understanding of the Trinitarian life, we see that the mystery of the Godhead is unveiled for us through the double mission of the Son and the Spirit. St. Irenaeus, in the second century, described this double mission as "the two hands of the Father"[3] that makes the discovery of God in history possible. The ineffable Mystery in whom "we live, move and have our being" (Acts 17:28) uses *two hands,* word and spirit, and not one hand only, in the process of divine self-communication.

The mission of the Spirit, the universality of grace, reaches out to all men and women of every place and time. The Holy Spirit calls them in their heart of hearts and seeks to transform them into images of the new Adam, Jesus Christ, even if, in the words of the Second Vatican Council, "through no fault of their own [they] do not know the Gospel of Christ or his Church."[4] But this mission of the Spirit is only one hand. To say this is all that is needed and to deny the mission of the Word proclaimed and made incarnate is to tie God's other hand behind his back, as it were. It is to bind God's tongue as the devil craftily did in our opening story.

The word of God in the Old Testament (in Hebrew, "dabar") possesses both dynamic and noetic elements. On one hand, it creates the world and sets history in motion, and, on the other hand, it manifests God's will, his salvific plan.[5] It is both revelation and power. Perhaps if it were not for that primordial fault, that original sin which mars our human nature, God very well might have saved us with just one hand. But somewhere back there, before recorded time, it all began to unravel. An original alienation took place. Sin not only negatively affected our relationships to God, to one another, and to all of creation, but also, deep within us, our hearts were pulled asunder and tossed into confusion by unruly desires, longings, and passions, each seeking its own independent way. In such a state our eyes became blind to God's plan. Our hearts grew cold to the transforming power of his love, his grace. God now needed his other hand, the mission of the Son, the Word-made-flesh, who came into the world to be its light, "a light that darkness could not overpower" (Jn 1:5).

The Second Vatican Council's Dogmatic Constitution on Divine Revelation tells us that God "sent his Son, the eternal Word, who enlightens all men, so that he might dwell among them and tell them the innermost realities about God (cf. Jn 1:1–18)."[6] God wants all men and women to arrive at a full awareness of his plan of salvation. God's self-communication through his Word seeks proclamation; it requires enfleshment. Incarnation, in fact, is the primary law of revelation.

Other religions may share images and symbols which are common to Christianity, but God's incarnation as an historic being—Jesus of Nazareth—is unique. As Mircea Eliade has observed, "since the incarnation of the Christ, the Christian is supposed to look for the interventions of God not only in the Cosmos . . . but also in historical events. . . . [The incarnation is] an audacious effort to *save the historical event* in itself, by endowing it with the maximum of being."[7] Against such spiritual vitality the mystery religions and gnosticism were utterly powerless. Giving reasons for its early and rapid growth, Christopher Dawson has written, "Christianity defeated its rivals because it was felt to be a historical and social reality, capable of transforming human life."[8]

Jesus enfleshed and proclaimed the good news of God's hidden plan. In Jesus Christ the sundering effects of sin were checkmated. As St. Paul tells us, "God wanted . . . all things to be reconciled through him and for him, everything in heaven and on earth, when he made his peace by his death on the cross" (Col 1:20). Jesus reveals "the way, the truth, and the life" (Jn 14:5). He clearly unveils God's other hand—the creative, unifying hand of grace, that is, the mission of the Spirit—that has always been at work in the world, but whose presence great numbers of the human race could only see through a mirror darkly.

This good news, Jesus tells his disciples, must be "proclaimed from the housetops" (Mt 10:27). Such proclamation, "far from being an attack on religious liberty" when presented without coercion or unworthy pressure, Pope Paul VI maintained, is both a right and duty.[9] It presents to our brothers and sisters the choice of a new way of life which they too may "consider noble and uplifting" (EN #80). In Chapter 7 of *Evangelii Nuntiandi,* the Pope asks: "Why should only falsehood and error, debasement and pornography have the right to be put before the people and often unfortunately imposed on them by the destructive propaganda of the mass media . . . ?" (EN, #80). The Word God spoke was Jesus!

Evangelization: The Mission Which Has a Church

The Church exists to evangelize, to proclaim the good news of the Word-made-flesh. "The pilgrim Church is missionary by her very nature," Vatican II tells us. "For it is from the mission of the Son and the mission of the Holy Spirit that she takes her origin. . . ."[10] Thus, Pope Paul VI points out in *Evangelii Nuntiandi* that, "having been born consequently out of being sent, the Church in her turn is sent by Jesus. . . . She prolongs and continues him. And it is above all his mission and his condition of being an evangelizer that she is called upon to continue" (EN #15).

In our mind's eye we often put the cart before the horse. We picture Jesus, first of all, establishing the Church to whom he then gave the mission of evangelization among a number of other important tasks and ministries. But *Evangelii Nuntiandi,* returning to the evidence of Sacred Scripture, tells us matter-of-factly that is not the way it happened. "The Church is born of the evangelizing activity of Jesus and the Twelve," Paul VI states (EN #15). It is the mission of evangelization which has the Church, not the Church which has the mission. Every task and every ministry within the Church serves this continuing mission. All ministries, whether in the area of missionary extension or pastoral care, whether in outreach to the unchurched and inactive Catholic, whether in the areas of family life, catechesis, preaching, international life, peace, justice and liberation—all ministries converge to serve the one "primary and essential mission" of evangelization (see EN #29, 42, 44, 45).

Ministry perceived from the perspective of evangelization takes on a new dynamism, a new purpose and focus. Given the principle of entropy, the law of inertia, it is so easy for Church leaders, and members as well, to slip into a maintenance mentality. Our churches can easily provide the comfortable pew where we simply bask in the consoling news of God's love and plead that he lend an attentive ear to our self-interest and private concerns. Ministry within the churches then becomes a matter of pastoral maintenance and customer satisfaction. Parishes become suburban country clubs of the saved. Members develop a consumer mentality regarding weddings, baptisms, and funerals. Paying their dues, they simply expect the Church to supply the needed religious and social services.

Only when we begin to realize that God calls us together to be Church (Ekklesia), that he gathers us together in communion and fellowship as members of Christ's body (koinonia) for the purpose of mission, of bearing witness to his hidden plan (see Col 1:26), only then are we really and truly Church. Vatican II describes the Church "as the universal sacrament of salvation,[11] simultaneously *manifesting* and exercising the mystery of God's love for man."[12] The marks of the early Church "gathered together" in Acts 2:42—teaching, fellowship, breaking bread, and prayer—served to make the disciples "witnesses" of the risen Lord (see Lk 24:48 and Acts 1:8). The communion of life and fellowship the early Christians shared with the risen Lord and with one another manifested the continual unfolding and incarnation of the Gospel mystery. "Everything is not contained in the command to 'go' and teach. There is also the prayer that 'they may be one *as*' the Father and the Son are one '*so that* the world may believe' (Jn 17:21–23)."[13] The Church's fundamental task is simultaneously both to be evangelized and to evangelize, both to become and to share the good news (see EN #15).

The Double Mission and the Two Moments of Evangelization

So far, we have seen that the good news must be proclaimed and that this proclamation of the Word-made-flesh in Jesus Christ constitutes the very reason *why* the Church exists. It is important for us now to realize that this proclamation is an ongoing process involving two moments or dimensions which unfold from "the two hands of the Father," namely the mission of the Son and the mission of the Spirit. Proclaiming the Gospel in word and deed constitutes the first moment. It is the explicit or *ad extra* dimension of the evangelization process which corresponds to the mission of the Son, the Word-made-flesh. Living the Gospel mystery by faithfully responding to the promptings of grace within our hearts constitutes the second moment. This is the *ad intra* or interior dimension corresponding to the mission of the Spirit through which God shares with us the hidden energy of this life and love.

Warning against formulating any partial or fragmentary definition of evangelization (see EN #17) Paul VI offers a one sentence description which incorporates these two moments. "The Church evangelizes," he says, "when she seeks to convert, solely through the power of the message she proclaims, both the personal and collective consciences of people, the activities in which they engage, and the lives and concrete milieu which are theirs" (EN #18).

The purpose of evangelization, he adds, is not just to reach out to "ever wider geographical areas," but to bring about "this interior change" affecting the human race's "criteria of judgment, determining values, points of interest, lines of thought, sources of inspiration and models of life, which are in contrast with the Word of God and the plan of salvation" (EN #19).

Evangelization is an ongoing process having a twofold dimension which involves both becoming and sharing the good news. It thus includes several essential elements which the Pope lists as: (1) the renewal of humanity, (2) Christian witness, (3) explicit proclamation of the Word, (4) inner adherence, (5) entrance into the community, (6) acceptance of signs, and (7) apostolic initiative (see EN #24). This whole process continues today under the influence of the Holy Spirit who is both "the principal agent of evangelization," impelling us to proclaim the good news and causing us to accept the word of salvation in the depths of our consciences, and "the goal of evangelization," stirring up "the new creation, the new humanity of which evangelization is to be the result" (EN #75).

THE CONTENT OF EVANGELIZATION

Having reflected upon the nature of evangelization, we turn our attention now to its content. Once again, let me introduce this part with a story:

We refer to an episode in the legend of Parsifal and the Fisher King, who alone held the secret of the Graal. The Old King was suffering from a mysterious malady that affected everything around him. The palace and gardens were falling into ruin. Animals no longer bred, trees bore no more fruit, the springs were drying up. Many doctors had tried to cure the Fisher King, all without the least success. The knights were arriving day and night inquiring about news of the King's health. But one knight—poor, unknown and even slightly ridiculous—paid no attention to courtly custom: his name was Parsifal. He made straight for the King's chambers and, addressing him without preamble, asked: "Where is the Graal?" In that very instant everything is transformed: the King rises from his bed of suffering, the rivers and fountains flow once more, vegetation grows again, and the castle is miraculously restored. Those few words of Parsifal propound the central question, the one question that can arouse not only the Fisher King but the whole Cosmos: Where is the supreme reality, the sacred, the Centre of Life and the source of immortality, where is the Holy Graal? No one had thought, until then, of asking that central question—and the world was perishing because of lack of imagination and absence of desire for reality.[14]

Salvation in Jesus Christ

" 'Where is the Graal?' No one had thought, until then, of asking that central question—and the world was perishing. . . ." In Chapter 3 of *Evangelii Nuntiandi* we are told the center of the message we must proclaim is that "in Jesus Christ, the Son of God made man, who died and rose from the dead, salvation is offered to all" (EN #27). This salvation, Pope Paul VI explains, is "liberation from everything that oppresses man but which is above all liberation from sin and the Evil One" (EN #9). It is not some immanent salvation restricted to the framework of temporal existence, but "a transcendent, eschatological salvation . . . [reaching] fulfillment in a communion with the one and only divine Absolute" (EN #27).

The "two hands of the Father" reach forth inviting us to share in a most intimate communion of life and love, not only with the Mystery "in whom we live, move, and have our existence" (Acts 17:28), but also with one another and with all of creation. This new life of intimate communion Jesus called the kingdom of God. Jesus in his teaching announces salvation by proclaiming this kingdom. Thus, we hear in that magnificent one-line summary of his teaching found at the beginning of Mark's Gospel: "The time is fulfilled. The kingdom of God is at hand. Repent, and believe the good news" (Mk 1:15). In *Evangelii Nuntiandi*, furthermore, we read this kingdom "is so important, that by comparison, everything else becomes 'the rest,' which is given 'in addition.' Only the kingdom therefore is absolute, and everything else relative" (EN #8).

"Only the kingdom therefore is absolute," Pope Paul VI is telling us, "and everything else relative." Do we hear all the implication of this statement? What, then, is this kingdom? The Pope tells us that it is adherence to revealed truths, to a program of life, adherence to the "new world," to the new manner of being and living in community, which the Gospel inaugurates (see EN #23). It is a non-territorial, eschatological kingdom. In practical terms, it is what would occur if everyone faithfully kept the two great commandments. In Jesus, the kingdom is the dynamism of God's love. It is grace! It is the power of God erupting in time and transforming our world as attested to by Jesus' words and deeds, parables and miracles. It is the revelation of what God is working to bring about in our lives, of God's plan for the human race.

In the early post-resurrection period the evangelists did not hesitate to identify Jesus with both the good news and the kingdom (e.g., Mk 8:35; 10:29). In St. Paul's letters the content of his message is no longer the kingdom of God, but "the Gospel of Christ" (e.g., 1 Thes 3:2; Gal 1:7) which is "the power of God saving all who have faith" (Rom 1:16). And the Gospel is described as "that mystery hidden from ages and generations past but now revealed to his holy ones . . . the mystery of Christ in you, your hope of glory" (Col 1:26–27). For St. Paul, Jesus Christ is the Gospel, its message and content.

Furthermore, God's plan of salvation is *fully* revealed in the paschal mystery of Jesus Christ—in his dying, rising, returning to the Father, and sending the Spirit. The paschal event is, in fact, the heart of the good news. All four Gospel accounts lead up to it. It is the Gospel Paul received and handed on (see 1 Cor 15:3–5). It is the mystery into which we are baptized (see Rom 6:3–4), and we remember it, celebrate it and are ritually united to it at every Eucharist. Sharing in Christ's dying and rising, we are given new life (Rom 6:4) and we dare hope to become like him, he who is "the last Adam . . . a life-giving spirit" (1 Cor 15:45). By appropriating Christ's paschal mystery in our own lives, by putting on the mind and attitude of Christ (Phil 2:5), we indeed become "a new creation." In the Spirit of the risen Lord we become "a spiritual person" (1 Cor 2:15), because it is through the Spirit that we are given power for the development of our inner selves (Eph 3:16). In the Spirit, the "principal agent" and "goal" of evangelization, we ourselves are being evangelized.

Conversion of the Heart

The kingdom Jesus proclaimed and inaugurated in his person, by his paschal mystery, is first of all an inner reality, a matter of the heart. The ancient Hebrews had looked for the restoration of the Davidic kingdom as an external and territorial reality. Jesus told Pilate, "My kingdom does not belong to this world" (Jn 18:36). Indeed, during his public ministry Jesus taught his disciples, "The kingdom of God is within you" (Lk 17:21). The kingdom of God first takes root within our hearts, indeed within our souls.[15]

Returning to the summary of Jesus' teaching in Mark's Gospel we read, "The kingdom of God is at hand. Repent" (Mk 1:15). Such repentance or conversion implies a change of mind and heart, a change of attitude. It requires a complete reversal of one's way of judging, valuing, acting. Bringing about "this interior change," Pope Paul VI tells us, is the purpose of evangelization (EN #19). This inner transformation of "both the personal and collective consciences of people" (EN #18) is the only sure foundation upon which to build a better political, economic, and social order. The Pope then adds that "the best structure and the most idealized systems soon become inhuman if the inhuman inclinations of the human heart are not made wholesome, if those who live in these structures or who rule them do not undergo a conversion of heart and outlook" (EN #36).

Knowledge of this inner world of the heart, the soul, is what we most sorely need today.[16] The very word "soul" has come upon hard times in contemporary Christian circles. Serious consideration of it has perhaps been side-stepped because of the overly individualistic, pietistic and dualistic notions that have surrounded the classical religious imperative "to save one's soul."

A fitting corrective to this long-standing preoccupation has emerged over this past century in the constantly growing body of Catholic social teachings. Our own Catholic bishops have not been afraid to lead the way in this area with their many statements on issues of social, political and economic justice and with recent pastoral letters addressing "The Challenge of Peace" and the U.S. economy. Within this context, however, we must not allow such laudatory efforts to implement the kingdom of God among us and in a concrete, external and practical way divert our attention from the continuing need of the human heart for healing, integration, wholeness, for meaning, love and communion with the Absolute—the Absolute whom Jesus himself taught us to call "Abba, Father."

St. Augustine once said, "Our hearts are restless until they rest in you, O God!" The Fathers and great mystics of our tradition show us that this inner world of the heart, the soul, is just as real as the inner workings of our bodies which medical science has so beneficially explored in recent centuries. The interior world of the soul possesses a structure common to all members of the human race as the universality of archetypes, images and symbols attest. Here precisely is found the beauty and hidden power of Jesus' teachings which do not depend upon any given system of thought, but are rather timeless and applicable to all ages. As Mircea Eliade has observed,

> . . . although Biblical and Christian symbolism is charged with a historical and—in the last analysis—a "provincial" context (since every local history is provincial in relation to universal history concerned in its totality), it remains nevertheless universal like every coherent symbolism. [17]

The symbolism of this inner world of the soul finds fruitful expression in the works of the Fathers, such as Tertullian, Irenaeus, John Chrysostom, Cyril and Augustine, and in the writings of the great mystics such as John of the Cross, Teresa of Avila and Catherine of Siena.

The emptiness and hollowness so evident in the lives of many people today are by-products of our overly rationalized, scientific and positivistic approach to life. Exclusively concentrating on extroverted attitudes and ignoring the needs of our inner world has created a vacuum which must be filled. In desperation people turn to drugs, alcohol, sexual promiscuity, and even to war to escape their inner isolation. The forces of sin and evil tear us apart within and throw our lives out of balance and into confusion. Deaf to the Spirit's promptings and blind to God's presence within our heart of hearts, this lack of personal integration finds expression in all our external activities and relationships. The accumulated effects of such sinfulness, then, become enfleshed in social, economic, and political structures.

EVANGELIZATION IN THE U.S. CATHOLIC CHURCH TODAY

It remains for us to ask now, "How does this nature and content of evangelization uniquely relate to the context of the U.S. Catholic Church?"

The Need for Foundational Evangelization

There is evidence in our society today of a deep spiritual hunger witnessed to in recent years by the popularity of new spiritual movements, courses in spirituality, journal keeping, religious cults, and the successes of Christian fundamentalism. At the same time there are structures that need changing in order that we might live in a more just and peaceful world. Many Catholics along with their fellow citizens of this great land have spent their lives in the pursuit of this end. We need only recall the Catholic Worker movement, civil rights, Vista volunteers, the peace movement, the U.S. bishops' statements on the burning social issues of our time and their recent pastorals. All of these have well understood the need to put Christ's teaching into action.

Oftentimes this dual thrust toward interior spiritual renewal and concrete social action appear to arise out of opposing visions of the Gospel message. A proper understanding of the kingdom of God tells us such cannot be the case. Both thrusts are necessary and constitutive of the evangelization process; they mirror the double mission of the Son and the Spirit, the "two hands of the Father" at work in the world. Some Catholic social activists are calling today for a North American theology of liberation. I sincerely believe we need a new, more encompassing imagery. I feel we need, if we are to label it, a theology of the new creation, a theology of the transformation of consciousness, of spiritual integration, a theology of building the kingdom in both its internal and external manifestations.

With Parsifal we need to ask the central, all-transforming question, "Where is the Graal?" While it is certainly necessary for theologians and others within the Church to explore all sorts of new questions put to us in recent decades by a rapidly changing world, we must never forget the central question. As we examine every tree in the forest of life we cannot afford to forget to keep in focus the Tree of Life that stands at its very center.

Father Patrick Brennan, president of the National Council for Catholic Evangelization, has stated that what we need today is *foundational evangelization*. This involves keeping ever in mind the fourfold task outlined in NCCE's Vision Statement: "To evangelize is to proclaim Jesus as the Word of Truth, to reveal the Kingdom of God, and to invite people to Christian discipleship, and to minister as instruments of the Spirit in the process of individual and ecclesial conversion."[18] "Where is the Graal?" "God spoke his one word. . . . The word he spoke was Jesus."

The Rediscovery of Narrative: An American Contribution

With regard to the nature of evangelization I have tried to employ throughout this chapter what I personally consider the unique American contribution, namely narrative theology, the rediscovery of stories and the role of imagination and symbol in nurturing Christian faith and values. Philip Keane, S.S. tells us: "In stories a type of learning is possible which we cannot achieve through discursive processes."[19] Perhaps this is why the Gospels point out: "All these lessons Jesus taught the crowds in the form of parables. He spoke to them in parables only" (Mt 13:34). The Old Testament, too, is full of stories.

While doctrinal formulations and ethical principles are certainly necessary to give clarity and form to the Christian life, these rational abstractions and impersonal rules do not really motivate. They appeal only to the intellect, the cognitive self. They do not tickle our fancy or capture our imaginations. Stories, images, and symbols appeal to the whole person: intellect, will, imagination and feelings. They are also universal, appealing to every culture while transcending the limitations of historical time and place. Perhaps Jesus in his method of teaching realized something we are just now rediscovering, something we lost in our rationalistic journey through the Enlightenment and the Age of Science.

Narrative helps us both tap and address the spiritual riches of our pluralistic, multi-cultural society. The magnificent patch-work quilt of peoples and cultures that is the United States should be viewed as nothing less than the workings of the Holy Spirit in our time, bringing about what St. Paul wrote to the churches of Galatia: "All of you who have been baptized into Christ have clothed yourselves with him. There does not exist among you Jew or Greek, slave or freeman, male or female. All are one in Christ Jesus" (Gal 3:27–28).

Congratulations must certainly be extended to the black bishops of the United States for their recent pastoral letter on evangelization entitled "What We Have Seen and Heard."[20] They have effectively set forth the spiritual treasures and needs of the black community in the United States. All the various cultural communities that form the multicolored fabric of American society must share their stories, the stories of their people and their own unique journey of faith. Not to do so, not to listen in awe and reverence to these stories and to be enriched by them, is surely a failure to clothe ourselves with Christ and to become one in him.

CONCLUSION

Our crying need today is to rediscover the total picture, the "Totus Christus" spoken of by St. Augustine. We must rediscover the vast rich heritage of faith that is our unique, magnificent legacy within the nearly two thousand year old Roman Catholic tradition. Let us be proud of our heritage, let us treasure these gifts, but let us also continue to be ever mindful of the words of Jesus to the Twelve when he sent them on their first missionary journey, "The gift you have received, give as gift" (Mt 10:8).

We continue to need doctrinal formulations and ethical principles; we need our catechisms of the faith, but they along with all our religious practices and ministries become empty and lifeless unless they are rooted in the very life-blood of the evangelizing mission. In the 1960's and 1970's, in the wake of Vatican II, we broke out of the pietistic individualism that primarily marked our spiritual lives in the post-Enlightenment period. Renewed biblical studies made the inspired written word of God come alive. We rediscovered the social implications of Jesus' teaching. Today, we still need to recapture the rich and dynamic spiritual vision of the Fathers and the great mystics; with them we need to explore once again the interior world of the soul. Their teachings were not aberrations of the Gospel message but rather an ever deepening understanding of its implications. Only when we see, understand, and appropriate the entire Gospel vision—this two thousand year long process of evangelization—shall we be adequately prepared to journey forth unto the third Christian millennium.

Maranatha. Come Lord Jesus!

NOTES

1. Adapted from William J. Bausch, *Storytelling: Imagination and Faith* (Mystic, Conn.: Twenty-Third Publications, 1984), pp. 115–16.

2. See *Lumen Gentium, #16*: "Those also can attain to everlasting salvation who through no fault of their own do not know the Gospel of Christ or his Church, yet sincerely seek God and, moved by grace, strive by their deeds to do his will as it is known to them through the dictates of conscience." Also, *Gaudium et Spes, #22* and *Ad Gentes, #3.*

3. "Against the Heresies," 5, 36, 2 (SC 153, 458, 460) as cited by Kiliam McDonnell, O.S.B., in "A Trinitarian Theology of the Holy Spirit?" *Theological Studies* 46 (1985), p. 206.

4. *Lumen Gentium, #16.*

5. See Rene Latourelle, S.J., *Theology of Revelation* (New York: Alba House, 1966), p. 30.

6. *Dei Verbum, #4.*

7. Mircea Eliade, *Images and Symbols: Studies in Religious Symbolism* (New York: Sheed and Ward, 1969), p. 170; emphasis in the original.

8. Christopher Dawson, *Religion and World History* (New York: Sheed and Ward, 1975), p. 108.

9. See EN #80. See also *Dignitatis Humanae, #4.*

10. *Ad Gentes, #2.*

11. *Lumen Gentium, #48.*

12. *Gaudium et Spes,* #45—emphasis mine.

13. L. Legrand, J. Pathrapankal and M. Vellanickal, *Good News and Witness: The New Testament Understanding of Evangelization* (Bangalore: Theological Publications in India, 1973), p. vi.

14. Adapted from Mircea Eliade, *Images and Symbols: Studies in Religious Symbolism* (New York: Sheed and Ward, 1969), pp. 55–56.

15. See Carroll Stuhlmueller, C.P., *The Jerome Biblical Commentary* 44:125, where, after offering three translations of the preposition, he adds: "In any case, the kingdom is not merely an immanent presence of the Spirit; it has an external as well as an internal manifestation." See also John A. Sanford, *The Kingdom Within* (New York: Paulist Press, 1970), p. 48.

16. See *Gaudium et Spes,* #14: "When a man recognizes in himself a spiritual and immortal soul, he is not being mocked by a deceptive fantasy springing from mere physical or social influences. On the contrary he is getting to the depths of the very truth of the matter."

17. *Images and Symbols,* p. 168. See also John Sanford, *The Kingdom Within,* p. 21.

18. Bylaws for the National Council for Catholic Evangelization (Approved in Convention on June 14, 1983), Article II.

19. Philip S. Keane, S.S., *Christian Ethics and the Imagination* (New York: Paulist Press, 1984), p. 66.

20. "What We Have Seen and Heard: A Pastoral Letter on Evangelization from the Black Bishops of the United States" (Cincinnati, Ohio: St. Anthony Messenger Press, 1984).

DISCUSSION QUESTIONS

1. In light of Vatican II's teaching on the universality of grace, why is it still necessary to send forth missionaries and explicitly proclaim the Gospel?

2. What do you believe is the primary task of Catholic education—to evangelize or to offer quality education? Explain your answer.

3. How would things change in your parish or area of ministry if everyone involved were to view *all* ministry as serving the primary mission of evangelization?

4. Do you feel that the contemporary spiritual renewal movements within U.S. Catholicism sufficiently incorporate Catholic social teaching? Is social action possible without interior conversion?

5. Do you see the teachings of the Fathers of the Church and the writings of the great mystics as having any bearing on the way we live our faith today? Or do you feel they belong to a more primitive, less enlightened age which can contribute nothing to our contemporary world?

6. What are some of the stories that have shaped your life of faith from childhood to the present? What are some of the stories our secular society and culture tell us about life and its meaning—from the worlds of politics, sports, advertising, the media?

FOR FURTHER READING

David Bohr, *Evangelization in America* (New York: Paulist Press, 1977).
  Traces the historical and theological development of the Catholic Church's understanding of evangelization, beginning with the New Testament. Gives special attention to the evangelizing efforts in the history of U.S. Catholicism.
———, "Evangelization: A Ministry of the Word? or the Chief Focus and Energizing Center of All Ministries?" in *Dimensions of the Word: Exploring a Ministry,* Gerard F. Baumback, ed. (New York: William H. Sadlier, Inc, 1984), pp. 9–34.
  Documents the evolution in the Roman Catholic Church's understanding of evangelization from Vatican II through *Evangelii Nuntiandi* and Pope John Paul II's *Catechesi Tradendae.*
James H. Provost, ed., *The Church as Mission,* Permanent Seminar Studies No. 2, Canon Law Society of America (CLSA: Washington, D.C., 1984).
  A series of eight articles synthesizing the basic categories that are central to an understanding of the Church's *mission* from the perspectives of theology, liturgical studies, sociology and canon law.

THE METHODS OF EVANGELIZATION

Alvin A. Illig, C.S.P. and Six American Evangelists

The question of 'how to evangelize' is permanently relevant, because
the methods of evangelizing vary according to the different circumstances of time, place and culture, and because they therefore present
a certain challenge to our capacity for discovery and adaption.

On us . . . rests the responsibility for reshaping with boldness and
wisdom, but in complete fidelity to the content of evangelization,
the means that are most suitable and effective for communicating the
gospel message to the men and women of our times.

These words are from Chapter 40 of *Evangelii Nuntiandi*. I will suggest five
principles to help us reflect on effective methods of evangelization.

1. When Christ gave us his great commission in Matthew 28:19–20,
"Go, therefore, and make disciples of all the nations. Baptize them in the name
of the Father, and of the Son, and of the Holy Spirit. Teach them to carry out
everything I have commanded you . . ." he did not tell us how to do it. We
were commissioned and sent to evangelize, but not given methods for evangelization.

I believe one of the reasons the apostles fled to the upper room and
slammed the door behind them was because they were frightened by the charge
Christ gave them. You see, Christ did not give them a clue on how to carry
out his command, on how to evangelize. Throughout the Gospels the Lord
rarely if ever tells us how to do his work, just that we are to do it. If he had
told us how, we would probably still be focusing on methods and materials
that would have been effective for the peoples of the eastern end of the Med-
iterranean world two thousand years ago, rather than developing methods that
are effective for today's Americans.

Evangelizers of today, as the evangelizers of the past, are empowered
with the knowledge that "he who wills the end wills the means." If Christ tells
us to evangelize, he will enlighten and strengthen us to do it. With the power
of the Holy Spirit, we can find the more effective methods and materials to
evangelize this community here and now with the human assets and liabilities

each evangelizer brings to the task. We can depend on Christ's help, but we must take some initiative. We must begin, even though we know we are inadequate and our gifts insignificant to the task.

2. In designing methods and materials for evangelization, the community to be served must be kept in mind: for example, the inactive Catholic, the unchurched American, the black community, the Hispanic community. However, when choosing particular tools for evangelization, the charism of the evangelizer is also an extremely important factor. The personality, the uniqueness, the creativity, the sensitivity of the evangelizer must be honored.

There is no one style of Catholic evangelization. There are as many styles as there are evangelizers. Such diversity is important because the communities we are trying to reach have a multitude of styles. Each one of us can reach people with Christ's message that others cannot reach. Each one of us, using our own special talents, background, education, experience, heritage, language, culture—all working together—build God's kingdom on earth. No one of us can do the task. Working together, however, we can do a great deal.

3. In addition to a diversity of styles, there must be a multiplicity of methods and materials. One approach will appeal to one person, another approach will appeal to someone else. A multiplicity of methods and materials designed for inter-personal dialogue and for mass communications, for peer-to-peer personal witnessing and for the work of national offices can complement one another and more effectively capture the imagination of those we are trying to evangelize. We are to be "catholic" in creating methods and materials.

We Catholic evangelizers are, for the most part, fairly well educated and somewhat sophisticated, yet we are often dealing with unsophisticated and less well educated people. We must have the courage to design and use very popular, quite simple, and at times fairly emotional approaches to share the Gospel. In Chapter 4 of *Evangelii Nuntiandi*, Pope Paul VI holds in high esteem what he calls "popular piety." He writes:

> [Popular piety] manifests a thirst for God which only the simple and poor can know. It makes people capable of generosity and sacrifice even to the point of heroism. . . . It engenders interior attitudes rarely observed to the same degree elsewhere: patience, the sense of the cross in daily life, detachment, openness to others, devotion (EN no. 48).

4. In the current bestseller on American management, *In Search of Excellence,* Thomas J. Peters and Robert W. Waterman urge that organizations wishing to excel display a bias for action: a preference for doing something—anything—rather than sending a question through cycles and cycles of analyses and committee reports. [1]

A bias for action must be part of our evangelizing strategy. The Catholic community is not short on mission theology. It is not short on mission theory. It is not short on mission history. It is not short on the examples of missionary lives. While theory is extremely important, evangelizers know a time arrives when the next step called for is activity.

Evangelizers should look upon themselves as the "marketing people" for today's Catholic Church—the ones who employ contemporary methods and materials to call people to conversion in the Lord Jesus Christ. Evangelizers are action-oriented people, doers of the Gospel. Jesus, the greatest of all evangelizers, used three action words when he commissioned us: "Go," "Make," and "Teach."

5. A clear distinction must be made between the message and the messenger. Mary, the mother of the Lord Jesus Christ, was a messenger; her son was the message. We are today's messengers. Christ must always be the message. "There is no true evangelization if the name, the teaching, the life, the promises, the kingdom and the mystery of Jesus of Nazareth, the Son of God, are not proclaimed" (EN no. 22).

Effective methods and materials for evangelization are simply helps to us who come to "preach Christ crucified—a stumbling block to Jews, and an absurdity to Gentiles; but to those who are called, Jews and Greeks alike, Christ the power of God and the wisdom of God" (1 Cor 1:23–24).

The messenger does gently impact on the message because of the unique qualities of each messenger. We believe in both "ex opere operato" (by the work itself) as well as "ex opere operantis" (by the work of the worker). The good messenger does not tamper with the message, but rather strives to be faithful to that authentic message.

The following reflections are five examples of the diversity of methods and materials for Catholic evangelization today.

WITNESS OF LIFE
by Tom and Lyn Scheuring

(No. 41 of *Evangelii Nuntiandi*)

Since Vatican II lay persons are beginning to get a clearer sense of their responsibilities as baptized Christians. We are discovering that through our baptism we too enter into the mission of the Church, which is the mission of Jesus.

When Jesus opened the scroll in the synagogue and read the passage from Isaiah 61, he was beginning to outline his mission. This passage as it appears in Luke 4:18, and mirrored again in Luke 7:22, has become meaningful to the two of us. The Word of God says something clear about how we are called as baptized Christians.

When we were first married we desired to be lay missionaries, but there were no Catholic opportunities for us twenty years ago. That desire, however, never left us. The longing to do evangelization work among the materially poor only continued to grow in our hearts. We kept looking for other avenues or possibilities to enter into a ministry like that. Finding none, and after much prayerful discernment, we finally stepped out in faith and began our own ministry a little over four years ago.

At that time it was primarily through serving in a poor parish in San Antonio as "Lay Ministers of Evangelization" with our three children that we saw the need for a ministry that comprised two main aspects: first, one that provided materially poor parishes with qualified persons to assist in the faith-building ministries of the parish, complementing and integrating the social outreaches; and second, one that provided qualified lay persons an opportunity for short term (at least one year), full-time evangelistic ministry among the poor. Stepping out in faith, we put together a proposal where we would recruit, train, and place qualified lay persons in poor parishes to assist the pastor in the ministry of evangelization.

After sharing this proposal with Cardinal Cooke (we had been from the New York area and planned to return), he invited us to research the beginning of LAMP MINISTRIES—Lay Apostolic Ministries with the Poor. We visited with the three ordinaries of the metropolitan dioceses (Cardinal Cooke, Archbishop Gerety, and Bishop Mugavero), chancery officials, pastors, and others. The warmth and encouragement of the ordinaries was a great support to us. Without their affirmation, obviously, we wouldn't have begun LAMP.

Beginning LAMP was an extremely challenging process which forced us to strengthen our trust in the Lord. More than once, when speaking with a pastor about our plans for LAMP, a typical conversation would begin, "Well, whom are you with?" and I would respond, "My wife and my children." He would look at me rather puzzled, having expected me to say a religious community or a diocesan office.

We inherited no one's mailing list and no one gave us a blueprint. Somehow we knew we had to respond to a call in our hearts, to be committed to evangelistic ministry with the poor, and we knew it had to be done in unity with the Church. It is unusual for lay persons to begin an organization to provide pastoral ministers for parish service, and we knew that the grace for this ministry would come from unity with the ordinaries of the dioceses in which we would serve.

Beginning and continuing LAMP MINISTRIES is not without risk. I (Tom) work full-time, and Lyn and others part-time. We have to raise all the funds for our ministry. The parishes provide room, board, a small stipend, and medical insurance for the LAMP Minister in the parish. In addition, we spend time building community which is very important in the support of the LAMP

Ministers. We have weekly meetings, monthly training days, and semi-annual training weeks.

A couple of years ago we were invited to speak to all the major seminarians in the Archdiocese of New York. At one point, I was struck by the material security they had. I said to them: ''If what we are doing (LAMP MINISTRIES) doesn't work, we do not just get reassigned! We do not have any money to fall back on if we're out of work.'' Once again, the risk being taken is highlighted as well as the encouragement and support lay people need when trying to break new ground in lay ministry.

Actually, we don't even like to speak of ''lay'' ministry. Granted, the lay people, clergy, and religious have different types of service, but we are all called to ministry. LAMP is not restricted to lay persons; it is simply that they need more opportunities for service and for training. We are delighted to have some religious sisters serving as LAMP Ministers and we look forward to the possibility of brothers and priests serving with us. We also see how essential it is to train youth to serve others, to stretch their hearts in compassion for those who suffer. Called LAMPLIGHTERS, these youth play an integral part in LAMP MINISTRIES. Together we are Church and share in the mission of Jesus.

What the LAMP Ministers do in the parish depends on the needs the pastor sees as well as the particular gifts of the minister. A common service is home visiting. Moreover, we train the LAMP Ministers to be catalysts to draw the parishioners into the service they are doing, so that when they leave, the ministry can continue through the parishioners themselves. A LAMP Minister, serving in one of the poorest parishes in Brooklyn, got together a number of the elderly people who came to daily Mass. Once a week he had a prayer meeting with them at which they interceded for the needs of the parish. One of his other services was to visit the shut-ins. In the course of these visits he met a lady who had been bedridden for a number of years. She was very despondent, couldn't sleep, and walked with great difficulty. Periodically he would visit and pray with her. He also got some of the people from his weekly intercessory group to visit and pray with her. Within a few months the woman was sleeping eight hours a night, walking around, and became a much happier person. We saw this as the healing power of a loving presence, and how parishioners, when given the direction, can evangelize each other and bring each other to wholeness through the presence and power of the Holy Spirit.

In our training of LAMP Ministers we stress the need for a faithful prayer life, daily Eucharist, poverty of spirit, and unity among the parish staff and among other LAMP Ministers. We don't believe any witness of life will more clearly mirror God than the witness of unity, of people united in the heart of Jesus reaching out with his loving concern to others with his message of joy and freedom. The witness of life as lived by the early Christians still has the greatest power: "See how they love one another."

ON PREACHING AND THE LITURGY OF THE WORD
by Rev. Laurence Brett

(Nos. 42 and 43 of *Evangelii Nuntiandi*)

In this section of his apostolic exhortation, Pope Paul VI spoke of a "sensitivity for reading God's message in events."[2] He displayed the sensitivity of which he spoke. In looking at the "necessity of preaching" and "the Liturgy of the Word," he first assessed the challenges that confront both elements in modern times, and then affirmed a truth drawn from "God's message," the Sacred Scriptures, that counters those obstacles.

Without laying claim to a similar sensitivity, I would like to follow his method. I will begin by assessing the challenges of the present (as I see them), and then reaffirm that truth which His Holiness posited. Finally, I would suggest some proposals that might make that truth, that teaching, operative.

THE LITURGY OF THE WORD

The Challenges

When it comes to "the Sacred Scriptures, the source of wisdom which . . . leads to salvation,"[3] the chief obstacle confronting us is the fact that a Catholic approach to the Bible is not the prevalent attitude, whether among the churched or the unchurched. The perception still persists that there is no "Catholic approach" to the Bible at all, or that Catholics do not believe in Scripture. It is a biblical literalism that colors most people's approach, and the simplicity of such a fundamentalism is becoming ever more attractive. Drawing upon this, some groups, revealing an anti-Catholic bias, further the notion that Catholic doctrine is not based on the Bible and even falsifies God's Word.

Consequently, large numbers are being drawn away from the Church. This loss reflects an ever-deepening hunger for the Scriptures, "the word of truth."[4] Proving St. Jerome's axiom that "ignorance of the Scriptures is ignorance of Christ,"[5] many sincere people feel they must leave the Catholic Church in order "to know him clearly."[6]

A Truth Reaffirmed

His Holiness described the Mass as "the feast of the Lord" as he discussed the Liturgy of the Word. In so doing he recalled that Vatican II referred to "the treasures of the Bible" as "rich fare."[7] That truth later emerged in the General Instruction of the Roman Missal, and we learn: "In the Mass both the table of God's word and the table of Christ's body are prepared."[8] In order to show how both "tables" are "so closely connected with each other that together they constitute but one single act of worship,"[9] I would offer these suggestions.

Proposals

1. In the construction or renovation of our churches, let the lectern resemble a table, its original form, and by its placement and materials be clearly set in balance with the altar-table.

2. Four principal focal-points should emerge within our sacred space: the altar-table, and, on an axis to it, the place of reservation for the Eucharistic Bread; the lectern-table, and, in axis to it, a place of reservation for the Bread that is God's Word. Such a *locus reservationis,* distinct from, but related to, the *locus actionis,* would accomplish the following:

(a) it would set the Word in balance with the Eucharist, a balance flowing from the "single act of worship";

(b) it would recapture the ancient Catholic tradition that honored the book with procession, lights and incense;

(c) it would honor the tradition of Judaism, which enshrines the Scriptures in every synagogue, thereby recalling our "share in the rich root of the olive" to which we "have been grafted";[10]

(d) it would parallel the esteem which other Christian churches have given to the Bible; and,

(e) it would clearly indicate the lectern-table as a *locus actionis,* a place of doing.

3. A reverence, not unlike that given to the Most Holy Eucharist, must accompany the ministry of the Word, the basis for the training of all who minister. The care with which the readings are *done,* the silence that attends, and the obvious preparation for this table—all must be in evidence.

4. Bible studies should be begun in every parish, as a "devotion" to the Word not unlike the traditional devotion accorded to the Blessed Sacrament.

Share The Word[11] was intended as such: preparing for, or leading from, the central act of the community's worship, placing the study of God's Word within the context of eucharistic worship. I am pleased to report that the issue currently being printed is at a press-run of 220,000, and that interest in the television format of *Share The Word* has drawn the interest of almost two thousand communities. Yet more needs to be done to answer the basic hunger that sees God's Word as nourishment.

THE NECESSITY OF PREACHING

The Challenges

The poor quality of Catholic preaching is a major cause for defection from the Church. Perhaps His Holiness' description of our age as "this time of uncertainty and confusion" has had its part to play.[12] An expanded lectionary demands a wider knowledge of Scripture, and biblical studies of the past have not allowed the homilist to keep pace with recent advances in the field. The limitations on time in modern parishes, and increased demands upon one's time, have made the task of careful preparation almost an impossible one. The overwhelming obstacle that I have noticed among homilists is the fear of failure. Sensing such failure, they fail, or at least imagine that they do.

A Truth Reaffirmed

Referring to "the necessity of preaching" and "the need to be convinced of this," His Holiness reaffirmed two truths derived from his namesake, Paul of Tarsus. The first is that "faith comes from hearing,"[13] and the second is that such faith "rests not on human wisdom but on the power of God."[14]

The first truth relates to "the necessity of preaching," connecting preaching with the faith it elicits. Pope Paul VI described the homily as "inserted in a unique way into the Eucharistic celebration." It comes between Gospel and Creed, between proclamation and profession of faith, and joins the two. As His Holiness observed, the homily should be "profoundly dependent on Gospel teaching" and "faithful to the magisterium."

The second truth addresses the fear of failure. The homily is "the bearer of the power of God." Fear must be cast aside so that the preacher may "speak with full confidence."[15] Recall what the Scriptures reveal. Moses, when called, raised the objection that he had "never been eloquent" and was "slow of speech."[16] Jeremiah claimed that he was "too young."[17] Isaiah felt himself "doomed" from the start because he was "a man of unclean lips."[18] And Paul openly admitted, in writing, that when he spoke he was "unimpressive and his word makes not great impact."[19]

How, then, impress modern preachers that the Lord will be with them as the Lord was with prophets and apostles?

Proposals

May I suggest the following possibilities.

1. We already possess in this country an untapped source for good hom-

ilies, namely those already given or being given. Could not the homilists of today be encouraged to submit their own works to a central committee for judgment, emendation, and distribution to other homilists, with recognition of the source?

2. There are three stages to a good sermon: preparation, delivery, and feedback. The faithful are involved, and only passively so, in one. Could they not be actively involved in the other two?

As for the *preparation:* I envision a support group of those willing to share their insights, or several groups on a rotational basis. Pope Paul said that there are "innumerable events in life . . . which offer the opportunity for a discreet but incisive statement of what the Lord has to say in this or that particular situation." Who better to analyze those situations than the laity "in the midst of the world?"[20]

As for *feedback:* Who better to indicate that "the word of God is at work within those who believe"[21] than those to whom that word is addressed? A support group of believers might best assess what Pope Paul called "the pastoral effectiveness" of the homily.

3. His Holiness ended this apostolic exhortation with a prayer and a blessing. Saint Paul is heard to ask, when dealing with preaching God's "word in its fullness,"[22] "Pray that I may speak it clearly."[23] A support group, gathered in prayer, whether together or singly, especially comprised of those who cannot participate fully in the worship of the community, such as the elderly or those confined by illness, might feel their contribution to the ministry of the Word by their prayers or sufferings suffused in prayer.

In the Liturgy of the Word, as in preaching within that liturgy, a love for the Word of God must rise to the fore in Catholic thought and worship, as in daily life itself. As a final note, need I remind you that Pope Paul VI, in this very exhortation, himself supplied an example? There are only 82 brief articles in *Evangelii Nuntiandi*. But there are almost 100 quotations (44) and references (54) here to the Sacred Scriptures, the Word of God.

"May the word of Christ, rich as it is, dwell within you."[24]

CATECHETICS
by Ms. Patricia Barbernitz

(No. 44 of *Evangelii Nuntiandi*)

Catechetics can be an effective means of evangelization. The good news is that if you do catechetics well, you are evangelizing in a very real sense.

Consider the outreach to parents that is part of most effective religious education programs. Parents are so concerned that their children have the very best, and they will do almost anything the catechist suggests as helpful for their children. Dean Hoge has documented the fact that a major reason for adults coming to the church for the first time, or returning to active membership in the church is family.[25] Parents want religious education for their children and they want to set a good example for the child by their own church attendance.

The parent meetings or sacrament preparation programs we have for parents are usually good opportunities for evangelization. Inactive Catholics or others who are not currently involved in a church are ripe for a welcoming person who pays attention to them, challenges them to be the better person they want to be, and helps them in realistic ways with their children. If the sessions simply teach new information or stay on the level of activities, they miss their evangelizing potential. If, on the other hand, they invite the parents to a deeper personal faith response which they can then share with their children, the new information and the activities are focused and can support ongoing evangelization and conversion in the whole family.

CCD programs designed for children and teenagers show the concern we instinctively feel for each member of the church. Regardless of age or sacramental experience, these young people need to be evangelized. Parents discussing textbooks for children phrase the question in other terms, but it is the same question: Are the materials we use promoting conversion and leading to personal commitment? *Evangelii Nuntiandi* puts it this way, "No one will deny that instruction must be given to form patterns of Christian living and not to remain only notional" (No. 44). It is not enough that texts contain information. They must aid the catechist by challenging the student to community experience, service, and prayer.

Current directions in youth ministry give other examples of the instinctive sense that educators and administrators have that catechetics reaches its desired goal only when it is evangelizing. We minister to teenagers and young adults through dances, drama, and music as well as discussion sessions and retreats. The message for them must be adapted to their age, culture, and aptitude while focusing on experience, intelligence, and heart. We know that if hearing the message of our faith does not lead to action, commitment, and personal conversion, then it has not really been spoken or heard adequately.

In a sense, we are beginning to appreciate once again the charismatic gift of teaching. For a good catechist, the act of teaching is prayerful and a work in which the teacher is hearing, learning, and being perfected along with the student. Catechesis is a ministry of the Word, one in which all the actors are receiving and responding to the Spirit who is directing and inspiring. This appreciation of teaching as gift can be the difference between catechesis which uses its evangelizing potential and catechesis which focuses on an impersonal study of theology or religion.

Catechesis is sharing faith, which means personal commitment, conversion, and acceptance for both the catechist and the student. In Catholic schools, CCD programs, and other religious education settings, we can choose to lead people to conversion. Leaders in such groups will never replace parents or basic life experiences but they can be significant influences in the evangelization of those they are teaching.

The clearest expression of this partnership between catechesis and evangelization is in the Rite of Christian Initiation of Adults. The conversion inspired by evangelization is the absolute measure for the RCIA. The flow of the formation periods and rites in the catechumenate process shows the natural development of conversion and becomes a model for understanding and helping anyone experiencing a deepened faith. It reminds us that catechesis both flows from the conversion and leads to it. The RCIA makes it clear that all catechesis should be connected to conversion.

The good news message is never adequately transmitted simply in words. It must always be inherently rooted in community, inspire service, and lead to worship. It must take form in a way of life that is open to ongoing conversion. This is the answer to the questions about the role of doctrine in RCIA, or in catechisms, or teen programs. Of course, we must have content; people need to know what Catholics believe. Of course, the information of our faith is important and must be shared. But if the catechesis does not also evangelize—if it does not lead to faith, to commitment, to conversion—then something is missing. Catechesis does not fulfill its promise unless it is also evangelization.

USING THE MASS MEDIA
by Mr. Adan Medrano

(No. 45 of *Evangelii Nuntiandi*)

"The Church would stand guilty before Our Lord if she did not use these powerful instruments" (EN, no. 45). These strong words of Pope Paul VI urge us to use the media, for through them, as the document states, we can "reach the multitudes." In an equally forceful manner, Pope Paul also raises a special media challenge: "to penetrate the conscience and enter the soul of the individual in all his (or her) unique individuality" (EN, no. 45).

Evangelii Nuntiandi addresses two aspects of media: their ability to reach and their ability to inspire. The first speaks of a delivery system and the second of a process of artistic creation.

As delivery systems, our communications media are as efficient as they are myriad: broadcasting, cablecasting, satellite, home media, and personal media. To quote statistics about the numerous hours that we spend using media would be to underscore a clearly evident fact. I only urge that our use be characterized by a spirit of religious poverty. Let me explain what I mean.

A system of communication which is the major vehicle for expressing ideas, providing social cohesion, and evolving dominant myths has a great responsibility. Our U.S. communications system, for better or for worse, is commercial and consumer-oriented. The forces of the marketplace rule. The trade press reports that today, more than at any other time, our communications policy is one of laissez-faire, deregulation, marketplace determination. The result of this policy for us as non-commercial, non-profit entities is that, in media, if you can pay you can pray. The converse is evident.

Pray-TV is becoming more and more expensive. In Los Angeles, a half hour on Sunday at 6:30 A.M. costs $10,000. These high prices for religious ghetto time are a recent phenomenon. They are the result of ever-increasing competition among religious broadcasting organizations. Ministries have bid the prices for religious ghetto time upward as they compete against each other for time slots in important markets. Praise the Lord, the 700 Club and Jimmy Swaggert are some of the better known ministries.

This is a trend toward decay. Competing to be the highest bidder in an effort to preach the Gospel degenerates the moral power of truth and of love. It is also counter-Gospel to ignore the plight of people who, having a need to express their particular ideas and values, do not have the possibility of paying the price. I specifically mean minorities, the poor, the disenfranchised.

Therefore I believe it is in the true spirit of our Gospel vocation and of our baptismal commitment to ask these questions:

1. Do the poor and marginalized in our communities have access to TV and radio?

2. Does the TV and radio programming schedule reflect their richness?

3. As we use or plan to use media, are our efforts redemptive of the system or do we play the game in an effort to "spread the word"?

4. Is the present policy of deregulation in the best interest of peoples who are disenfranchised?

Questions like these are our guides to using media with a spirit of religious poverty.

Evangelii Nuntiandi confronts the second aspect of media, the ability to inspire, with a very special challenge: "to enter the soul." The future of the United States, and indeed of the world, more and more depends on the state of our collective soul. We are acutely aware of the massive buildup of war weapons. This buildup is possible because we believe more in fire power than we do in the real power of self-giving love. Other aspects of our life in this country also cry out for redemption: the misuse of our environment, prison systems filled with minorities and the poor, inadequate care of the elderly. We sorely need to be healed by the meek and gentle spirit of Jesus.

Through media you and I can play a significant role in this healing. Because we publicly profess to be vocational guardians of civilizing values which nurture our God-likeness we can respond with power to the challenge: "enter the soul." The key word to describe our media role is "resonance." If we believe that we are sons and daughters of a God whose spirit we breathe, then media allows us to resonate with the Divine in the other. Media can help us recognize the Spirit which dwells in our souls. That Spirit pours forth blessings in a creative, magnificent, unpredictable fashion. It is predictable only in its fruits of justice, peace, joy, and love.

When we deal with media, TV and film in particular, all too often our attention is placed on manifestations of neurotic behavior like pornography and violence. Our well-intentioned and proper efforts in the past have been countered by First Amendment arguments and we have been perceived chiefly as censors.

I believe it is right and proper that we exercise review of current film and TV fare. I also think we should relate creatively with artists who work in video, film, and radio. In the long run they will shower upon American society a multitude of redemptive images: celebration of life, blessedness of the environment, the naturalness of sexuality, the bond of the human community, and the power of truth.

As a negative example, consider M-TV which really should be called EMPTY-TV. The gravest problem with M-TV is not that it is violent, although it indeed is, and not that it trivializes sex, which it does. The gravest problem with EMPTY-TV is that it lacks a soul. It copies shallow, shiny techniques which were invented by serious media artists ten years ago to reveal extraordinary beauty and truths.

Let us ally ourselves with media artists who pioneered video and film images so powerful that they revealed the glories of the human soul. Jonas Mekas and Ed Emschweiller electrify the viewer with movements of color and sound which celebrate transcendent beauty. Juan Downey pierces through South American stereotypes to capture stark faith. Barbara Kopple bares the soul of coal miners with such simplicity that humanity is ennobled and complex issues are seen through the harmonizing prism of brotherhood and sisterhood.

Many of these artists are isolated and starving today. That is indeed unfortunate. I believe that they explore the questions we explore and that they express the Spirit we experience. Their productions make the mind more critical and the heart more sensitive.

Besides relating to these artists, let us strongly support media artists in our own communities: to be not only efficient deliverers of a message but creators of images which make insight possible. These insightful images are part of what I call the media vernacular—images which can help us resonate with the Spirit who will inspire us and lead us to silent prayer. The path to a rich and expressive media vernacular lies in the training of our artists and in freeing them to express their visions.

When using communications as a delivery system, we can show how powerful is poverty by being mindful of the questions I posed earlier. Let us encourage our artists to create noble images that resonate with the Divine in the other, images that reveal to other souls the God who is already breathing inside their human heart.

Media systems deliver messages very well. But media artists reveal, inspire, and revive true joy.

PERSON TO PERSON EVANGELIZATION
by Ms. Gertrude E. Morris

(No. 46 of *Evangelii Nuntiandi*)

Person-to-person communication is the most elemental and basic form of evangelization. Combining faith and action, sharing the faith is the common responsibility and joy of all Christians. In the normal vocation of family, work, and social life, we can live out the precepts of our faith through our conduct. We can accomplish the mission of Christ's Church by doing the ordinary in an extraordinary manner. We can incarnate the living Word of God into flesh by being his present hands, feet, and heart in today's world.

When converts are asked what drew them to the Church, the common answer is another person—a Catholic relative, friend or associate whose life witness attracted them, and who invited them to worship services. One-to-one evangelization is available to us all—wherever we are, whoever we are, whatever we do—in the course of our everyday lives. Each of us is called to live Christ, called to that radical transformation in him where we encounter another human being as sister or brother to be reverenced and given the good news of God's saving love through word and experience.

Here in the United States, we are fortunate to have a diversity of peoples and a variety of cultures among us. God has blessed us with the opportunity to experience his incarnation in a rainbow of colors, languages, and traditions. We can touch and be touched by him freshly and in delightfully unexpected ways when we refute the sinful, human-imposed barriers that separate us and recognize each other in the power of his love. Evangelization based on that love is an ongoing, lifetime, life-giving process.

The one-to-one mode of evangelization becomes more powerful in a group setting. Individuals bonded together by faith—praying and studying together, telling their own journey/stories and acknowledging the truth of God's healing presence in their lives—become pockets of Christianity and are better able to reach out to others and draw them into living, caring community. Even though some individuals are blessed with the unique charism for proclaiming and witnessing as solo evangelizers, the parish for most of us is the ground from which our outreach efforts spring. It is the parish community that nurtures, encourages, and inspires us to evangelize.

The National Office for Black Catholics' One-to-One In Christ program has been conducted in many parishes throughout the country. Parishes that serve their mission best are concerned with the inward growth of their people and the needs of their surrounding communities. Every area of their parish life has its evangelizing component, its outreach dimension carefully thought out and developed. They take into consideration the actual people whose lives they touch, especially their language, signs, and symbols. Persons are not attracted to a setting in which they do not feel culturally affirmed. Effective parishes have vibrant liturgies, opportunities for growth and learning in small group settings, communal and meditative prayer, involvement in civic and community affairs and active ministries to the hungry, the unemployed, prisoners, elderly, youth, homeless, and hopeless.

Parishes such as these demonstrate an awareness that Christ showed his concern for the physical as well as the spiritual needs of the community, an awareness that one cannot share what one does not have, and an awareness that the sense of powerlessness in the face of today's overwhelming evils and problems can only be overcome by immersion in the death/resurrection mystery in a community of prayer, sustenance, and support. In the black community constant contact with and nourishment from the Church has not been a luxury but a necessity and a deeply felt hunger.

The parish that meets these challenges is the one that successfully evangelizes by attracting and keeping its people. Leadership training and ongoing study of Scripture and the tenets of the Catholic faith in an atmosphere of mutual respect and sharing are essential. The parish community becomes an extended family where one's truest self, one's deepest definition is realized: that of a loved child of God. It is out of this identity that one is impelled and compelled to draw others. Enlightened by his truth, one can help others to overcome the negative definitions of self operative in society and in the world. It is out of this truth that one can develop a global mission to end the oppression that contradicts the intrinsic worth of each person.

Evangelizing on a person-to-person level most often comes out of careful planning and creative involvement rooted in a prayerful, caring parish that is aware of the history, gifts, and desires of its community. Door-to-door canvassing, revivals, street ministries, summer youth Bible classes, ecumenical prayer services, and open-door celebrations are proven ways of reaching *out* if at the same time we are reaching *in* for continued growth.

Catholics have to be aware of the opportunities for evangelizing that surround us. Many parishes are located in areas where there are almost twice as many unchurched as church-affiliated. Many parishes have schools with heavy concentrations of non-Catholic students. Others have social programs open to the entire community, food and clothing banks as well as day care and services for senior citizens. These are our neighbors to whom we *owe* the good news. With love, dedication, planning, and commitment, we can share our faith as well as our resources with our neighbors, our brothers and sisters in Christ.

When we hesitate or are reluctant, we have to seriously ask ourselves, "Why?" We must be aware that they, knowing who we are and what we profess to be, are asking, "Why not?"

NOTES

1. See Thomas J. Peters and Robert H. Waterman, Jr., *In Search of Excellence* (New York: Warner Books, 1982).

2. *Evangelii Nuntiandi*. Quotations without notes are from Articles 42 or 43.

3. 2 Tim 3:15.

4. Eph 1:13.

5. *Comm. in Isaias, Prol.: PL* 24, 17.

6. Eph 1:17.

7. *Constitution on the Sacred Liturgy*, Art. 51.

8. *GIRM*, No. 8.

9. *Ibid.*

10. Rom 11:17.

11. *Share the Word,* a magazine written by Fr. Laurence Brett and published by the Paulist National Catholic Evangelization Association, 3031 Fourth Street, NE, Washington, D.C. 20017, presents a weekly Bible study of the Church's Sunday lectionary readings.

12. *EN,* Art. 1.

13. Rom 10:17.

14. 1 Cor 2:5.

15. 2 Cor 3:12.

16. Ex 4:10.

17. Jer 1:7.

18. Is 6:5.

19. 2 Cor 10:10.

20. *EN,* Art. 70.

21. 1 Thes 2:11.

22. Col 1:25.

23. Col 4:4.

24. Col 3:16.

25. See Dean R. Hoge, *Converts, Dropouts and Returnees* (Washington, D.C., USCC, and New York: The Pilgrim Press, 1981), especially Chapters 2–4, and 7–8.

DISCUSSION QUESTIONS

1. Why must contemporary Catholic evangelizers be creative and innovative?
2. What can be done to integrate the social and evangelistic outreach efforts in Catholic parishes?
3. What are your expectations of a homily? Are they being met?
4. In your opinion, what connections are there between evangelization and catechetics?
5. How is the Gospel present in programs our families view on television today?
6. Why are Catholics (why am I) generally reluctant to evangelize on a person-to-person level?

FOR FURTHER READING

The following books offer helpful background reading regarding methods of evangelization:

William J. Bausch, *Storytelling: Imagination and Faith*. Mystic, Conn.: Twenty-Third Publications, 1984.
Les Brown, *Television: The Business Behind the Box*. New York: Harcourt, Brace, Jovanovich, 1973.
James W. Fowler, *Stages of Faith: The Psychology of Human Development and the Quest for Meaning*. New York: Harper and Row, 1981.
Aidan Kavanagh, O.S.B., *On Liturgical Theology*. New York: Pueblo Publishing Co., 1984.
Sharing the Light of Faith, The National Catechetical Directory for Catholics of the United States. Washington, D.C.: USCC Publications, 1979.

These resources document successful strategies and methods for evangelization:

Glenn C. Smith, ed., *Evangelizing Adults*. Washington, D.C.: Paulist National Catholic Evangelization Association and Wheaton, Illinois: Tyndale House Publishers, Inc., 1985.
————ed., *Evangelizing Youth*. Washington, D.C.: Paulist National Catholic Evangelization Association and Wheaton, Illinois: Tyndale House Publishers, Inc., 1985.
Alvin A. Illig, C.S.P., *Six-Week, Parish Based, Clergy/Laity Evangelization Program*. Washington, D.C.: Paulist National Catholic Evangelization Association, 1983.

THE BENEFICIARIES OF EVANGELIZATION
Louis J. Luzbetak, S.V.D.

THE QUESTION

Our question is simple enough: To whom are we to proclaim and witness the Gospel? More specifically, whom are we *American Catholics* supposed to reach?

The identification of the beneficiaries of evangelization is one of the most important, most basic, and most useful questions that anyone concerned with evangelization could possibly ask. It is important and basic because it tells us *where* evangelization must take place; it is important because it tells us much about *how* we are to evangelize.

The Gospel message must be convincing and believable not only to the preacher and witness of the good news but also to the recipient of the message. We must, therefore, know *whom* we are addressing, be it in proclaiming the Gospel or witnessing it. As St. Augustine put it centuries ago in his *De Doctrina Christiana,* a person will be moved to action

> if what you promise him is what he [already] likes, if the danger of which you speak appears real, if your censures are directed against something he hates, if your recommendations are in harmony with what he embraces, if he regrets what you say is regrettable, if he rejoices over what you claim is a reason for joy, if his heart is sympathetic toward those whose misery you describe, if he avoids those who you advise should be avoided . . . not merely imparting knowledge about things that ought to be done but rather moving them to do that which they know must be done [IV:12].

Evangelization, although primarily the work of the Holy Spirit, observes the basic laws of human communication. Before we can understand a message, it must somehow be compatible with our psychological frame of mind and our particular cultural experience. Before individuals are moved to action—and that is what evangelization is all about—they must be led from their already felt-needs to those still not felt, from the known to the still-unknown, from the appreciated to the still-unappreciated. Of one thing we can be sure: long before the evangelizer has appeared on the scene, God in his loving Providence was already at work. The evangelizer must now build on *God's* foundation. In so doing, the evangelizer must communicate as much as possible not on his or her own wavelength but on that of the beneficiary of evangelization. The starting point in evangelization is a cultural, sociological, and psychological analysis of the needs of the particular beneficiaries of evangelization (Luzbetak 1963; Hesselgrave 1978; Holland, Henriot 1980; Schreiter 1985), be it done in a simple unsophisticated manner or scientifically, a task impossible unless we first identify the beneficiaries. The advice I constantly give to missionaries who come to me with their missiological problems can be reduced to a single formula: "Get the answers to your problems *from* and *with* your people"— that is, get them with and from the beneficiaries of your evangelization. This is not to deny that at times the evangelizer must play the role of the prophet and be counter-cultural (*Evangelii Nuntiandi* no. 65).

In any case, the evangelizer must never, I say never, lose sight of the fact that the "language" both Creator and creature "speak" best and love most of all is the *cultural language,* the communications system of the society, subsociety, or, as the case may be, a further subdivision of the society or subsociety being evangelized. There is no more effective way to communicate and no more genuine way of expressing one's love for God and neighbor than in terms of the ways and values of the beneficiaries in question, whether it be an ethnic group, a gang of delinquents, the inmates of a state penitentiary, the professional and educated class of a diocese, or the unemployed, the terminally ill, the divorced, or the alienated lapsed Catholics of one's parish. Yes, look for the answers to your liturgical, catechetical, and other evangelization problems inside the souls of your people and do so together with them. The best evangelizers are, after all, not the best *preachers* but the best *listeners.* To listen, of course, is impossible, unless we first know *who* our "people" are— who the particular beneficiaries of *our* evangelization happen to be.

But before going on to the identification of the beneficiaries of our American evangelization efforts, I would like to look a little more closely, even if only very superficially, at what is meant by "cultural language." At times, the term "culture" is used by anthropologists and sociologists rather loosely, and generally from a particular perspective. Today more and more the term is being described as the symbolic system of a social group, the social group's shared verbal and non-verbal system of communication. This happens to be the only system by which a social group can really understand the Gospel, evaluate its message, and be able to live by. We might also very usefully view culture—as many, if not most, anthropologists do—as a socially shared design for living, as a tried and more or less successful system for coping with life, as the total set of norms learned from one's group for best dealing with the given physical, social, and ideational environment. This is the "language" that is so dear to God, the language used by the Holy Spirit in the Scriptures, the language that the God of history uses when he speaks to us, and it is the language that we must use in evangelization.

Some years ago such an attempt was made by Carl F. Burke, described in his book with the apt title *God Is for Real, Man* (1966). Youths of the lowest rung are led to Christ by using their own set of assumptions, values, attitudes, and goals. Judas is described as a "stoolie" in Jesus' "gang." "The Lord is my shepherd" becomes "The Lord is like my probation officer"—and why not? After all, the probation officer happens to be the youths' only friend. One could hardly say "The Lord is my Father" instead of "The Lord is my shepherd" because "father" connotes to this group of beneficiaries of evangelization nothing more than "a drunken good-for-nothing."

This is not to deny the existence of human commonalities. There is a common humanness created by God himself, whether we are speaking of people in Washington, D.C. or of people in the heart of New Guinea. We do not deny this human commonality but rather are struck by the fact that the Creator so delights in human diversity. Unless we identify the concrete beneficiaries of those being evangelized, we shall not be able to respect that diversity, that luxurious human pluriformity, nor shall we be able to communicate the good news in the only cultural language understandable to them, the language of their very souls.

Having answered the question *why* the evangelizer should be concerned about identifying the beneficiaries, let us look more closely and see *who* they are.

THE GENERAL ANSWER: ALL HUMANITY AS BENEFICIARY

Vatican II and Evangelii Nuntiandi

If there is anything that Vatican II documents and Paul VI's exhortation *Evangelii Nuntiandi* tell us, it is that the mission of Jesus of Nazareth and his Gospel have a unique, universal, and worldwide character. The opening sentence of the Dogmatic Constitution on the Church (*Lumen Gentium*), one of the two most important documents of the Council, sums up the whole tenor of the historic assembly.

Christ is the light of *humanity;* and it is, accordingly, the heart-felt desire of this sacred Council, being gathered together in the Holy Spirit, that, by proclaiming his Gospel to *every creature* (cf. Mk 16:15), it may bring to *all* men that light of Christ which shines out visibly from the Church (no. 1; italics added).

Evangelii Nuntiandi is no less clear and emphatic.

> For the Church, evangelizing means bringing the good news into *all strata of humanity,* and through its influence transforming *humanity* from within and making it new: "Now I am making *the whole of creation* new" (Rev 21:5) (no. 18; italics added).

Evangelii Nuntiandi leaves no doubt whatsoever that the mission of the Church is indeed to nothing less than "To the whole world! To all creation! Right to the ends of the earth!" (no. 50). Karl Rahner in his article "Toward a Fundamental Theological Interpretation of Vatican II" (1979) regards Vatican II as the most significant event in Church history since the Council of Jerusalem. It was then, in 49 A.D., that the infant Church inaugurated a theologically new era passing from being a Jewish Christianity to something that was Gentile, Graeco-Hellenic and European, abandoning such sacred Judaic practices as circumcision, the sabbath, and laws regarding unclean food, not mere externals but traditions with deep theological consequences. The Second Vatican Council was the official beginning of a no less theologically radical understanding of the Church, an understanding that Rahner sums up under "*world* Church," that is to say, a Church whose *life* is *supra*-cultural, no longer Western, but a Church at home equally everywhere, as Asian and African in its *self-understanding* as it is European, and not only potentially as before but actually (even if at the moment still only imperfectly and rudimentarily so).

Before this new "world Church" era was inaugurated, the Church may have been a worldwide Church, but more in the sense of a big European corporation with a big, worldwide export program of a European-packaged Christianity, with a strictly Western management and a self-understanding that was definitely European. At Vatican II, the Church for the first time officially thought, judged, decided, spoke, and acted as a true world entity, as a single people of God, with the bishops acting in a truly worldwide collegiality. This new direction was not a contradictory change, an aberration of some kind, but the result of growth and precedent, the result of previous insight and hope, an actualization of an existing potential. It nevertheless took a Vatican II to steer Peter's bark in this radically new direction.

What has not changed at Vatican II and in *Evangelii Nuntiandi* is the unique position of Jesus and his Gospel, the basic Christian belief that "at Jesus' name *every* knee must bend in the heavens, on the earth, and under the earth, and *every* tongue proclaim to the glory of the Father: Jesus Christ is Lord" (Phil 2:10f), that the Church has no choice but to "make disciples of *all* nations" (Mt 28:19), that "Jesus Christ is the same yesterday, today, and forever'' (Heb 13:8)—*for all times and places*—''for there is *no other* name in the *whole* world'' (Acts 4:12).

Although Vatican II showed deep respect for non-Christian religions by recognizing that they were a part of God's own design and therefore could be instruments of salvation in cases where someone through no fault of his or her own did not and in fact could not know Christ, and although Vatican II left some difficult theological questions unanswered, it nowhere suggested that non-Christian religions in themselves and apart from Christ were an optional way of salvation. The beneficiaries of evangelization were indeed as wide as the world itself.

Crosscurrents

The uniqueness, universality, normativeness, and finality of Jesus for all societies and cultures is, of course, unacceptable to not a few modern radical theologians. Neither time nor the purpose of the present paper, however, will allow us to do more than to offer some examples of what we mean by crosscurrents, theological views that run counter to the official teaching of the Catholic Church. Long before Vatican II and the *Evangelii Nuntiandi* there was, for instance, Ernst Troeltsch with his claim that Christ was but one among many other founders of great religions, and that Christianity was ''true'' only in the Christian context. Then, in the 1960s, an atheistic Christianity raised its head for a brief moment in the form of the so-called death-of-God theology. Shubert M. Ogden (1961) argued that to believe in Jesus Christ was in the last analysis nothing but ''to understand oneself authentically''—a self-understanding that, of course, occurs in all religions and by no means only in Jesus and in the faith of his followers. John Hick (1977, 1980, 1981), in turn, claimed that Jesus was purely human and that he was ''Christ'' only in the sense that ''Christs'' are to be found in all religions.

Crosscurrents within Roman Catholicism would include, for instance, the views of such liberal thinkers as Paul Knitter, Raimundo Panikkar, and Gregory Baum. Knitter (1978, 1985) feels impelled to question the uniqueness of Christ. It is interesting to note that the title of his recent book *No Other Name?* (1985) designedly ends with a question mark. Like Hick, Knitter contends that religions other than Christianity have saviors too. To him, a religion is ''true'' if it is *theocentric*—that is to say, *theo*centric rather than *Christo*centric. To Raimundo Panikkar (1981, 1978, 1972), ''Christ'' is synonymous with ''God the Son,'' ''the Word,'' ''Logos,'' and ''the Alpha and Omega'' but not with ''Jesus of Nazareth.'' Jesus was indeed Christ, but Christ is not to be identified with the person Jesus. The name that is above every other name (Phil 2:9) is not ''Jesus'' but ''Christ,'' and all religions in some way recognize the same ''Christ,'' ''Logos,'' and ''Son of God''—the mythic Christ that sanctifies and saves, even in non-Christian religions. This "Logos" is merely called by other names. No wonder Panikkar can say, "I 'left' as a Christian, I 'found' myself a Hindu and I 'return' a Buddhist without ever having ceased to be a Christian" (1978:2). In Gregory Baum's view, the preaching of the Christian message to convert members of other religions to Christianity is "a hidden form of aggression, a disguised attempt to triumph over other religious cultures" (1974:82). Consequently, "a rethinking of our theological tradition is necessary. Theologians must examine the possibility that the Church's missionary message exercises its salvational power where people in fact are, in their own cultural environment, enabling them to cling more faithfully to the best of their religious tradition and live the full personal and social implications of their religion more authentically" (1974:86). In other words, Baum seems to be saying: Leave Christ out of the picture; be satisfied with making the Hindu a better Hindu, a Moslem a better Moslem; evangelization is a tyranny.

Despite such crosscurrents, we cannot and must not limit our evangelization efforts to our own country and to our own culture (*Ad Gentes; Evangelii Nuntiandi* nos. 18, 50, 51, 53). The whole world is entitled to share in the faith of American Catholics. Yes, nothing less than "the *world* is our parish" (Wesley).

THE BENEFICIARIES IN THE UNITED STATES

General Observations

Let us look a little more closely at the *American* scene. Paul VI in *Evangelii Nuntiandi* identified five major categories of beneficiaries of evangelization, categories that are more or less valid throughout the Catholic world, and therefore also in the United States: (1) the active Catholics (no. 54); (2) the inactive Catholics (no. 56); (3) fellow-Christians who are not in full communion with Catholics (nos. 54, 77); (4) non-Christians (no. 53); (5) the unchurched (no. 57). None of these categories should be overlooked. In fact, as we have seen, we must as much as possible communicate the good news on the wavelength of the beneficiaries in question.

These five categories, however, as useful as they may be, form only the horizontal lines of a grid. To describe the concrete American scene, further delineation would be necessary. A whole set of cultural, sociological, and psychological subdivisions will be needed to form the vertical rows. Take as an example the first category, active Catholics. As is only too obvious, not all so-called active Catholics can be put into the same basket and treated alike. Among such active Catholics, you will find, for instance, dozens of ethnic groups, each with its own traditions, ways and values, aspirations, and unique soul; you will find youths and young adults with their way of looking at life and with aspirations and hopes peculiar to their generation; you will find urbanites, suburbanites, inner city people, and people living in rural areas with their subcultures; and there are the illiterates and the highly educated with their particular needs. There are, for instance, the handicapped active Catholics; there are the retarded, the alcoholics and drug adicts, and the mentally ill. These and many other considerations must be taken into account by the evangelizer. As obvious as all this may seem, it is unfortunately not so obvious in practice.

In the Gospel Jesus tells John's disciples, "Go back and report to John what you hear and see: the blind recover their sight, the cripples walk, lepers are cured, the deaf hear, dead men are raised to life, and the poor have the good news preached to them" (Mt 11:4). But who are the poor in the United States? The "poor" certainly are those we *normally* understand by "the poor"—the hungry, the homeless, the unemployed, the "street people," those deprived of the basic necessities of life, the immigrant farmer and refugee, and many many others—those with whom the Lord identified most closely and with whom we as his followers have cast our lot. The "poor" of the Bible represent a great variety of "poverty" (Léon-Dufour 1973:436–438). In fact, even the middle class and the wealthy can be "poor." Penniless or rich, you may be "poor," and the good news must be preached and witnessed to you in terms of *your* poverty, in terms of the type of liberation *you* need. Think, for instance, of the lonely and forgotten in our homes for the aged, the alienated and the seriously depressed or terminally ill sitting alone in their delapidated, or plush, apartments; they are all "poor" even if they happen to have all the money in the world; think of the juvenile delinquents, runaways, and the hardcore criminals; think of the pain of a broken family, penniless, middle class, or wealthy (they are all "poor"); think of the deaf, the mute, the blind, the alcoholics and drug addicts; think of the family that has lost someone through suicide or some other calamity—and we might go on and on. Yes, "the poor you will *always* have with you" (Mt 14:7), poor in different ways perhaps but genuinely poor nonetheless—all hungry for and entitled to the Bread we call Jesus Christ. To all these the good news must be preached, each in a slightly different way, but always in the way Christ would preach to them—in a language they could understand, in the language of the poor.

THE AMERICAN SCENE

The General Context

There is no country, large or small, that is as heterogeneous as the United States. The differentiation that we are speaking about has been primarily the function of the steady stream of immigrants and refugees, literally from all parts of the earth, a flow that began two centuries ago and has continued to this day. No less than seventeen million European immigrants passed through Ellis Island alone between 1892 and 1954. In fact, half of the American population today have either gone through Ellis Island themselves or their parents have. Millions have come, and are still coming, from Latin America and the Caribbean; others have come and are coming from the Orient, more recently especially from Southeast Asia, and others, still, from the Philippines. There are the native Americans, the Indians, who have been here long before any white man. Then, of course, there are the twenty-six million Afro-Americans, our black brothers and sisters, native to the land longer than most whites, who form some of the most important cultural groups in the land. American Catholicism has always reflected much of this heterogeneity. As late as 1960, statistics showed that no less than half of the Catholics in the United States were themselves foreign-born or had foreign-born parents. With the number of Hispanics steadily growing, in the hundreds of thousands, the Catholic Church in the United States can expect to remain an immigrant Church for many years to come.

Socio-economically, immigrant Catholics of the past were mostly poor, hard-working Europeans, usually with hardly more than an elementary education. They were blue-collar workers, underpaid, but somehow always hopeful—hopeful not so much for themselves as for those to follow them. They were mistrusted, often hated, and sometimes discriminated against even by lawmakers. The many churches, schools, institutions, and organizations that still exist today are monuments to a great faith and to great sacrifices. Understandably, American Catholics of the past developed a ghetto or fortress mentality, were very defensive, and focused their evangelization primarily on themselves—on the nurture of active Catholics and on the preservation of their faith.

Today American Catholics are of the middle class, perhaps too "middle"; generally they are as educated as any other middle class Americans, they are politically strong (with many senators and congressmen, and many political leaders on the national, state, and local levels), and after two centuries of mistrust and discrimination, Catholics have even had a president.

Despite our heterogeneity, we are not a melting-pot, and never have been. Some sociologists describe America more as a pressure cooker, or, better still, as a stew pot, that is, the potatoes remain potatoes, the beef or pork remains beef or pork, the carrots, turnips, and onions remain carrots, turnips, and onions—whatever goes to make up this remarkable tasty stew remains to a large extent what it was before, each ingredient, however, contributing to the distinctive aroma and taste of the stew while itself absorbing the aroma and flavor of all the other ingredients. That is the basic context in which American evangelization of today and tomorrow must take place: both the individual ingredients and the common flavor are important.

THE AMERICAN SCENE TODAY

Active Catholics

It is very difficult to say how many so-called active or practicing Catholics there are in the United States—I would venture to say somewhere perhaps between fifty and fifty-five million. It is strange that the country that can tell us how many toothpicks were produced last year and how many cigarettes were smoked in the last ten years cannot tell us how many Catholics there are. The *Official Catholic Directory* in this regard is thoroughly unreliable since it depends for its statistics on the good will of busy pastors and uninterested associates. What is of concern to us is to make sure that these so-called active Catholics are active evangelizing and witnessing their faith.[1] Also of concern to us should be not to forget to evangelize the evangelizer, including the hierarchy, priests, deacons, seminarians, religious, lay ministers and lay leaders. Bishop E. Walsh, M.M. was certainly concerned when he reminded his fellow-missionaries:

> The task of a missioner is to go to a place where he is not wanted, to sell a pearl whose value, although of great price, is not recognized, to people who are determined not to accept it even as a gift. . . . To accomplish this he need not be a saint but he must come close to passing for one. And in order to achieve this hoax, he must do so many things that a saint does, that it becomes for him a serious question if the easiest way is not simply to be a saint in the first place and be done with it. (Cited from Bishop Andrew G. Grutka, *Grateful Reflections of a Bishop* 1977:11)

Nominal Catholics

The problem of nominal Catholicism is a worldwide concern. Although frightening, Gallup statistics have shown that about a quarter (twenty-four percent) of all U.S. Catholics should not even be labeled as nominal Catholics but rather simply as unchurched. The reasons for the large number of inactive Catholics are many.[2] Sometimes trivial excuses are offered, but often the reasons are serious indeed. The sad part is that while some Catholics abandon their faith on account of unavoidable situations (e.g., mobility due to employment), many do so for reasons that could have been corrected but were not (e.g., the overall impersonalism of some priests and parishes). Regrettable too is the fact that many parishes do not have a budget or an organized program for contacting nominal Catholics and inviting them back.[3] With almost nineteen thousand parishes in the United States and some fifty million-plus active Catholics, the potential to bring a large number of the fifteen million inactive Catholics back to the Church is there. It is sometimes said that very few Catholics leave their Church for theological reasons, a claim I personally would question. We Americans are actually swimming in heresy. I mean the heresy of secularism, materialism, hedonism, sexism, extreme personalism (i.e., nobody and nothing counts except me), scientism (i.e., an idolatrous worship of science and technology), satisfaction with a purely civil religion that neutralizes most of the Gospel, and a greedy rather than just economic system, allowing profit to decide what should or should not be done. This is the air we breathe day in and day out in America. That the spiritual health of so many of us should be affected should not surprise us but should rather spur us active Catholics on to ever greater and more meaningful action and witness.

Ecumenism

Ecumenism is mutually enriching. It is the first step to interdenominational understanding and, we hope, in God's time, Christian unity. (Gallup statistics have shown there are approximately seventy-five million Protestants in the United States.) Through respectful dialogue and cooperation wherever possible we can learn much from one another.[4] While Catholics might lead their Christian brothers and sisters not fully in communion with them to appreciate, for instance, Christian sacramental life more than they do, Catholics in turn might learn to believe and appreciate what Catholics already hold, that the Bible is indeed the Word of *God*. Catholics might also learn, for instance, much about true Christian fellowship. Both Catholics and Protestants can teach each other much about the centrality of Christ in our lives and about an asceticism built around the active presence of the Holy Spirit. And what could be more enriching than to see members of Christ's own body weep together over their brokenness and disunity.

Non-Christians

For a good number of years now, American Catholics were represented by no less than six to seven thousand missionaries all over the world—something, of course, that we can rightly be proud of and in fact we should increase our efforts to provide evangelizers for distant lands. What does make me wonder is why we seem so unconcerned about the twelve million non-Christians in our own backyard? Yes, there are twelve million Moslems, Hindus, Buddhists and other non-Christians here in the United States. The largest body of non-Christians are, of course, our Jewish brothers and sisters, about six million in all. Respectful dialogue and cooperation wherever possible, especially with those of the Jewish faith, could bring many mutually beneficial insights into our faiths.[5] The Jew might teach us something about God as our Father and, in fact, teach us much about Jesus' own innermost Jewish feelings and values. We Christians, in turn, could make Jewish people appreciate more and more that one of their sons was indeed a great prophet and teacher meant for all humankind, meant also for them.

The Unchurched

In a monumental study by Gallup, *The Unchurched American* (1978), forty-one percent of all Americans over the age of eighteen (some sixty-one million adults in all), and eighteen percent of Catholics (the so-called nominal Catholics, numbering eleven million) do not belong to any organized religion or have not worshiped in a church, synagogue, or temple for six months or more. Like nominal Catholics, the unchurched give a variety of reasons for their lack of interest in joining a church, synagogue, or temple. The reasons should be studied, since they may give the evangelizer a clue as how best to approach these potential beneficiaries:[6] sixty percent of the unchurched, for instance, feel that organized religion has lost its spiritual purpose; fifty-six percent say that it is too concerned with organizational as opposed to theological or spiritual issues; almost half (forty-nine percent) feel that churches and synagogues are not effective in finding meaning to life. On the other hand, the evangelizer should be greatly encouraged by such statistics as:

Seventy-five percent of the unchurched pray to God;
Seventy-four percent want religious education for their children;
Sixty-eight percent believe in the resurrection of Christ;
Sixty-four percent believe in the divinity of Christ;
Fifty-seven percent believe in an afterlife;
Twenty-four percent have experienced a particularly powerful religious insight
    or awakening.

Also very encouraging is the fact that fifty-two percent can see a situation right now where they could become active members of a church or synagogue. Father Alvin A. Illig, C.S.P., commenting on these statistics rightly points out:

> The great challenge to us Catholics is not that the unchurched exist in great numbers. The great challenge is how do we inspire our Catholic people to develop more effective ways to enter into dialogue with unchurched Americans. . . . (Special Newsfeature, National Conference of Catholic Bishops, Ad Hoc Committee on Evangelization)

CONCLUSION

Christ is the light of the *world*, and the good news is for *all* humankind despite the differences in ways and mentality, with their own soul and special needs. The proclamation and witness of the good news must be tailored as much as possible to this human pluriformity. The best evangelizer, therefore, is not the best *preacher* but the best *listener*. The best evangelizer is the one who has identified his or her beneficiaries, knows their felt-needs, and evangelizes accordingly.

NOTES

1. An excellent diocesan program of evangelization that might well serve as model for others is that of the Archdiocese of Cincinnati, described in a brochure entitled *Witness to Christ* distributed by the Paulist National Catholic Evangelization Association, 3031 Fourth Street, N.E., Washington, D.C. 20017. Other useful materials are available from the same source, e.g., "Creating in the Catholic Community a Receptive Atmosphere for Catholic Evangelization."

2. Reasons why American Catholics leave their Church are succinctly spelled out in brochures by Alvin A. Illig, C.S.P., "Getting a Handle on Evangelization in America," and "Another Look: A National Ministry for the Inactive Catholic." For a sociological study of inactive Catholics see *Converts, Dropouts, Returnees* by Dr. Dean Hoge (1981), available from the United States Catholic Conference, Washington, D.C. For the recent (1985) Gallup figures, see *Attitudes of Unchurched Americans Toward the Roman Catholic Church,* conducted for the Paulist National Catholic Evangelization Association. (This NCEA publication includes in its Technical Appendix two very practical considerations: "The Inactive Catholics/How Do We Reach Them?" and "New Personalized Parish Program for Inactive Catholics."

3. A very useful book is William McKee, C.SS.R, *How To Reach Out to Inactive Catholics,* a Ligouri Publication (1982).

4. See paper by Alvin A. Illig, C.S.P., "What Catholics and Protestants Can Learn from One Another about Evangelization," available at the Paulist National Catholic Evangelization Association, Washington, D.C.

5. For the controversy on whether those following the Jewish tradition should be evangelized, see Gerald H. Anderson, "The Church and the Jewish People: Some Theological Issues and Missiological Concerns," *Missiology* 1974, 3:279–293; and Eugene J. Fisher, "Interpreting *Nostra Aetate* through Postconciliar Teaching," *International Bulletin of Missionary Research,* vol. 9, 1985, pp. 158–165.

6. Useful one-sheet papers on evangelizing the unchurched are "Ser-

vices a Diocesan Office for the Evangelization and Religiously Alienated Could Develop for Parish Use" and Alvin A. Illig, C.S.P., "Fourteen Principles for Evangelizing the Unchurched American," both available at the Paulist National Catholic Evangelization Association, Washington, D.C. See especially the 1985 Gallup study referred to above in Note 2.

DISCUSSION QUESTIONS

1. Why be so concerned about identifying the particular beneficiaries of evangelization?
2. Name the five basic beneficiaries.
3. Name some of the special groups of beneficiaries in America.
4. Discuss some of the approaches to these special groups that you feel are needed and possible.

FOR FURTHER READING

D.J. Hesselgrave, *Communicating Christ Cross-Culturally.* Grand Rapids: Zondervan Publishing House, 1978. A practical, non-technical introduction to intercultural communication of Christianity. Excellent and not too technical. 511 pages.

J. Holland and P. Henriot, *Social Analysis: Linking Faith and Justice.* Maryknoll, N.Y.: Orbis Books, 1983. A practical handbook for those interested in social action as a form of evangelization. The authors show how the evangelizer can concretize the Gospel of the poor through careful analysis of actual needs and social structure. 118 pages.

L.J. Luzbetak, *The Church and Cultures: An Applied Anthropology for the Religious Worker.* Pasadena, CA: William Carey Library, Publishers. 4th WCL Printing 1984. A basic introductory course in anthropological concepts and principles useful for cultural and subcultural evangelization. 431 pages.

R.J. Schreiter, *Constructing Local Theologies.* Maryknoll, N.Y.: Orbis Books, 1985. Shows how by identifying and clarifying the basic theological and culturological characteristics of a particular society, the evangelizer is to proceed in constructing a living theology for the people concerned. 178 pages.

B. Quinn and J. Bookser-Feister, *Apostolic Regions of the United States: 1980.* Atlanta: Glenmary Research Center, 1978. The United States is divided into nine regions according to the types of beneficiaries of evangelization concerned. With a useful bibliography. 53 pages.

REFERENCES
(Those not mentioned in *Notes* or *For Further Reading*)

G. Baum and Ch. W. Forman
  1974 "Is There a Missionary Message?" in *Mission Trends No. 1*, pp. 75–86. Edited by G.H. Anderson and Th. F. Stransky, C.S.P. New York/Paramus/Toronto: Paulist Press and Grand Rapids: Eerdmans.

C.F. Burke
  1966 *God Is for Real, Man: interpretations of Bible passages and stories as told by some of God's bad-tempered angels with busted halos to Carl F. Burke*. New York: Association Press.

J. Hick
  1977 "Jesus and the World Religions," in *The Myth of God Incarnate*, John Hick, ed. SCM Press, 167–185.
  1980 "Whatever Path Men Choose Is Mine," in *Christianity and Other Religions*, J. Hick and B. Hebblethwaite, eds. Philadelphia: Fortress, 171–190.
  1981 "On Grading Religions," *Religious Studies*, 17:451–467.

P. Knitter
  1978 "A Critique of Hans Küng's *On Being a Christian*," *Horizons*, 5:151–164.
  1985 *No Other Name? A Critical Survey of Christian Attitudes Toward the World Religions*. Maryknoll, N.Y.: Orbis Books.

X. Léon-Dufour
  1973 *Dictionary of Biblical Theology*. (rev. ed.) Leon-Dufour, ed. New York: Seabury Press.

S.M. Ogden
  1961 *Christ Without Myth*. New York: Harper & Row.

R. Pannikar
  1972 "The Meaning of Christ's Name in the Universal Economy of Salvation," in *Evangelization, Dialogue, and Development*, M. Dhavamony, ed. Rome: Gregorian University Press, 195–218.
  1978 "The Category of Growth in Comparative Religion: A Critical Self-Examination," in *The Intrareligious Dialogue*. New York: Paulist Press, 53–73.
  1981 *The Unknown Christ of Hinduism*. Maryknoll, N.Y.: Orbis Books (rev. ed.), 1–30.

K. Rahner
1979 "Towards a Fundamental Theological Interpretation of Vatican II," in *Catholic Mind,* September 1980, 44–56; *Theological Studies,* December 1979, 716–727.

The Princeton Religious Research Center and The Gallup Organization, Inc.
1978 *The Unchurched American.* Princeton, New Jersey.

THE WORKERS FOR EVANGELIZATION

Marsha Whelan

Recently a bishop spoke to me about *Evangelii Nuntiandi*. He had just finished meditating on it for a week, taking a different chapter each day for his prayer. And he said to me, "It is all here."

After six years of involvement in evangelization ministry in the Archdiocese of Miami, I share the view of that bishop; it is "all here" in *Evangelii Nuntiandi*. Pope Paul VI's apostolic exhortation is one of the most significant documents of the Catholic Church in the twentieth century. As more and more people become aware of it, read it, understand it, and make its vision their own, it will be a major influence in transforming our country and our American culture.

Part of the "all here" in the document is a chapter on the workers for evangelization. Pope Paul writes not only about the workers but also about their different tasks in a Church which emphasizes shared responsibility and collaboration. Each of us must understand our own tasks in evangelization as well as the tasks of others in order to support and encourage each other to fulfill our vocation as baptized Catholic Christians.

Pope Paul VI begins with reflections with these seven points which establish the context for the work of evangelization:

- the Church as missionary in her entirety
- evangelization as an ecclesial act
- the perspective of the universal Church
- the perspective of the local church
- adaptation and fidelity in expression
- openness to the universal Church
- the unchangeable deposit of faith

(EN nos. 60–65)

In reflecting on the Church as missionary in her entirety Paul VI restates what appeared in *Ad Gentes* from Vatican II: ". . . the whole Church is missionary, and the work of evangelization is a basic duty of the people of God."[1] We know from the very beginning of Chapter 6 that each of us has a role in evangelization.

84

Effective evangelization, however, calls for a balance in the relationships that exist in the Church in order to preserve her unity as well as to preserve her fidelity to the message and to the people to whom the message must be transmitted. A balance must be maintained between the universal Church and local churches, between adapting the message so people can hear it and fidelity to the expression of the message. The responsibility for maintaining these delicate balances rests with the Church leadership—the Pope with his fellow bishops and the clergy who assist the bishops.

THE EVANGELIZERS

Pope Paul VI begins his reflection on the actual workers for evangelization by commenting first on those who share in the sacrament of orders and then on religious and laity. While seemingly hierarchical, this approach stems from responsibilities rather than from status, position, power, or state of life. All baptized Catholics are called to evangelize, to carry on the mission of Christ. If Church leaders do not grasp hold of their responsibilities, however, the laity will be less effective in their mission. Pope Paul VI highlights the integral relationship among all workers for evangelization when he writes,

> The whole Church therefore is called upon to evangelize, and yet within her we have different evangelizing tasks to accomplish. This diversity of services in the unity of the same mission makes up the richness and beauty of evangelization (EN no. 66).

Paul VI ascribes to the Pope the evangelizing task of preacher of the good news of salvation and teacher of the revealed truth. He says, "The full, supreme and universal power which Christ gives to his Vicar for the pastoral government of his Church is thus especially exercised by the Pope in the activity of preaching and causing to be preached the good news of salvation" (EN no. 67). Pope Paul VI witnessed masterfully to his evangelizing task by producing the document *Evangelii Nuntiandi*.

As Pope Paul develops his vision for the workers of evangelization he states clearly that his teaching and preaching mission is shared with his brother bishops:

> The Second Vatican Council wished to reaffirm this when it declared that "Christ's mandate to preach the Gospel to every creature (cf Mark 16:15) primarily and immediately concerns the bishops with Peter and under Peter" (EN no. 67).

Preaching the good news of salvation in America primarily and immediately concerns our three hundred and ninety bishops. They have the responsibility to see that the Gospel is transmitted to all people of the United States.

Another evangelizing task belonging to the bishops is that of teacher of the faith. As Paul VI writes,

> In union with the successor of Peter, the bishops who are the successors of the apostles receive through the power of their episcopal ordination the authority to teach the revealed truth in the Church. They are teachers of the faith (EN no. 68).

That faith, the basic content of evangelization, stems from a covenant relationship with our God. It is a faith that mirrors in all of our human relationships—as individuals and as a community—that intimate relationship we share with our living and personal God. Our doctrines and dogmas, worship, prayer, community and Christian service are meant to reflect this covenant relationship with a God who loves intimately and unconditionally. Teaching that fundamental faith is the responsibility of our American bishops.

A further evangelizing task of the Pope and bishops deals with the effective communication of the Gospel. As Paul VI writes,

> On us particularly, the pastors of the Church, rests the responsibility for reshaping with boldness and wisdom, but in complete fidelity to the content of evangelization, the means that are most suitable and effective for communicating the Gospel message to the men and women of our times (EN no. 40).

The responsibility for finding effective methods to share the Gospel rests with our bishops.

The bishops, linked with the Holy Father in their leadership role in evangelization, are also linked to the priests and deacons in the diocese. The clergy share the leadership role of the bishop at the parish level. Reflecting on the clergy, Pope Paul writes, "They are educators of the people of God in the faith and preachers, while at the same time being ministers of the Eucharist and the other sacraments" (EN no. 68).

Paul VI sums up his reflection on those who share the sacrament of orders—the Pastor of the universal Church, the bishops who head the local churches, and the priests and deacons who are united with their bishop—with a clear statement of their task:

> . . . as pastors, we have been chosen by the mercy of the Supreme Pastor, in spite of our inadequacy, to proclaim with authority the

Word of God, to assemble the scattered people of God, to feed this people with the signs of the action of Christ which are the sacraments, to set this people on the road to salvation, to maintain it in that unity of which we are, at different levels, active and living instruments, and unceasingly to keep this community gathered around Christ, faithful to its deepest vocation. And when we do all these things, within our human limits and by the grace of God, it is a work of evangelization that we are carrying out (EN no. 68).

This paragraph tells us that fostering the inner spiritual growth and life of the ecclesial community and promoting unity is the major evangelization task of the clergy.

An evangelizing task of Church leadership at all levels is to keep the people of God faithful to their vocation. And what is that vocation? According to Paul VI:

Evangelizing is in fact the grace and vocation proper to the Church, her deepest identity. She exists in order to evangelize, that is to say, in order to preach and teach, to be the channel of the gift of grace, to reconcile sinners with God, and to perpetuate Christ's sacrifice in the Mass, which is the memorial of his death and glorious resurrection (EN no. 14).

The Catholic parish is the locus in which most of us live out this vocation. We gather in the parish to hear the word, to be taught, to share the bread of life, to experience together God's love, to share intimate life. It is from the parish that we are sent into the world: ''Go into the whole world and proclaim the gospel to every creature'' (Mk 16:15). The gathering, the teaching, the preaching, and the sending is the evangelizing task of the parish clergy as outlined by Paul VI.

Paul VI links the parish clergy to another group called to assist them in their task—the laity who minister within the Church. They minister in numerous areas such as liturgy, religious education, youth education, and outreach as well as to the handicapped and imprisoned. While most of these ministers are volunteers, some receive formal training as lay ministers and others are paid members of the parish staff. Commenting on lay ministers within the Church, Pope Paul VI writes,

. . . the laity can also feel themselves called, or be called, to work with their pastors in the service of the ecclesial community, for its growth and life, by exercising a great variety of ministries according to the grace and charisms which the Lord is pleased to give them.

> . . . side by side with the ordained ministries . . . the Church rec-
> ognizes the place of non-ordained ministries which are able to offer
> a particular service to the Church (EN no. 73).

It is important that this group understand their role of keeping the community faithful to its deepest vocation. In terms of evangelization that means changing the status quo within the Church from one of Catholic "maintenance" to one of forming missionary Catholics who will be a powerful leaven in the world.

A perusal of the Kenedy Directory reveals some interesting data about this Church leadership group which I have discussed thus far. The number of bishops, priests, deacons, religious sisters and brothers totals about 188,000. This number seems small compared to the total Catholic population of fifty-two million. The data reveal that Church leaders who carry out evangelization tasks comprise .004% of the total Catholic population. Even if we tripled the 188,000 and said that number included laity involved in Church ministry we would end up with about one percent of the total Catholic population. If all baptized Catholics are workers for evangelization, the remaining ninety-nine percent must have a very important role. The Lord gives the largest task to the most numerous group: he calls them to use their gifts and talents to evangelize all strata of American society.

THE LAITY

In the beginning of the document Paul VI defines evangelization as ". . . bringing the good news into all the strata of humanity, and through its influence transforming humanity from within and making it new . . ." (EN no. 18). Later he gives us a clue as to who will do it and how it is to be done:

> . . . if the preaching of the Gospel is to be effective, she must ad-
> dress her message to the heart of the multitudes, to communities of
> the faithful whose action can and must reach others (EN no. 57).

Paul VI says we need to address the message to the hearts of the fifty-two million American Catholics so they can reach others with the good news which can transform all strata of humanity.

Imagine our Catholic parishes on a Sunday morning. Do we see people from all strata of humanity in America? Yes—they are rich, poor, and everything in between; they come from all walks of life. They earn a living in virtually every kind of job and some are jobless. They live in every kind of neighborhood and some are homeless. They are well educated and they are illiterate. They socialize with all kinds of people and some are lonely. They are black and brown, yellow and white, and anything in between. They speak every kind of language. They are immigrants and exiles as well as political and economic refugees. They are sons and daughters of the American Revolution and they are native Americans. They make up the communities of believers; they are the ones who share ''intimate life,'' listening to the Word of God, living fraternal charity, sharing the bread of life. They are the ones whose ''intimate life'' ''only acquires its full meaning when it becomes a witness, when it evokes admiration and conversion, and when it becomes the preaching of the good news'' (EN no. 15). They are the ones sent to America. They are the laity.

Pope Paul VI writes clearly about the evangelizing work of the laity:

> Lay people, whose particular vocation places them in the midst of the world and in charge of the most varied temporal tasks, must for this very reason exercise a very special form of evangelization.
>
> Their primary and immediate task is not to establish and develop the ecclesial community—this is the specific role of the pastors—but to put to use every Christian and evangelical possibility latent but already present and active in the affairs of the world. . . . The more Gospel-inspired lay people there are engaged in these realities, clearly involved in them, competent to promote them and conscious that they must exercise to the full their Christian powers which are often buried and suffocated, the more these realities will be at the service of the kingdom of God and therefore of salvation in Jesus Christ . . . (EN no. 70).

Lay people especially are called to evangelize our culture ''. . . as it were upsetting, through the power of the Gospel, mankind's criteria of judgement, determining values, points of interest, lines of thought, sources of inspiration and models of life, which are in contrast to the Word of God and plan of salvation'' (EN no. 19). What other Church in America can say it touches all strata of humanity? What other Church can say it has fifty-two million people to send? What would be the impact if this ''sleeping giant,'' the Catholic Church in America, woke up to a new vision of evangelization?

While we are imagining our 19,000 Catholic parishes on a Sunday morning, let me pose another question. Whom don't we see, at least in any great numbers? We don't see those who are unable to come because they live in institutions—prisoners in correctional facilities, the elderly in nursing homes or congregate living facilities, the mentally and emotionally ill who are unable to cope. How do we share that ''intimate life'' of God with them? How do we unceasingly keep them faithful to their deepest vocation? Do we really believe they can and do evangelize their world?

We don't see some of our brother and sister Catholics who make us feel uncomfortable because we do not know how to cope with them—the mentally retarded, particularly those living in institutions or group homes, the physically handicapped and the deaf, blind, and crippled. How do we share "intimate life" with them? How do we make them aware of their deepest vocation? Do we believe they can and do evangelize their world?

We don't see some of our brother and sister Catholics who feel uncomfortable with us—those who are separated and divorced and/or remarried, those involved in abortions, the gay community and many immigrants, exiles and refugees. How do we share "intimate life" with them? How do we keep them faithful to their deepest vocation? Do we really believe they can and do evangelize? Are we the older son in the story of the prodigal son or do we rejoice when our brother or sister returns home?

Perhaps these are the first groups to which we need to extend a hand of friendship. Our American black bishops have given us a beautiful gift in their pastoral letter on evangelization, *What We Have Seen and Heard*. In it we read:

Let us who are children of pain be now a bridge of reconciliation.[2]

The Gospel message is a message that liberates us from hate and calls us to forgiveness and reconciliation. . . . Reconciliation can never mean unilateral elevation and another's subordination, unilateral giving and another's constant receiving, unilateral flexibility and another's resistance. True reconciliation arises only when there is mutually perceived equality. This is what is meant by justice.[3]

Do we see those missing on Sunday as equals and do they see us as equals? All of us stand before our God as equals; all of us are invited into an intimate relationship with God. We are poorer without our missing brothers and sisters. Our world is poorer without their evangelizing efforts.

RELIGIOUS

Another group that Paul VI focuses attention on as workers for evangelization are the religious. They too are involved with the mission and inner life of the ecclesial community through various ministries which are more and more shared with the laity. Twenty years after Vatican II, I see the religious as a link between Church leadership and the laity concerning the future of evangelization.

Paul VI writes of the gift of religious to the Church:

At the deepest level of their being they are caught up in the dynamism of the Church's life, which is thirsty for the Divine Absolute
and called to holiness. It is to this holiness that they bear witness.
They embody the Church in her desire to give herself completely to
the radical demands of the beatitudes (EN no. 69).

Religious challenge the world and *the Church herself* because of their public
commitment to live solely for Christ. Religious men and women highlight the
universal call to holiness, a call rooted in prayer and action. The Gospel message which gives light in their prayer also moves them to loving action in their
communities, neighborhoods, and work places. Their prayer acquires a richer
meaning when it stirs the radical demands of the beatitudes.

Religious also give example of life lived in Christian community. The
prayer and action is not just lived individually; it is a community witness which
challenges all Church members to live that prayer and Gospel action as a total
community of believers.

In the years since Vatican II, the religious in our country have taken to
heart the call of Vatican II to renew their lives and witness to holiness. They
have gone back to the roots of their founders and foundresses as well as examined the American scene in which they are called to live out their charisms.
Many religious have reflected on the question posed at the beginning of *Evangelii Nuntiandi:* namely, do we find ourselves "better equipped to proclaim
the Gospel and to put it into people's hearts with conviction, freedom of spirit
and effectiveness?" (EN no. 4).

This questioning and probing among religious has not come without criticism, nor has it come free from pain and struggle both from within and outside
of religious communities. It has not come without the inner struggle of being
confronted with the Gospel message and allowing oneself to be transformed
by that message. As a result some religious remained in the same ministry and
others moved into new ministries and joined others in their struggle for freedom, justice, peace, and liberation from all kinds of oppression. The pain and
the struggles are a witness to the cross and that followers of Jesus must travel
the road to Calvary to reach resurrection.

In a Church that calls all of its members to holiness and to the transformation of all strata of humanity, religious give witness that it is possible to
open one's heart to the transforming Gospel message and, in turn, transform
the world according to Gospel values. Each of us will experience a similar
process as we let ourselves be confronted by the Gospel and take up our own
evangelizing tasks.

WHAT NEEDS TO BE DONE AND WHAT TRAINING IS NEEDED

Paul VI does not give specific reflections regarding training except to say "serious preparation is needed" (EN no. 73), especially for those engaged in the ministry of the Word. I believe the critical need for the American Church is clear: reaching the fifty-two million laity in America (ninety-nine percent of our Catholics) and awakening them to their evangelizing task. This requires that all others in the Church take up their evangelizing tasks. Signs of this new era of evangelization are beginning to occur at every level of the Church.

The Extraordinary Synod held in Rome in November and December 1985 is one such sign. It has given Church leadership the opportunity to reflect on the past twenty years and address whether or not the Church is better equipped to proclaim the Gospel message. At the level of our own episcopal conference, the NCCB Ad Hoc Committee on Evangelization is being reactivated and committee members presented a broad vision statement on evangelization which the full body of bishops passed unanimously at the November 1985 meeting. Similarly, the American black bishops have given Americans our own document on evangelization in *What We Have Seen and Heard.* On diocesan levels, more evangelization offices are being established and more dioceses are joining the National Council for Catholic Evangelization. At the parish level, at least in the Archdiocese of Miami, more pastors and priests are taking an interest in evangelization. Our diocesan evangelization training programs for parishes are full as is our schedule for the year.

Despite these signs of hope, many things remain to be done if our culture is to be transformed. I would like to offer a few suggestions, again at each level within the American context beginning with the Bishops' Conference. I urge the bishops to support national groups such as the National Council for Catholic Evangelization who assist the bishops in fulfilling their primary responsibility for evangelization. I also urge them to place evangelization as a top priority within the American Church.

I urge bishops to evangelize actively in the dioceses: encourage people to read *Evangelii Nuntiandi;* support the NCCB Vision Statement on Evangelization; circulate and urge people to read *What We Have Seen and Heard;* develop a plan for evangelization in the diocese if you do not already have one; educate your clergy and religious in their roles and tasks in the evangelization process; provide the resources for them to accomplish their tasks; preach on evangelization and call forth your clergy to do the same to assist you in your task. Evangelization takes root through diverse and persevering efforts. Moreover, parish priests need to evangelize not only through their own ministry but also by enabling others to witness and proclaim the good news of salvation to the world in which they live.

The renewal of preaching is a critical task ahead in order to equip Catholics to evangelize. In addressing the topic of the Liturgy of the Word in the chapter entitled "Methods for Evangelization" Paul VI states:

> This preaching, inserted in a unique way into the Eucharistic cele-
> bration, from which it receives special force and vigor, certainly has
> a particular role in evangelization, to the extent that it expresses the
> profound faith of the sacred minister and is impregnated with love
> (EN no. 43)

Preaching is an evangelizing tool and is effective to the extent that the preacher communicates a "profound faith." An effective preacher deals with such questions as, "How have I really experienced the saving act of Jesus' death and resurrection in my life? How has Jesus freed me from sin?" This "profound faith" needs to be communicated in our Sunday preaching to the fifty-two million because it helps them begin to reflect on their own lives and identify the healing love of Jesus in their experience.

More specific training is needed for our Catholic laity once they have been awakened to their mission. Let me reflect on my experience in the Archdiocese of Miami. We began our evangelizing program with the intention of training people for specific outreach ministry such as home visiting and door-to-door evangelization. We discovered that all who came to the training did not have the gift necessary for these specific tasks. However, the training still met their needs because it gave them the skills to proclaim the Gospel in the everyday world in which they live—in their families, neighborhoods, work places, and social groups. These Catholics are the majority of the fifty-two million; they are called to evangelize in the everyday circumstances of their lives. Paul VI says in this document that witness of life is important but it must lead to the actual proclamation of the Gospel. Generally our people do not know how to do that. Our people need training to effectively proclaim the good news of salvation.

What does that involve? First, it involves helping people identify and reflect on the experience of God in their life. I am referring here to conversion experiences. Second, Catholics need to be able to articulate simply and clearly the ways in which God has changed their lives. Third, they need to be able to share that with others in a meaningful way. Fourth, they need to be able to share the basic content of the good news as found in Scripture and the Catholic tradition. Finally, they need to discover that the circles in which they travel are just the places the Lord Jesus wants them to be to proclaim the message.

As a Church we are indeed fortunate to have many lay Catholics teaching in our schools, working in our parishes, and ministering in our hospitals and social service agencies. We need to train and empower them to take over the administration of these as the numbers of priests and religious decrease. However, these laity comprise only a small percentage of the fifty-two million Catholics. We also need to affirm and train those lay Catholics teaching in our public institutions, working in "a secular environment," and ministering in secular hospitals. They need to know that they are the ones who are essential for the transformation of all strata of American society.

CONCLUSION

Jesus said to his disciples:

I do not pray for these alone. I pray for those who will believe in me through their word, that all may be one as you, Father, are in me and I in you: I pray that they may be one in us that the world may believe that you sent me . . . I living in them, you living in me that their unity may be complete. So shall the world know that you sent me and that you love them as you loved me (Jn 17:20–23).

These words from John's Gospel capture for me the essence of our evangelization mission. As a community of believers, we are called to mirror the relationships of the God community—Father, Son, Spirit. We share God's life through his gracious gift so that the world sees in us the reflection of a God whose heart longs for union with all God's creatures. Because we share in God's covenant love through baptism, we are called to invite others to share it; God's love is meant for all. Sharing the good news of God's love will not happen without all the workers for evangelization—it is a matter of people's salvation.

NOTES

1. Austin Flannery, O.P., ed., "Decree on the Church's Missionary Activity," No. 35, *Vatican Council II* (Northport, New York: Costello Publishing Company, 1975).

2. American black bishops pastoral on evangelization, *What We Have Seen and Heard* (Cincinnati, Ohio: St. Anthony Messenger Press, 1984), p. 8.

3. *Ibid.,* pp. 6–7.

DISCUSSION QUESTIONS

1. In what ways do you see yourself as servant of the Gospel message? In the past year, how have you been faithful in transmitting it to others according to your particular evangelizing task?

2. Who in your life keeps you faithful to your deepest vocation to evangelize? How is this done?

3. What can your parish community do to assist you in fulfilling your evangelizing task? What can your bishop do?

4. What can you do to assist your parish community in its evangelizing task? What can you do to help your bishop in his evangelizing task?

5. How do you experience salvation concretely in your life? How do you share that experience with others? What would help you to do that more effectively?

FOR FURTHER READING

"Decree on the Apostolate of the Lay People" from *Vatican Council II* (Northport, New York: Costello Publishing Company, 1975). This decree highlights each lay person's baptismal vocation in the lay apostolate. It includes discussion on lay spirituality, the family, and young people as well as the need for appropriate training.

"What We Have Seen and Heard": A Pastoral Letter on Evangelization from the Black Bishops of the United States (Cincinnati, Ohio: St. Anthony Messenger Press, 1984). A comprehensive and insightful vision of evangelization gives rise to a need for effective evangelizers.

Section II

The Broad Horizon
of Catholic Evangelization

CONVERSION: THE UNDERLYING DYNAMIC OF EVANGELIZATION

Robert D. Duggan

INTRODUCTION

In a crucial passage of *Evangelii Nuntiandi,* Paul VI asserts that "interior change" is the purpose of evangelization, "and if it had to be expressed in one sentence the best way of stating it would be to say that the Church evangelizes when she seeks to convert, solely through the divine power of the message she proclaims, both the personal and collective consciences of people, the activities in which they engage, and the lives and concrete milieu which are theirs" (#18). It would be difficult to find a more sweeping statement than this of the centrality of conversion in the Church's mission to evangelize. If, indeed, it is conversion that is the underlying dynamic of evangelization—and we believe that is in fact the case—then a sustained reflection on conversion is not only appropriate but called for in a collection such as the present one.

In this essay we wish to consider the rich understanding of conversion which our tradition affords us, with the conviction that a better grasp of that elusive, mysterious reality will result in a more fruitful praxis of evangelization as well. The issue is an important one, because we are exposed regularly to ideas about conversion which are defective, incomplete or even erroneous. The issue is also a complex one, and its consequences are significant. If one misperceives the nature of the conversion experience, pastoral agendas can be off target, ecclesial structures deformed, and God's children led astray rather than in the paths of the Gospel. No more graphic illustration of this can be offered than the horrible events of November 18, 1978. On that day, 912 members of the People's Temple, a religious sect whose adherents had undergone a "conversion experience," gathered at the community's main pavilion and one-by-one consumed a strawberry flavored drink mixed with heavy doses of cyanide, tranquilizers, and pain-killers. "It is time to die with dignity," James Jones told his followers. And the converts came forward in orderly procession—infants first, followed by entire families—to play out the last bizarre act in a conversion journey that had gone from trust to madness.

Jonestown was admittedly a limit situation. But conversion, even healthy and authentic conversion, has always operated at the limits of "common

sense.'' The early Christians sang joyful songs as they entered the amphithea-
ter to die; Francis of Assisi's conversion led him to strip naked before the
bishop in the town square; Luther's conversion led him out of the Church of
his birth; Spanish conquistadores ''converted'' the natives of the New World
under the threat of death. The examples could be multiplied many times over,
but the point should be obvious: In dealing with conversion we treat a volatile
reality with explosive potential. Lest it destroy the very faith it is meant to
evoke, the ministry of conversion which we exercise in evangelizing must be
based on sound understandings and solid tradition.

AN AMERICAN IMAGE OF CONVERSION

The reflection on conversion which this essay suggests is particularly appropriate in a collection which strives to capture the distinctively American
manner in which *Evangelii Nuntiandi* is to be received. Christian people of
every time and place have had their unique ways of understanding conversion
and of evangelizing in light of that understanding. The American people, however, are second to none in the cultural importance they attach to a religious
conversion experience. Ours is a nation whose founders sought a place of freedom to live out the consequences of their religious faith, and our cultural my-
thology is inextricably linked to many of the great biblical conversion motifs.
The New England Puritans nurtured on John Bunyan's *Grace Abounding to
the Chief of Sinners,* his spiritual autobiography, developed a deep sensitivity
to religious experience through their constant preoccupation with the inner
workings of grace. Under the psychological sophistication and theological acu-
men of Jonathan Edwards, a refined image of the conversion experience received a distinctively American stamp. It was this image which the Great
Awakening of the last century saw translated into revivalism, an evangelization strategy which flows directly from a particular vision of conversion.

That characteristically American approach to conversion and evangelization is deeply imbedded in the national consciousness, thanks to a series of
powerful preachers from Billy Sunday to Billy Graham. This approach, which
can be aptly described as a ''fundamentalist understanding of conversion,'' is
constantly reinforced in the media, with stories of dramatic conversions to ex-
otic religious cults and with intense personal witnessing from prominent
''born-again'' personalities, eager to share their conversion experience with
others.

Our reflection from the American perspective cannot ignore this fundamentalist understanding of conversion, since traces of its influence are to be
found within our Catholic communities as well. But the breadth of the theological and ascetical traditions to which we as Roman Catholics are heirs al-

lows us to critique its adequacy, noting its shortcomings and offering richer alternatives.

The image of conversion operative in the fundamentalist perspective is powerfully evocative, charged as it is with religious story and symbol that resonate with the high drama of great figures from the pages of Scripture and heroes of the Christian faith throughout the centuries. Who could fail to admire the example of a St. Paul or Francis of Assisi? But fundamentalist conversion is also a two-edged sword: its very drama is its own undoing. Because it stereotypes the "born-again" experience in such powerful terms, it sets up an unattainable ideal as the norm for every believer. Like every stereotype, it betrays the very reality it purports to describe. Because it reduces the conversion experience, in a sense, to its "essentials," great clarity is achieved. The fundamentalist expects one who is born again to be able to pinpoint and describe the *moment* of transformation. But its description is so rigidly enforced that the variety of religious experience is suppressed and narrowed excessively. Whatever does not fit the classic pattern—a time of suffering which leads to a moment of crisis, an awakening in that moment both to sin and to personal salvation from Jesus, and a transformed consciousness characterized by joy and peace of soul—is disqualified and excluded from consideration as authentic spiritual conversion.

The emphasis is on the *event,* to the detriment of the *process.* The experiential base is exaggerated to the point of demanding a focused, explicit awareness and a charged emotional tonality. The hidden quiet workings of the Spirit are ignored or minimized, and the gradual awakening as faith develops seems discounted entirely. Such is the classic American image of conversion within the fundamentalist context.

A ROMAN CATHOLIC IMAGE OF CONVERSION

We call attention to this stream of our American heritage, not only that it might serve as a counterpoint to our rich and, we believe, more nuanced Catholic understanding, but also because it has not failed to have an impact on the shape which Catholic evangelization has sometimes taken in our country. While the fundamentalist perspective is not without its merits, as we have indicated, our remarks would like to suggest the advantages of rooting our praxis of evangelization more thoroughly in the best of contemporary Catholic theological reflection on conversion.

A BIBLICAL THEOLOGY OF CONVERSION

One of the great strengths of Catholic theology today is that it has recovered its scriptural roots. Reflection on conversion, too, has profited from this return to the sources of faith, especially in the pages of Sacred Scripture. Unlike the fundamentalist reading of Scripture, however, Catholic theology has incorporated the critical approaches of contemporary scholarship in its retrieval of the biblical data. This means that a Catholic biblical theology of conversion recognizes that there is no single understanding of conversion normative for all of Scripture. Rather, there are many understandings operative, some complementary and others that seem to compete. The Jewish Scriptures contain classic prophetic notions of conversion that reflect an evolving personal sense of sin, together with a progressive interiorization of the idea of return to covenant fidelity. Also present in the Jewish Scriptures are the Deuteronomic writings whose theology of conversion stresses more the repetitive cycle of grace-apostasy-punishment-repentance, as well as later, more legalistic notions of conversion as obedience to the Torah or the performance of cultic ritual.

It is in the Christian Scriptures, however, that a contemporary biblical theology of conversion has been most richly nourished. There, too, scholarship has recognized various strata in an evolving understanding which stretches from John the Baptizer's cry for *metanoia* to the Johannine corpus' developed reflection on the dynamics of faith. The conversion preached by John the Baptist was a reviviscence of the prophetic demand for purity of heart. But his linkage with a once-and-for-all water rite and his strong eschatological focus on the One who comes was a distinctive break with all that preceded him.

By his own baptism in the Jordan, Jesus affirmed the rightness of John's message, but he thereby also enacted prophetically Israel's repentance and acceptance of salvation—its conversion. This "source experience" for Jesus became the *raison d'être* for his joyful proclamation of the good news, which sets off his call for *metanoia* (Mk 1:15) from the grim warnings of the Baptist. The call for conversion on the lips of Jesus, in fact, took the form of a proclamation of God's reign and an invitation to enter into its reality. By word and deed, in the parables he told and in the lived parable of his ministry, Jesus made present the human possibility of an entirely different kind of existence, which he termed the kingdom or reign of God. By embodying the gracious love of a God whose unconditional offer of salvation was available to all, Jesus made conversion a matter of fellowship and discipleship with him in that kingdom.

A biblical theology of conversion moves from this level of the first disciples' following of the earthly Jesus, to the decisive shift which occurred in the Easter event. Henceforth, conversion was to Jesus as the Christ, the risen One. He who proclaimed the kingdom becomes himself the object of proclamation, and conversion assumes new meanings in the experience of the post-resurrection apostolic community. From there, one can trace the developing theologies of conversion within the different communities responsible for the formation of various Gospel and epistolary traditions. The Matthean community's preoccupation with Church order resulted in different emphases than those found in a Lucan community, with its universalist perspective and its more developed pneumatology. Pauline and Johannine theologies of conversion similarly show different concerns and emphases.

The result of all this contemporary scholarship has been a tremendously invigorating stimulus to those concerned with the mission of evangelization in the modern world. A much more nuanced scriptural vision allows a kind of reflection which is open to a variety of pastoral options. By showing how different understandings of conversion even within the New Testament era resulted in different pastoral emphases and ministerial initiatives, we are encouraged to greater flexibility and creativity in our own efforts. By highlighting the interrelationships between these factors, we are encouraged to a more critical reflection on our own praxis and the vision which underlies it.

A LITURGICAL THEOLOGY OF CONVERSION

We move now to a second contribution which Catholicism brings to reflection on conversion and evangelization. From earliest times our tradition has looked upon liturgy as the primary embodiment of the faith of the Church. Creed, dogma, teaching are all derivative in the sense that they attempt to articulate an experience of faith which is first lived at worship. *Lex orandi, lex credendi,* the Latin adage which attempts to capture this insight, means that a reliable guide to the belief of the Church can be found in the lived faith of the Church at prayer. For our purposes, we turn to two primary liturgical sources in our effort to derive a thoroughly Catholic understanding of conversion. The rites of baptism and penance are the Church's two major rituals of conversion which promise to yield important data for those who wish to minister more effectively to the conversion experience. We suggest that a careful reading of the Rite of Christian Initiation of Adults (RCIA) should be a primary source for Catholic evangelizers, inasmuch as its whole focus is the Church's care for the conversion journey of those whom she evangelizes. Secondly, but also importantly, the Rite of Penance (RP) which deals with continuing conversion should be allowed to focus our understandings of conversion and shape our ministry of pastoral care.

We cannot explore in detail the richness of the RCIA's vision of conversion and evangelization, any more than we were able to exhaust the contributions of biblical theology. But a schematic overview of what the RCIA can teach us about conversion will hopefully be suggestive of the possibilities in a more careful review.[1] Analysis of the Introduction and prayers of the RCIA reveals that a Catholic liturgical theology of conversion is summarized in the following six points:

(1) Conversion is understood as entrance into a convenantal relationship.

At root, the conversion experience is a matter of human response to divine initiative. This implies the priority of the divine call, but it also underlines the element of human freedom in accepting or rejecting that call. In addition, using the metaphor of covenant highlights the fact that conversion deals with an interpersonal relationship in which there has been a mutual commitment by both parties. The polarities of this image help to contextualize the tensions of growth, as well as reinforce the need for constant renewal of fidelity amidst the developments of a changing relationship.

(2) Conversion is radically Christocentric. This affirmation which is repeatedly made in the prayers and rites of the RCIA reminds us both of the foundation and of the direction in every authentically Christian experience of conversion. It is to Jesus Christ that one turns, none other. The transformation called for is a "putting on" of the Lord Jesus Christ, so that ultimately one may proclaim with St. Paul that "I no longer live . . . Christ lives in me" (Gal 2:20). By proposing the paschal mystery of Jesus as the heart of conversion, the RCIA speaks to a fundamental pattern of experience which must be assimilated in the process of spiritual growth. In fact, the closest the Rite comes to an actual definition of conversion is found in the Introduction (#8) where it refers to a person's "sacramental sharing in the death and rising of Christ."

(3) Conversion is a thoroughly sacramental experience. This is to be understood in two senses. First, the interior spiritual reality of transformation into Christ must of necessity be embodied. Ours is a profoundly incarnational faith, and we instinctively insist that spiritual experience be enfleshed in the lived reality of daily existence. There is no room for Gnostic dualism in this vision. Conversion, we are told, is sacramentalized in the converted life. Second, conversion is sacramental in the sense that participation in liturgical ritual is integral to the experience. The celebrations of the conversion journey provided in the RCIA are not mere window dressing. They express and effect what they signify. By giving voice to the awakening of the Spirit's life in an individual, the rites celebrated become constitutive ingredients of the developing conversion, not only articulating that experience but supporting and building it as well.

(4) Conversion is an essentially ecclesial event. The RCIA reminds us that conversion occurs "step by step in the midst of the community" (#4). Any conversion experience that remains individualistic and leads to religious privatism is defective in this view. The Christ to whom we turn is found in his body, the Church, and to escape from God's people is to flee from God. Our evangelization, then, is a call not just to an experience of Jesus as personal Lord and Savior. It is to an encounter with the living Christ incarnate in the Church of every age. Conversion, according to the RCIA, involves developing more and more ties to a particular community of believers and making that foundational commitment to God via a whole network of interpersonal relationships. Conversion is also ecclesial in the sense that the entire community is undergoing change, not just

the newcomer. The Rite stresses that the faithful must accompany and support the new member by sharing their own conversion journey.

(5) Conversion is understood as a spiritual journey. This insight of the RCIA uses the image of journey to convey the developmental nature of the transformation involved. Conversion is a process, not just an event. Unlike the fundamentalist stress on the decisive *moment* of encounter with Christ, the RCIA recognizes the gradual nature of growth in faith, without denying the importance of marker events as well. A journey has beginning, middle, end. Similarly, conversion unfolds sequentially in an individual's life. There are seasons and rhythms, and it is in the nature of things that this unfolding experience should ebb and flow. One should not harbor the expectation of a "spiritual high" indefinitely. Prolongation of such a state would more likely be the result of pathology than healthy growth. In fact, the "down" times are as much a part of conversion as the periods of exhilaration. Evangelization strategies aimed at artificially sustaining only one dimension of the conversion journey miss seasons of growth that are equally important. The journey theme also reminds us that conversion is a lifelong process, not something that ends with formal membership in the Church.

(6) Conversion is a comprehensive reality involving transformation of the whole person. One of the most helpful insights of the RCIA is this reminder that every dimension of the human person is affected by the conversion experience. The social sciences speak of holistic growth as involving cognitive, affective and behavioral components. This same balanced perspective can be verified in the RCIA's approach to conversion. Cognitive development is a constant concern of the Rite. What is at issue here is not mere indoctrination, however. Conversion is about acquiring "know-how" as much as it is about the acquisition of new knowledge. New learnings must include the appropriation of a specific tradition, but this entails an intuitive feel for the "Catholic thing" as well as mastery of Church teachings. Affective growth is expressed in the Rite in a variety of ways, but ultimately is a reminder that conversion is about falling in love—with God and with God's people. This means that as part of conversion one begins to speak the language of love, prayer, both in the intimacy of solitude and in the exuberance of communal ritual. Conversion also means behavioral change, a break with sin, adoption of a specifically Christian ethic, and recognizable fruits embodied in the life of charity. Apostolic zeal, the witness of personal values, action for justice, responsive love, these are the ways in which conversion is lived out in the holistic understanding of the RCIA.

The constraints of a brief essay prevent us from a more detailed analysis of the RCIA's understanding of conversion and its implications for our praxis of evangelization. In the space remaining we would like to focus on another primary liturgical source for reflection on the topic of conversion, the Rite of Penance. Like the RCIA this ritual was one of the last and most mature fruits of Vatican II's liturgical renewal. Its pastoral-theological Introduction is quite developed, its prayers and ritual forms are richly elaborated, and its lectionary is extensive. Where the RCIA focuses on the conversion experience of those entering the Church for the first time, the RP is focused on the conversion experience of the already baptized. Thus it nicely complements the RCIA and offers help with another group of persons who are the beneficiaries of evangelization, Catholics themselves. The insights of this document should be particularly valuable to those who minister to inactive Catholics and who are currently exploring pastoral structures for a more effective evangelization effort on their behalf.

What, then, does the RP tell us about ongoing conversion in the life of the believer? One of the most striking features of the renewed ritual mandated by Vatican II is the use of a new name to describe the sacrament: the Rite of Reconciliation. The choice was not a casual one, as is evident from the fact that the Introduction devotes its opening paragraphs to an extensive reflection on the mystery of reconciliation in the history of salvation and in the life of the Church. By this change in terminology we are invited to a deeper awareness of how conversion involves the restoration of a reciprocal relationship between the penitent and God. The former terminology of ''penance'' or ''confession'' (which are only parts of the total sacramental experience) emphasized the human component alone. To speak of the effect of the sacrament only in terms of forgiveness of sins also exaggerates this focus on individualistic purification. Reconciliation, however, evokes a balanced understanding of conversion as a response to the divine gift. The new ritual further redresses the imbalance by highlighting this divine initiative in yet another way. Each form of the Rite now includes a Liturgy of the Word which precedes the sacramental action. Christian conversion, it seems, is at root our response to the Word which invites us to salvation. As with so many other areas of the Church's life in the post-Vatican II era, this restoration of the Word of Scripture to a place of prominence in the RP has called attention to its crucial role in the dynamics of ongoing conversion. A significant relationship is only possible between those who come to know one another deeply, and the restructured RP constantly signals how crucial is the Word proclaimed in leading a penitent to know the Lord more clearly, to follow him more nearly, to love him more dearly.

Another feature of the renewed RP worth considering is the prominence it gives to the ecclesial/social dimension of both sin and reconciliation. Something important is being said in this about conversion as more than just an interior reality. It involves also reshaped relationships with the community and the larger world. In countless ways the Rite stresses that reconciliation to God happens through reconciliation to the Church. Conversion to God is mediated by a communal experience, one in which both the penitent and the Church discover the Spirit at work as they reach out to one another. But lest conversion lead the

Church and her members only to turn in on themselves, the Rite also stresses that authentic reconciliation leads to heightened awareness of the broader social needs. Conversion, we are reminded, enables one to "work with all men of good will for justice and peace in the world" (#5). One is reminded of Paul VI's definition of conversion with which we opened this essay.

The Introduction to the RP contains its own descriptive definition of conversion. Using the traditional Scholastic framework of the "parts" of the sacrament (contrition, confession, penance/satisfaction, absolution), the Rite nonetheless reveals a thoroughly contemporary understanding of the process of conversion. Here conversion is described as "a profound change of the whole person by which one begins to consider, judge, and arrange his life according to the holiness and love of God. . . . For conversion should affect a person from within so that it may progressively enlighten him and render him more like Christ" (#6a). The focus here, in this section on contrition, is not on an introspective preoccupation with sin and guilt. Rather, healthy conversion has the sinner look to the Lord, where sin is seen as a betrayal of covenant love rather than narrowly perceived as a personal defeat. The perspective is religious, not merely psychological, and offers a strong reminder that conversion is more than feelings. The essence of conversion, in this view, is an experience of God which transforms, one that lifts us out of our sinful self-preoccupation and "turns us around" by a taste of God's unconditioned offer of love.

The second "part" of the sacrament, confession, further specifies an essential element in the conversion process. Historically, this component of the ritual was more an act of praise ("confessio laudis") than a self-accusatory recitation of personal faults. But even with this latter emphasis which the RP still preserves, there is evidence of a recovery of the earlier tradition. The "Proclamation of Praise," though separate now from the time for self-accusation, has been made integral to the Rite. This element of confession (whether of praise or of sin) makes some important contributions to our understanding of conversion. Interior contrition alone results in a truncated experience of conversion. As embodied creatures in the world, our inner states cry out for expression in human terms. Our ecclesial identity likewise requires ecclesial recognition—both by us and by the community—of our conversion experience. Regardless of what form it takes, our "confessio" is a way of allowing our conversion to enter the world in a decisive way and become "real" in a more full manner. Cultural and liturgical factors will continue to shape the sacrament's particular expression of this dimension of conversion, but the underlying necessity is unmistakable. In fact, in a ministry of evangelization directed at ongoing conversion, it seems important to provide opportunities for "confessio" both of human evil and of divine goodness. The pastoral structures of this "confessio" likewise would need to be both individual and communal if we are ministering to a balanced experience of conversion.

The third "part" of the sacrament, penance/satisfaction, further unfolds this imperative that interior conversion be given outward expression. The "penance" referred to here is a way of manifesting the transforming power of the Spirit in one's life, not a punishment for misdeeds. To be complete, conversion must issue forth in the fruits of a Spirit-led life. Focus on this element in the process reminds us that "ordinary life" is the locus of all true conversion. Authentic conversion leads us not just to longer hours of prayer in the Church, but to a deeper immersion into this world, its joys and hopes, its griefs and sorrows. The Rite of Penance offers a perfect example here of the wedding of liturgy and life, reflecting how the conversion experience leads to a reconciled Christian existence in the world, an "ordinary life" that is a "holy sacrifice, truly pleasing to God" (Romans 12:1).

After focusing on these three "acts of the penitent," the Rite describes the final "part" of the sacrament, absolution. Here, too, something significant is being said about conversion. For the Christian, conversion is not complete unless it finds a responsive embrace in the bosom of the Church. The priest's absolution is the present liturgical form to express this. Like all the parts of the sacrament, however, this ritual element is indicative of a much broader reality involved in the conversion process. "Pax cum Ecclesia," peace with the Church, was one ancient way of describing the final resolution of the conversion experience. Understood merely in a juridical sense of receiving absolution, the expression trivializes conversion. But for one imbued with a deep appreciation for all that the Church is meant to be in the life of the believer, the expression is a fitting culmination to the Rite's overview of conversion. Peace with the Church, in this view, is peace with self, others, all creation, and God. It is final and complete conversion, an evocative symbol of that total reconciliation which awaits us on the final day.

AN INVITATION

Much, much more could be drawn from the Catholic tradition to enrich our understanding of conversion, and numerous implications for a ministry of evangelization could be elaborated. But this essay is meant to be suggestive rather than exhaustive. We have tried to show how conversion, the underlying dynamic of evangelization, can be approached from a variety of perspectives. We began by describing the American fundamentalist notion of conversion, which we found wanting. We then turned to the Scriptures and the lived faith of the Church at worship as two sources from which to gain enlightenment. We have left untouched the extensive reflection on conversion available today in teachings of the magisterium, in contemporary systematic theology, and in the social sciences. Those, too, merit careful attention and study by evangelizers. What we have done, hopefully, is to frame the issue of conversion as crucial to the task of evangelization, and to introduce the reader to a process of reflection that will lead to an improved praxis of evangelization. It is for the reader, now, to continue what has been begun here.[2]

DISCUSSION QUESTIONS

1. What was your most powerful personal experience of someone undergoing conversion? How would you describe it in terms of the categories suggested above? What role did some form of evangelization play in that experience?

2. What are some implications for evangelization of the foundational role of the Word in the conversion experience? How does the relational and interpersonal character of conversion suggest the Word should be proclaimed for effective evangelization?

3. Do the visions of the RCIA and the RP suggest any differences in the conversion experiences of the unbaptized and the already baptized? How would the ministry of evangelization be affected by these differences?

4. Can you envision for your parish a pastoral structure which might be a kind of restored "Order of Penitents," modeled on the RCIA, but directed specifically to inactive Catholics? What kind of evangelizing experiences would be appropriate for such a situation?

5. Are there any other liturgical experiences which help you to understand better the nature of Christian conversion? Do they offer any insight into how good sacramental celebrations can contribute to the task of evangelization?

6. Where would you go to find guidance from magisterial teaching in coming to a better understanding of the conversion experience and its implications for evangelization? What theologians offer help in this regard? Do the social sciences have anything to contribute in this area?

FOR FURTHER READING

1. Edward K. Braxton, *The Wisdom Community*. New York: Paulist, 1980. Chapter Three of this book contains a very readable introduction to the foundational work of Bernard Lonergan on conversion. The entire work suggests a pastoral model for communal conversion.

2. Walter E. Conn, *Conscience: Development and Self-Transcendence*. Birmingham: Religious Education Press, 1981. A challenging study of how developmental psychology and Lonergan's theoretical reflections on conversion ground a distinctive view of conscience as the basic form of personal authenticity. The focus is on foundational ethics, but the implications for conversion and evangelization are significant.

3. James Dallen, *The Reconciling Community: The Rite of Penance*. New York: Pueblo, 1986. The finest pastoral-theological commentary available on the contemporary Rite of Penance. This book presents insights invaluable to anyone contemplating an outreach to inactive Catholics or a renewed praxis of the sacrament among active parishioners.

4. Robert D. Duggan, ed., *Conversion and the Catechumenate*. New York: Paulist, 1984. This is an interdisciplinary collection of essays on the conversion experience as it unfolds in the context of the restored catechumenate. Included are the perspectives of ascetical theology, sacramental theology, systematics, sociology, developmental psychology and biblical theology.

NOTES

1. See the author's extended analysis of conversion in the RCIA in *Ephemerides Liturgicae* 96 (1982) 57–83, 209–252; 97 (1983) 141–223.

2. In addition to the works cited in the "For Further Reading" section, those interested in a deeper look at these issues might consider the following: (1) From a theological perspective: Robert Doran, *Psychic Conversion and Theological* Foundations (Chico, Cal.: Scholars Press, 1981); Donald Gelpi, *Charism and Sacrament: A Theology of Christian Conversion* (New York: Paulist Press, 1976); Rosemary Haughton, *The Transformation of Man: A Study of Conversion and Community* (New York: Paulist Press, 1967); Bernard J.F. Lonergan, *Method in Theology* (New York: Herder and Herder, 1972); Paul V. Robb, "Conversion as a Human Experience," *Studies in the Spirituality of the Jesuits* 14 (1982) 1–50; Edward Schillebeeckx, *Jesus: An Experiment in Christology* (New York: Seabury, 1979) 116–154, 219–229, 379–397; (2) From a social-scientific perspective: James W. Fowler, *Stages of Faith* (New York: Harper and Row, 1981); Arthur Greil and David Rudy, "What Do We Know About the Conversion Process?" Paper read at the annual meeting of the Society for the Scientific Study of Religion, Providence, R.I., 1981; Rosabeth Moss Kanter, *Commitment and Community: Communes and Utopias in Sociological Perspective* (Cambridge: Harvard University Press, 1972); John Lofland, "Becoming a World-Saver Revisited," in J.T. Richardson (ed.), *Conversion Careers* (Beverly Hills, Cal.: Sage, 1978), 10–23; John Lofland and Norman Skonovd, "Conversion Motifs," *Journal for the Scientific Study of Religion* 20 (1981) 373–385; James T. Richardson, "The Active vs. Passive Convert: Paradigm Conflict in Conversion/Recruitment Research," *Journal for the Scientific Study of Religion* 23 (1985) 163–179; David A. Snow and Cynthia L. Phillips, "The Lofland-Stark Conversion Model: A Critical Reassessment," *Social Problems* 27 (1980) 430–447.

DYNAMICS OF EVANGELIZATION
IN THE CATECHUMENATE

James B. Dunning

The *Rite of Christian Initiation of Adults* is the most radical rite since Vatican II because it raises basic questions about our very roots (in Latin, our "radices"). The catechumenate journey makes us ask: what is evangelization, what is catechesis, what are conversion, faith, mission and ministries, what is Church, who are your God and Christ? In raising those questions for new Christians, we raise them for all Christians. The vision of evangelization for catechumens presents a vision for all of us. What is that vision?

THINK ALCOHOLICS ANONYMOUS

Think Alcoholics Anonymous. When exploring the "dynamics of evangelization in the catechumenate," don't think inquiry class. Think AA!

We made a tactical mistake in reducing the *Rite of Christian Initiation of Adults* to RCIA. People hear that as one more Catholic alphabet and program. At least the term "catechumenate" points to a group of people, like diaconate. But because of former patterns of initiation, many identify catechumenate with inquiry class. Since we also have gamblers anonymous, over-eaters anonymous, and even prostitutes anonymous, why not inquirers anonymous, catechumens anonymous? Listen to an alcoholic's story.

A few years ago, I lay desperately sick on a motel floor in a southern city. I got the phone operator and pleaded, "Call Alcoholics Anonymous." Within ten minutes a man walked in, scooped me up in his arms and raced me to a detox center. There began the agony of withdrawal.

The stranger brought me back to life. This fallen-away Catholic told me the Father loved me. He had not abandoned me. He affirmed me in my emptiness. Later I learned this stranger had lost family and fortune through drinking. Every night he spends fifteen minutes reading a meditation book, praises God for his mercy, thanks him for what he has left, prays for alcoholics, then goes to his window, and blesses the whole world.

Two years later I returned to that southern city. I learned my friend was back on Skid Row. While looking for him, I met a wino who pleaded, "Man, can you gimme a dollar for wine?" I knelt and took his hands in mine. I kissed his hands, and he began to cry. He didn't want a dollar. He wanted what I wanted two years earlier—to be accepted in his brokenness. I never located my friend.

A few days later I was celebrating Eucharist. Midway through the homily, my friend walked in; but he soon disappeared. Two days later, I got this note: "You will never know what you did for me last week in Skid Row. I saw you kiss that wino's hands; you wiped from my eyes the blank stare of the breathing dead. When I saw you cared, my heart grew wings; and I threw my bottle down the sewer. You released me from my panic, fear and self-hatred. If you wonder who I am, I am every man and woman you meet. . . . Am I also you? Wherever I go, sober by the grace of God one day at a time, I will thank God for you."[1]

Would anyone suggest that lectures, classes, instructions could convey good news to those alcoholics on the motel floor and on Skid Row? Think AA. Think of sponsors scooping a drunk off the floor and kissing a wino's hand. Think of peers who have "been there," who are "every man and woman you meet" sharing stories about a God who accepts us in our brokenness and heals our fear, panic, self-hatred. Think doctrine; think of twelve steps of AA, not as abstract theory but lived truth about total dependence on a Power beyond us. Think of passing through stages of deepening conversion and commitment. Think of the alcoholics' bible, what they call the Big Book, full of the stories of their people who have journeyed from stupor to sobriety. Think of the commitment to the twelfth step of bringing the message of recovery to practicing alcoholics. Think of conversion in and through a community. Then think—evangelization of catechumens!

Listen to a catechumen's story. Her catechumenate director says that Jennifer (not her real name) suffered more trials than any person should be asked to bear. Born into an alcoholic family, she left home at an early age. A friend gave her a place to live. She married into wife abuse and was soon divorced. Later, she became engaged to a fine young man who was drowned while fishing with her ex-husband (against whom they could never prove anything). Through bureaucratic bungling, she lost her insurance and her home and was near despair. Through friends she entered a catechumenate where she learned, in her words, that "life is bigger than all those mishaps since I was brought into a community and baptized into Jesus who is my saving grace." One month after baptism she was raped, but she experienced healing because "I had accepted Christ into my life."

Would anyone suggest that lectures, classes, and instructions could convey good news to Jennifer, battered, abandoned, cheated and raped? Rather, think AA. Think CA, Catechumens Anonymous. Think sponsor, the key catechumenate minister, who scoops her up when she is bruised, kisses her hands, and takes the entire journey with her. Think about a community of peers gathered to share their stories of hurt and healing because they've "been there." Think of creed and commandment not as abstract theory but as a Christian's "twelve steps" of lived truth about a loving Power beyond us who became one of us and took up the cross of our brokenness. Think of catechetical periods and liturgical stages celebrating deepening conversion and commitment. Think of Bible, our Big Book full of stories of our people who have also journeyed from slavery to freedom and through death to life. Most important, think not classroom and catechism. Think chapel and community. Catechumens meet not just a book but living people, nourished Sunday after Sunday by the Word with life. Think of the newly baptized committed to share that Word with others, the "twelfth step" of Pentecost. Think of evangelization and conversion in and through a community of faith.

You say to yourself, "Not all catechumens (and not all Christians) have gone through hell like Jennifer!" Thank God! But there are different kinds of hell. Listen to another story, a poem by a young man at seventeen.

He wanted to say things, but no one understood.

He wanted to explain things, but no one cared. So he drew.

He drew the picture. It was a beautiful picture. When he started school
    he brought it to have as a friend.

It was funny about school. He sat in a square, brown desk like all the
    other square, brown desks and he thought it should be red.

His room was square, brown, like the other rooms. And it was tight
    and close and stiff.

The teacher told them to draw. He drew all yellow because it was the
    way he felt about morning. It was beautiful.

The teacher came. "What's this?" she said.

"Why don't you draw something like Ken's drawing? Isn't that
    beautiful?"

It was all questions.

After that he always drew airplanes like everyone else.

And he threw his old picture away.

When he lay out alone looking at the sky, it was big and blue and all of
    everything—but he wasn't anymore.

He was square inside and brown, and his hands were stiff, and he was
    like everyone else.

And the thing inside him that needed saying didn't need saying
    anymore.
It had stopped pushing. It was crushed. Stiff.
Like everything else.

One week after writing those lines, that young man committed suicide.

In a two year period, there were three suicides by catechumens in a parish in Texas. Indeed, not everyone's life is square and tight and stiff. Not all who are stiff commit suicide. But there are the walking dead, hardened by life, building walls of defense so they need not face what Albert Camus called the most profound question, "Why not commit suicide?" They are there in parishes and catechumenates. They clamor for quick, easy answers of literalism or fundamentalism so they can avoid more painful questions of meaning. Like that wino, they plead, "Gimme a dollar. Gimme a quick fix." The inquiry class, with lectures in old or new theology, plays right into their hands. Like that wino, what they really need is a catechumenate, friends who will kneel and kiss those hands. They really are not stiff and hard but broken. They need someone (who acts in the name of Someone) to accept them in their brokenness. They need good news, evangelization.

EVANGELIZATION: INTEGRATING THEME

That is why Pierre-Andre Liege insists, "The first task in the Church's mission . . . is evangelization . . . in all places where the good news has not yet been announced, a matter to be decided on *sociological* grounds as well as geographical ones."[2] If by sociological forces people are dehumanized so that "the things inside them don't need saying anymore," if they commit spiritual suicide and are square and tight and stiff, often they cannot hear the good news without all the humanizing forces of a catechumente. Paul VI puts it this way:

> Strata of humanity which are transformed: for the Church it is a question not only of preaching the Gospel in ever wider geographic areas or to ever greater numbers of people, but also of affecting and as it were upsetting, through the power of the Gospel, mankind's criteria of judgments, determining values, points of interest, lines of thought, sources of inspiration and models of life, which are in contrast with the Word of God and the plan of salvation.[3]

If a person of a culture has mainlined on consumerism, racism, sexism, nationalism or any addiction which hardens us to our own humanity and that of others, a purely cognitive approach normally does not heal. It takes the graced humanity of a Catechumens Anonymous. Unlike some religious cults which segregate initiates from family and friends, AA does not segregate but offers a new community to support the new identity of a person moving from resentment and self-hatred to acceptance and self-love. Likewise, a catechumenate offers a community to support the new identity of a person who now believes in such countercultural Gospel values as poverty of Spirit, fullness of mercy, thirst for justice, the making of peace. *If* school and culture produced the suicidal self-hatred and resentment of a stiff and hardened self, catechumenate counters that culture with sponsors and a community to support the new identity of a graced and loving self. Catechumenate thrived in the Roman Empire when culture assaulted Church. It died after the influence of the Edict of Constantine when culture and Church became one. It resurrected when pagan unbaptized mission lands and "pagan" baptized western Europe discovered evangelization is not a matter of geography but of living countercultural Gospel values. The cognitive approach of inquiry class is not enough for countercultural evangelization. We need the holistic approach and strong personal ties of a Catechumens Anonymous supporting new identity and values.

In this perspective, evangelization is the integrating theme for catechumenate and all Christian life. It's all about sharing and hearing good news. The RCIA document implies evangelization happens only during the first catechetical period, the precatechumenate (cf. nos. 9–11). Rather, in Paul VI's vision, evangelization is the umbrella for the entire mission of the Church; it happens in every period of the RCIA. Frequently, authors relate evangelization to initial conversion involving new identity and values and catechesis to the more reflective process of deepening understanding of conversion and living our communion with God. But Liege insists evangelization and catechesis are in constant dialogue. "It is like an extension of conversion to communion and back again. Conversion develops into communion but on condition that communion is ceaselessly animated by fuller conversion."[4] There are not two kinds of faith nor two successive stages of faith but two intertwined dimensions of faith, one living reality.

CATECHUMENATE: JOURNEY TO EMMAUS

I shall spend the rest of this essay naming specific dynamics of evangelization in the catechumenate. They happen throughout the journey, not just in precatechumenate. I offer seven imperatives, "market-tested" for ten years. For all seven, think AA. Think how they are modeled better in AA than in inquiry class.

They emerge from the dynamics of the Emmaus story. Two disciples walk down the road telling stories of what happened in Jerusalem. Since Luke writes some sixty years after Easter, most likely these are not stories just of Good Friday but of last Friday, the continued crucifixion of the early Church.

Therefore, they raise questions: What kind of Savior is this? Where is God now? A stranger joins them. If they had not welcomed the stranger, they would have missed the risen Lord. Two or three gather to walk in his name, and the stranger listens to the stories. Then he shares other stories of Moses and all the prophets which reveal a tradition of God bringing life out of death. Light breaks through. Conversion happens. They recognize him in the breaking of the bread and the shared brokenness. They celebrate at table, and leave on mission to bring good news to others.

The RCIA speaks of the spiritual journey of adults (cf. no. 4). Seven imperatives suggest it continues the dynamics of Emmaus.

1. *Let there be storytelling.* Like AA, let catechumens tell stories of crucifixion, ache, hurt and brokenness but also healing, ecstasy, love, gratitude. These are not just individual stories but cultural, e.g., the Hispanic story. Assumption: in stories we discover our God. John Shea:

> There are moments which, although they occur within the everyday confines of human living, take on a larger meaning. . . . It may be the death of a parent, the touch of a friend, falling in love, a betrayal . . . the unexpected arrival of blessing, the sudden advent of curse. But whatever it is, we sense we have undergone something that has touched upon the normally dormant but always present relationship to God.[5]

2. *Let there be questions.* Humans are meaning-making mammals; we ask questions: What is the meaning of all this? What is the purpose of my life? Can anybody love me? Why did I deserve this (cried in undeserved pain, sung in undeserved gift)? The questions can be entry point from loneliness to community, from control to wonder and gift, from self to God, from our story to the Big Story when we find we are not the answer to our own questions.

3. *Let there be a community of faith.* Let two or three gather in Jesus' name. Let the stories be shared with "strangers"; in them we find the risen Lord. Like AA, the catechumenate is rooted in peer ministry—sponsors, a small sponsoring community, parishioners who share faith, prayer companions, a community gathered in worship, people who have "been there" like Damien the leper. After years of frustration in reaching lepers with good news, they finally let Damien into their lives on the day he became a leper.

> That Sunday he got in the pulpit and did not begin with his customary "You lepers" but with "We lepers . . ." From that point on, his unsuccessful ministry is electric. . . . *He* is their story and once more a word has been made flesh, however leperous, and dwelt among people.[6]

Catechumenates offer a community of words made flesh.

4. *Let there be tradition.* Let the community hand on (in Latin, "traditio") its most precious gifts. Catechisms are not our most precious gift! The gifts are first the people: Moses and all the prophets, climaxing in Jesus, continuing in those touched by his Spirit. We hand on their stories especially through the lectionary, the Big Book offering the "curriculum" for the primary sessions, dismissal after homily on Sunday (not a weekday class). When doctrine is handed on, we hand it on like AA's twelve steps: as summaries of truth lived in stories.

5. *Let there be conversion.* Throughout the catechumenate, let catechumens recognize the Lord in the breaking of the bread, in shared brokenness and also shared thanksgiving. Many people joining our Church are not catechumens but baptized Protestants. Often they believe they are just changing churches. That may be true. If so, AA with its radical changes of identity and values is a poor model. But the baptized may also be tight and square and stiff; they may need to change images of themselves, their God and Christ. They may need to move from fundamentalism to meaning. If that is true, profound changes may happen throughout the journey.

6. *Let there be celebration.* Let there be welcoming, signing with cross, presentation of Bible, Creed and Our Father, signing the book of the elect, scrutinizing and laying on of hands, washing-immersing, anointing, breaking bread and drinking cup. Let catechumenate be truly Catholic—not just sterile words of classroom but sights, sounds, gestures of liturgy. Catechumenate restores the integral ties between catechesis and liturgy, word and rite.

7. *Let there be mission.* Let there be the "twelfth step." If all the baptized are gifted by God, if mission is simply giving the gifts away, throughout the catechumenate the candidates need missionaries who live the good news, especially in their homes and work. Throughout the process candidates are invited into mission so they can celebrate commitment on Pentecost. At rock bottom, the catechumenate journey is the Church's way of forming people for mission.

IMPLICATIONS FOR ALL EVANGELIZATION

These are some dynamics of evangelization in the catechumenate. They offer a vision for all evangelization, with implications: for renewal of Catholics, reception of baptized Protestants, reconciling alienated Catholics, welcoming new parishioners, for all sacramental preparation, for novitiates and the formation of all ministries. The content may differ because individual and cultural stories differ, but the dynamics are the same. We evaluate all we do in evangelization from the vision offered by the spiritual journey of the catechumenate.

A few examples. First, with this vision, how might we approach parish renewal, the on-going conversion of Catholics, or what some call adult education? Much of what we did after Vatican II in the name of adult education or "up-dating" centered on the cortex, an extremely cognitive approach. We used the school model, and gave courses on the documents of Vatican II, the new theology, new biblical criticism, new liturgy, new Church. But that approach was really old Church, centered on a teacher-pupil model not the peer ministry of AA, lectures not shared faith experience, theology not spirituality, classroom not chapel. It was informative, entertaining. Some people enjoyed it. They came to one series, learned what they wanted to know, and dropped out. At best, we offered a good education model.

With a vision of evangelization in the catechumenate, we move into programs of renewal with spirituality, conversion, deepening communion and not just education as the model. We would plan and evaluate programs using the seven imperatives. For example, "Let there be questions" assumes that for most people the resounding question is, "What is the purpose of my life?" and not, "What literary form is the first chapter of Genesis?" We do not invite Catholics seeking renewal into the catechumenate. Indeed, sponsors are renewed, but all Catholics are there for the sake of the catechumens. We would offer Catholics a similar journey in order to claim their baptism.

Second, those imperatives help us find ways to welcome Catholics returning to active Church practice and needing reconciliation. I refer here to those with scars and wounds, people with painful experiences of Church. "Let there be storytelling" means we don't begin with lectures on how good we are today. We begin with their stories of what hurt them. Let them dump the garbage. We simply listen and feel with them, making no judgments. Then we would hope to move on. "Let there be celebration" suggests the need for liturgies of healing and reconciliation, perhaps celebrated in stages like those of the catechumenate, *if* people want to celebrate their return publicly. Once again, because these people's stories and questions are usually so different from those of the catechumens, they deserve a separate track.

Third, what if we applied this vision to sacramental preparation, e.g., for infant baptism or marriage? "Let there be storytelling" means that preparation for baptism includes not just talk on the new ritual. We begin with the stories and questions of the parents. What are their hopes and dreams for themselves and their children? How are they living their baptism? Both for baptism and marriage, "Let there be a community of faith" means we offer people a community of peers, parents and married couples who couple-to-couple share their faith and experience.

Fourth, since the catechumenate journey is aimed at Pentecost, "Let there be mission" proclaims that the seven imperatives are ingredients in the formation of all the baptized for mission and ministries. How do we form missionaries? "Let there be stories and questions" prepared people especially for ministries of the Word. "Let there be communities of faith and traditions" enables ministries of community-building ("koinonia"). "Let there be celebration" leads to ministries of worship and liturgy. "Let there be mission" means especially living the Gospel in home, neighborhood, and work and in ministries of service ("diakonia") because the other imperatives have done the work of evangelization. Now there is good news to share. All of this is in light of "Let there be conversion": mission rooted in spirituality and not just education or "busy-ness."

I close with a testimony from an alocholic.

> When I walked into the friendly atmosphere of my first AA meeting, I knew I was where I belonged. Here were people who had thought and felt as I had. Here was the understanding I'd been searching for all my life. These people were my friends, and I felt their sincere interest in me. . . . AA has become a way of life and living for me. It has brought about a revelation of self, the discovery of an inner being, an awareness of God.[7]

Might that revelation happen for every catechumen and for all of us. Think AA.

NOTES

1. Adapted from Brennan Manning, *The Wisdom of Accepted Tenderness* (Denville, N.J: Dimension Books, 1980), pp. 60–63.

2. Pierre-Andre Liege, "The Ministry of the Word: From Kerygma to Catechesis," *Lumen Vitae* 17 (1962): 32–33.

3. Pope Paul VI, *On Evangelization in the Modern World* (Washington, D.C.: USCC Office of Publication, 1975), no. 19.

4. Liege, "The Ministry of the Word," p. 29.

5. John Shea, *An Experience Named Spirit* (Chicago: Thomas More Press, 1983), p. 98.

6. William Bausch, *Storytelling: Imagination and Faith* (Mystic, Connecticut: Twenty-Third Publications, 1984), p. 62.

7. *Alcoholics Anonymous* (New York: AA World Service, Inc., 1976), p. 355.

DISCUSSION QUESTIONS

1. Tell a conversion story from your own life, when your life changed, either suddenly or over a longer period, in a way that you would call a Christian conversion. What changed? Did any of the elements of the Alcoholics Anonymous process help make that change?

2. What are some of the "addictions" besides alcohol which hinder conversion today? How do those addictions affect you personally?

3. Talk with a catechumen in your parish. What is helping that person to hear the good news in the journey of the catechumenate?

4. Take the Emmaus journey. Tell the story of an event in your life about which you have some strong feelings, happy or sad. What questions did it raise for you? Who journeyed with you? Is there anything in our Gospel tradition that speaks to that time in your life? Did you experience some change you would call a conversion? If so, how did you celebrate that and share it?

5. Explore adaptations of the seven imperatives for: Catholics returning to the Church, sacramental preparation for infant baptism and marriage, and formation for ministries.

FOR FURTHER READING

New Wine, New Wineskins: Exploring the Rite of Christian Initiation of Adults, James B. Dunning. New York: Wm. H. Sadlier, Inc., 1981. Research paper written for the National Conference of Diocesan Directors of Religious Education. Explores theological assumptions behind the RCIA; describes dimensions of each of the four periods; draws out implications for other areas of Church life.

Rite of Christian Initiation: Historical and Pastoral Reflections, Michel Dujarier. New York: Wm. H. Sadlier, Inc., 1979. Offers a history of each of the liturgies of the RCIA and makes suggestions for adaptations.

Welcoming the New Catholic, Ronald Lewinski. Chicago: Liturgy Training Program, second ed. 1983. A good, basic introduction to the catechumenate, suitable for parishioners. Summarizes the catechetical periods and liturgical celebrations, with pastoral suggestions.

EVANGELIZATION AND THE AMERICAN CULTURE: PROCLAIMING THE GOOD NEWS IN A NEW KEY

Regis A. Duffy, O.F.M.

In the past year two very different books about missionaries and their work of evangelization have appeared. Both books deal with Jesuit missionary activity in roughly the same era of European colonization and trade expansion in the Americas and in the Orient. But here the similarity between the two books ends. Brian Moore, in his novel *Black Robe,* attempts a careful reconstruction of the reactions of the Huron, Algonquin and Iroquois Indians to evangelization by the French Jesuits, represented by the sincere but naive efforts of the fictional Father Laforgue.[1] To his credit, this young Jesuit eventually begins to appreciate the force of the Indian culture and his own cultural presuppositions in evangelizing the Indians.

In sharp contrast to this cultural insensitivity of some missionaries, Jonathan Spence narrates the remarkable effort at cultural adaptation in evangelization in his biography, *The Memory Palace of Matteo Ricci.* Unlike his fellow Jesuits in America, Ricci took the measure of the enormous cultural differences between the Chinese and his own European background. His first response was to absorb the culture and language of his adopted country to a remarkable degree. He then became a highly respected teacher of mnemonic skills needed to advance in the Chinese system of government exams. Ricci believed that his own expertise, highly valued in the Chinese culture, would open the door to effective evangelization. Spence recounts the evaluation of one well-known Chinese scholar and contemporary: "Now he can speak our language fluently, write our script, and act according to our rules of conduct. He is an extremely impressive man—a person of inner refinement, outwardly most straightforward. . . . Amongst people of my acquaintance no one is comparable to him. . . ."[2]

It is easy to appreciate the evangelical creativity and the cultural sensitivity of Father Ricci and, in doing so, to miss the underlying and more troubling question: When the proclamation of the Gospel does not seem to change anything in areas where it has been preached even for centuries, is part of the problem a cultural naiveté similar to Father Laforgue's? In other words, are the evangelizers capable of decoding both the richness of God's creation and the flawed traces of radical evil in the complex strands of their own or of a foreign culture? Without such sensitivity, can evangelizers effectively proclaim how God saves in this particular situation? Paul VI gives the question a more contemporary ring: "In our day, what has happened to that hidden energy of the good news, which is able to have a powerful effect on man's conscience? To what extent and in what way is that evangelical force capable of really transforming the people of this century?" *(Evangelii Nuntiandi,* 4).[3]

Paul VI's words, in fact, evoke a series of other questions: Do we avoid, for example, the errors of Father Laforgue in proclaiming the Gospel to a culture which we mistakenly think we know and have accurately assessed? Do we think, on the other hand, that we have successfully adapted our message to our American culture, in the spirit of Father Ricci, because of the relevancy of our religious education manuals or the frequency of our liturgies of the Word? Certainly questions such as these only sharpen the profile of the authentic Pauline evangelizer: "We at least are not like so many who trade on the word of God. We speak in Christ's name, pure in motivation, conscious of having been sent by God and of standing in his presence" (2 Cor 2:17).

My assigned task is to analyze paragraph 18 of *Evangelii Nuntiandi* from two perspectives: first, in relation to the rest of Paul VI's exhortation; secondly, within the context of our American culture. Interestingly enough, there is nothing in paragraph 18 that would not sound familiar to Fathers Laforgue and Ricci:

> For the Church, evangelizing means bringing the good news into all the strata of humanity, and through its influence transforming humanity from within and making it new: "Now I am making the whole of creation new." But there is no new humanity if there are not first of all new persons renewed by baptism and by lives lived according to the Gospel. The purpose of evangelization is therefore precisely this interior change, and if it has to be expressed in one sentence, the best way of stating it would be to say that the Church evangelizes when she seeks to convert, solely through the divine power of the message she proclaims, both the personal and collective consciences of people, the activities in which they engage, and the lives and concrete milieux which are theirs (EN 18).

Even the stress on the personal and collective consciences of the people and their milieux is part of the missionary wisdom of the centuries.

The pivotal connection in paragraph 18, of course, is between the two biblical terms, "good news" and "new." In English the two terms, derivatives of the same root, cannot match the much more challenging idea that the Greek New Testament usage conveys. When Paul, for example, speaks of the evangelized and initiated Christian as a "new creation" (2 Cor 5:17), the Greek adjective he employs (*kainos*) conveys the sense of a reality so new that its like has never been seen before. This "newness" already reflects the kingdom of God coming toward us. The term "good news" captures the radical surprise of those who welcome this new way of living and its ultimate goal, the kingdom of God.

Much like a weathervane, the connecting idea of the biblical "news" and "new" is, then, a sense of orientation and direction. Gospel proclamation and initiation present a road to be traveled whose destination is the peaceable kingdom of God. Even in the Old Testament the idea of conversion is often pictured in terms of a change of direction while "the way" in the language of the early Church becomes synonymous with following the Gospel.

When Paul VI speaks of the interior change that evangelization must effect in our society, his citation from the Book of Revelation ("Now I am making the whole of creation new") with its resonance in 2 Cor 5:17 sets the tone. The conversion that evangelization calls us to is a change of direction so unexpected and a transformation so profound that only the terms "good news" and "new" could describe it. When the Holy Father outlines the extent of this transforming evangelization in paragraph 18 ("both the personal and collective consciences of people, the activities in which they engage, and the lives and concrete milieux which are theirs"), he is only spelling out the implications of "good news" and "new."

These ideas are beautifully summarized in the words of the celebrant to catechumens entering the process of evangelization: "Now *the way of the Gospel* opens before you, inviting you to make a *new beginning* by acknowledging the living God who speaks his words of truth to people. You are called *to walk* by the light of Christ and to trust in his wisdom. Are you ready to *enter on this path* today under the leadership of Christ?" (*Rite of Christian Initiation of Adults,* par. 76, my emphasis).[4]

In both situating paragraph 18 in the larger context of Paul VI's exhortation and in teasing out its implications for our cultural situation, I propose, then, this biblical criterion of "new/good news" as a realistic frame of reference. To answer Paul VI's questions, cited above, about how much transformation we should expect from evangelization, we must take more seriously the biblical wonder of what God expects and effects among us.

FAIRY TALE OR KINGDOM?

As children, the joy of such fairy tales as *Snow White and the Seven Dwarfs* was entry into a special world and time which was different from daily experience. Although recent psychological writing has examined some of the unsuspected and more sinister dimensions of fairy tales, it remains true that there is a certain false security in even temporarily residing in a world where there is no real time and where good eventually triumphs over evil. Fairy tales have a legitimate place in the imaginative development of the growing person but what happens if the adult has not acquired a more responsible notion of time and a more realistic appreciation of the power of evil? "Once upon a time . . . and they lived happily ever after" can be the beginning and end of untransformed living.

Paul VI's teaching on the radical newness proclaimed by the Gospel has been carefully prepared in the early paragraphs of his exhortation. Jesus himself, as the good news of God (EN 7) proclaims a kingdom that makes all else relative (EN 8). The way in which this kingdom and its "kernel," salvation, is experienced is in "a radical conversion, a profound change of mind and heart" (EN 10). To prevent this conversion being understood in a privatized way, Paul VI then gives some very practical testing points: (1) the marginal and poor are evangelized (EN 12), and (2) gathered into a community "which is in its turn evangelizing" (EN 13). In fact, the unique profile of the Church, as this gathered community, comes into focus through evangelization (EN 15).

The connections between kingdom, conversion, and community so far have been fairly abstract, and therefore, safe. Once, however, paragraph 18 with its broad and challenging vision of transformed personal and collective conscience is sketched, the reader senses that Paul VI's vision is uncomfortably more biblical and radical than anticipated. In paragraphs 19 and 20 of his exhortation, he presents the cultural and social field in which all evangelization must take place.

In doing this, he makes several salient points that have very practical corollaries. First, evangelization must "affect" and "upset" our very way of thinking, planning, hoping, and striving (EN 19). Second, this profound reevaluation always happens within the cultural context that first framed these aspirations and hopes. To refer to our earlier examples, Laforgue and many of his contemporaries thought that evangelization could bypass a culture and thus save people. Ricci saw that people could only "hear" the Gospel challenge with all its ramifications within the culture that had molded their vision.

Paul VI was well aware of the danger of confusing superficial cultural changes effected by Christianity with the profound transformation that the Gospel demands ("not in a purely decorative way as it were by applying a thin veneer, but in a vital way, in depth and right to their very roots"—EN 20). More concretely, whether speaking of Italian or Brazilian culture as being "Catholic" or "Christian," we should pause and ask what the difference is between culture and Gospel. For many people there is obviously no difference. As a result, in such superficially Christian cultures radical forms of evil can be tolerated more easily because one too naively equates culture with Gospel. Thus, one suspects, the genocide practiced by the Nazis in the 1930's and 1940's was tolerated, if not colluded with, in the nominally ancient Christian culture of Germany more easily than it might have been in a so-called non-Christian culture. A more contemporary example is the high incidence of human rights violations in South American countries that are considered "Christian."

Paul VI's crucial distinction between Gospel and culture, between God's kingdom and our contexts, must be taken more seriously. On the one hand, evangelization and culture are not identical (EN 20). Therefore, to speak too easily of a "Christian culture" is ambiguous, if not misleading. On the other hand, evangelization cannot be done in a cultural vacuum. Gospel proclamation must not only borrow cultural elements but should ideally permeate a culture (EN 20). Paul VI is walking a tightrope here and we would do well to follow his example.

The early history of evangelization bears out Paul VI's teaching. In recent years a great deal of creative research on the social and cultural contexts of this period of evangelization has been done.[5] Wayne Meeks in describing what the term "social world of early Christianity" means for these researchers echoes Paul VI's careful balance of kingdom and culture: "It has a double meaning, referring not only to the environment of the early Christian groups but also to the world as they perceived it and to which they gave form and significance through their special language and other meaningful actions. One is the world they shared with other people who lived in the Roman Empire; the other, the world they constructed."[6]

Paul VI then moves from the context of evangelization to the evangelizers themselves. Any Christian who gives the "wordless witness" of a life praxis that provokes troubling Gospel questions is indeed an evangelizer (EN 21). Paul VI then offers examples of such deafening questions: "Why are they like this? Why do they live in this way? What or who is it that inspires them? Why are they in our midst?" (EN 21). These questions summarize two important ideas which we have been discussing—conversion and culture. First, conversion pivots on the questions asked or avoided. Notice that the questions set up a dialogue between the experience of the unconverted and those who witness. Second, these questions can only be heard and responded to within a culture that inevitably has values and visions never identical with the Gospel. In fact, two groups specifically mentioned by Paul VI as needing evangelization are possible examples of those who confuse conversion and culture: "baptized people who do not practice, or people who live as nominal Christians but according to principles that are in no way Christian" (EN 21).

Evangelii Nuntiandi then retrieves one of Christianity's oldest beliefs (Paul VI, in fact, calls it the "test of truth, the touchstone of evangelization"— EN 24): all are called to witness (and thus, be evangelizers—EN 21) and the truly evangelized always evangelize others in turn (EN 24). It is such transformed people who accept the Church "as the Word which saves" and who celebrate the sacrament honestly. Adherence to this shared new vision is adherence to the kingdom (EN 23).

From this brief review of Paul VI's teaching on the proclamation of the kingdom it is obvious that this event occurs only in a real world where a sense of the purpose of time and definitions of happiness are still deeply flawed. In contrast to the imaginary world of fairy tales, the kingdom and its radical newness do not assure the "happy ending" of such stories but, rather, God's troubling questions about our view of his world linked to his faithful promise to renew all that he has made. But such a review paradoxically brings us back to our starting point—Paul VI's questions probe the reasons why this does not seem to be happening in our own world and time. To attempt to answer his questions we must now examine how the evangelizing Christian community shapes its awareness of its mission within a complex cultural situation.

IMPOSSIBLE CONTEXTS?

In response to Paul VI's question about why evangelization does not seem to affect our world, we might pose another question: Is it realistic to expect a radical transformation of "the personal and collective consciences of people, the activities in which they engage, and the lives and concrete milieux which are theirs" within our complex and highly individualized American culture? As already noted, we are only beginning to appreciate how the social and cultural contexts of the ancient world shaped evangelization in the first century. But in the case of the American scene there is a huge and ever increasing body of anthropological, psychological, and sociological analysis that seems to offer some answer to Paul VI's question.

Robert N. Bellah and his colleagues have recently synthesized some of this research in *Habits of the Heart: Individualism and Commitment in American Life.*[7] For our modest purposes their work can serve as a guide in trying to answer our question concerning the possibility of effective evangelization within the American cultural scene. At the outset they provide us with a useful description of culture: "So long as it is vital, the cultural tradition of a people—its symbols, ideals, and way of feeling—is always an argument about the meaning of the destiny its members share. *Cultures are dramatic conversations about things that matter to their participants, and American culture is no exception.*"[8] In other words, culture always reflects shared values and vision.

Bellah and his associates isolate three such cultural conversations that have been going on since the founding of this country. They have labeled these strands biblical, republican, and individualist. Within each of these perspectives the themes of success, freedom, and justice take a particular cultural shape. The biblical focus, as seen in early Puritan colonial life, centers on an idea of covenant community transposed to civic and social life. American freedom, within this perspective, always has a strong ethical component, while individuals could not easily disassociate ideas of God and morality from either their private or their public lives.

The republican strand of American culture is exemplified in a person like Thomas Jefferson. His concept of a republic is one in which everyone participates. It was precisely because citizens were equal that they could share in the responsibilities which all social and civic life entail. Although the republican view also has a strong ethical component, its understanding of freedom includes that of religion. This religious dimension of freedom would not have been understood in the same way in early Puritan praxis. If such a participatory republic were to work, it also implied that everyone had to enjoy enough success to allow them to have the leisure in shaping this common life. Bellah cites Jefferson's dictum, "Love your neighbor as yourself, and your country more than yourself."[9]

The third cultural strand of individualism takes two forms, utilitarian and expressive. Ben Franklin represents a utilitarian individualism that advocates ambition and self-improvement. The resulting success of such attitudes in turn would help to form a certain type of society where the ordinary citizen enjoyed an assured measure of freedom and justice. Expressive individualism, as the label indicates, sums up the efforts of those who are not so much interested in material security as in self-development. Definitions of freedom and success are determined by the individual's ability to promote his or her emotional as well as intellectual life.

The complexity of American life has grown considerably since each of these cultural tendencies first began in our history. As Bellah notes, "The split between public and private life correlates with a split between utilitarian individualism, appropriate in the economic and occupational spheres, and expressive individualism, appropriate in private life."[10] The corollary of this situation is that one's definitions of success, freedom, and justice may have nothing to do with the larger community. Success in one's work life, e.g., may then be seen only as a means to financial security without having made any appreciable difference in or contribution to one's world.

This split between public and private life in our American culture leads to a crucial distinction between community and, to use Bellah's term, lifestyle enclaves. Community is used here in the sense of an integration of the public and private spheres of life. A group of social activists or religiously motivated people living together or even an ethnically cohesive neighborhood in a large city might serve as examples of community. Among such people there is still the possibility of sharing elements from the many dimensions of human life.

Lifestyle enclaves represent unique contemporary gatherings. They are unlike communities in two important ways: only the individual's private life is involved and fellow participants in an enclave share the same lifestyle.[11] A familiar example of lifestyle enclaves would be "yuppies," i.e., young singles whose leisure pursuits and consumption habits set them apart from other groups. Often enough they occupy apartments in high rent urban areas and dress in a consistent style that lends itself to parody. The proliferation of retirement villages, although often called communities, might be another example of lifestyle enclaves as "an appropriate form of collective support in an otherwise radically individualizing society."[12]

Imbedded in both community and lifestyle enclaves are values and a vision that are quite different. Bellah uses the immigrant communities in the late nineteenth and early twentieth centuries as a clear example of community. Ethnic, religious, and familial values could be preserved in new rural or urban settings because they were shared and reinforced within the group. Often enough their shared occupational and resulting economic lives helped to solidify these deeper values.

Lifestyle enclaves, on the other hand, reflect the markedly changed social and economic situation in post-World War II America. Upper mobility, changing occupational and familial structures, and the emergence of the so-called "youth culture" are but a few of the contributing factors favoring lifestyle enclaves. Members of enclaves are not ethnically or religiously bound in the same way as communities. While a person can have religious values and vision in either a community or a lifestyle enclave, one's functioning in either situation can be quite different.

If one asks, for example, who should be the recipient of my energy and talents, the religious answer will be influenced by convictions about an interdependence with others or search for an autonomous self. Those who would evangelize should take serious note of Bellah's remark that "the American understanding of the autonomy of the self places the burden of one's own deepest self-definitions on one's own individual choice. . . . But the notion that one discovers one's deepest beliefs in, and through, tradition and community is not very congenial to Americans. Most of us imagine an autonomous self existing independently, entirely outside any tradition and community, and then perhaps choosing one."[13] This tendency seems to be supported by the observation that many former communities have become, in fact, lifestyle enclaves.[14] One wonders if this could not be equally said of some parish and religious communities.

In any case, the practical result of this American penchant for radical self-autonomy is groups of good people whose sense of direction and mission is limited by their solitary position outside an authentic community. When Bellah and his colleagues look at the American who has roots in a community of memory, such as a Christian within an ecclesial community, they see a bifurcation that arises from this cultural situation. They describe this split identity in terms of two languages—that of the self-reliant individual and that of tradition and commitment within a community of tradition. As they note, the task of Church communities to negotiate between these two languages has become increasingly difficult.[15]

The evaluation that Bellah makes about the problems of love and marriage in the contemporary American situation apply to the larger problem we have been discussing: "Without a wider set of cultural traditions, then, it was hard for people to find a way to say why genuine attachment to others might require the risk of hurt, loss, or sacrifice. They clung to an optimistic view in which love might require hard work, but could never create real costs to the self. . . . What proved most elusive to our respondents, and what remains most poignantly difficult in the wider American culture, are ways of understanding the world that could overcome the sharp distinction between self and other."[16]

SAME THEME, NEW KEY

Singers know that the musical key or area in which they perform a song or aria crucially affects the outcome of their performance. The music remains the same but the musical transposition allows the tenor to feel comfortable in a range that a baritone would not. In much the same way, Gospel proclamation retains its unique message but the cultural, political, and social contexts do key the way in which that message is effectively proclaimed and heard.

Paul VI, in speaking of the particular way individual churches express themselves in their world, emphasizes that they "have the task of assimilating the essence of the Gospel message and of transposing it, without the slightest betrayal of its essential truth, into the language that these particular people understand, then of proclaiming it in this language" (EN 63). We have benefited from a few of the insights of Bellah and his colleagues in order to be able to measure the complexity of this task or, to continue our analogy, to select the right key for the same proclamation that is heard elsewhere in other keys.

Several corollaries immediately emerge from this brief dialogue. First, *American individualism can easily reduce the central Gospel message about the kingdom of God to a privatized notion of salvation.* In other words, while Jesus' teaching focuses on how God will gather his people, individualism may readily believe that the kingdom is a set of eternal private condominiums, and that salvation can be welcomed outside or despite the community of the Word. A relevant sounding teaching and preaching may talk about the oneness of the kingdom of God but our acculturated American ears may quietly filter out its implications. The way in which we phrase, then, the Gospel challenge to a one-sided individualism is crucial. After mentioning the other corollaries, I will return to this point with a suggestion about interactive language.

A second corollary of this cultural dialogue is *that the radical "newness" of conversion which evangelization announces can be more easily misconstrued within a lifestyle enclave that incorrectly believes itself to be a community.* The reader will remember that lifestyle enclaves may superficially appear to be communities but it is the lack of integration of the public and private dimensions of their living that betrays them. Their values and vision have been narrowed to the private goals of consumption and congenial living. This style of living is in sharp contrast to a call to a "new way of being" that has, as a costly component, an integration of what happens in our world and in our personal lives. Translated into pastoral terms, an affluent parish may hear the Gospel message about social justice but interpret this test of ongoing conversion solely in terms of financial support of the poor. Because of the way in which "sharing" is understood within such a lifestyle enclave, the sharing that gospel justice entails is conveniently minimized.

A third corollary is that *the evangelizer as witness cannot hope to assume this prophetic role if he or she is colluding with American "values" that are naively equated with Gospel values.* Paul VI laid much stress on the evangelizer as witness: "Modern man listens more willingly to witnesses than to teachers, and if he does listen to teachers, it is because they are witnesses" (EN 41). As already noted, such witnesses provoke questions that trouble the calm surface of our lives (EN 21). But such questions arise precisely because there is a tension between our respectable cultural values and the radical values and vision of the Gospel. To be an evangelizing witness means, then, to bring a sharp eye to our familiar world and ask questions of ourselves that we have not asked before: Does American aid to third world countries, e.g., reflect accurately the Gospel viewpoint and which viewpoint in practice is operative in our own sharing? Does the cultural value system of the average middle class American family easily allow for the mutual evangelization of parents and children that Paul VI calls for (EN 71)? If not, does this not say something important about the way in which evangelization is currently being carried out on the local, regional, and national levels of the American Church?

The heart of the matter seems to be whether we know how to speak in a language that not only can challenge the personal lives of our hearers but also, dialogue with the cultural contexts in which we must live and die. F. Fiorenza, using Habermas' familiar distinction between cognitive and interactive speech, rightly criticizes the one-sided propositional speech we use to the neglect of relational dialogue with our world: "The focus on the interactive dimension of the kingdom proclamation singles out how that proclamation challenges the normative values of society and entails commitments from its hearers so that its proclamation necessarily establishes and constitutes community."[17]

But is this whole discussion merely wishful theological thinking? Not at all. At its best, the catechumenal process of initiating candidates and reforming the baptized is an historical example of successful evangelization within sharply perceived cultural contexts.[18] The lengthy catechumenal period pivoted around a vital dialogue between the Word of God and both the cultural and personal contexts of candidates' lives. From the information available, at least some of this evangelization could be described as interactive speech, i.e., the challenge of Jesus' kingdom teaching in a tensive conversation with the values of a particular time.[19] A contemporary example, similar to the catechumenate, is the successful movement earlier in this century known as the Young Catholic Workers' Movement. Young workers learned to share the Word of God within their social and cultural situations and to tease out its implications for a shared commitment and a community of prayer and mission. The remarkable impact of this evangelizing movement on the hitherto untouched working world of the poor can be attributed, in part, to the decisive ways in which the Word of God, responsibly shared and appropriated within the workers' situation, spoke to "the personal and collective consciences of people, the activities in which they engage, and the lives and concrete milieux which are theirs" (EN 18).

When evangelization is effectively proclaimed, the kingdom of God is not separated from his promise of renewing and transforming all creation. In turn, we hearers of the Word can only listen within the cultural world that has shaped our personal and communal experience. We may indeed find ourselves caught in between the kingdom promise of true communion and the American temptation to lifestyle enclaves and rampant individualism. Paradoxically, this may be the best position in which to appreciate both the unearned healing of God's Word and the as yet incomplete transformation of his creation.

NOTES

1. B. Moore, *Black Robe* (New York: Dutton, 1985).

2. J.D. Spence, *The Memory Palace of Matteo Ricci* (New York: Viking, 1984), p. 255.

3. Hereafter, the apostolic exhortation will be noted as EN, followed by the paragraph number as given in the document.

4. Hereafter, noted as RCIA, followed by the paragraph number as given in the document.

5. See, e.g., G. Theissen, *The Social Setting of Pauline Christianity: Essays on Corinth* (Philadelphia: Fortress, 1982); W. Meeks, *The First Urban Christians. The Social World of the Apostle Paul* (New Haven: Yale University, 1983).

6. Meeks, *The First Urban Christians,* p. 8.

7. (Berkeley: University of California, 1985).

8. *Habits of the Heart. Individualism and Commitment in American Life* (Berkeley: University of California, 1985), p. 27, my emphasis. For purposes of editorial convenience, I shall cite this group of authors under the name of Bellah.

9. *Ibid.*, p. 31.

10. *Ibid.*, pp. 45–46.

11. *Ibid.*, p. 72.

12. *Ibid.*, p. 73.

13. *Ibid.*, p. 65.

14. *Ibid.*, p. 74.

15. *Ibid.*, p. 154–55.

16. *Ibid.*, pp. 109–10.

17. F.S. Fiorenza, *Foundational Theology: Jesus and the Church* (New York: Crossroad, 1984), p. 117.

18. See, e.g., R. Duffy, *On Becoming a Catholic: The Challenge of Christian Initiation* (San Francisco: Harper & Row, 1984), pp. 1–60.

19. This can be seen in Hippolytus' *Apostolic Tradition*, c. 16, where the lists of work and professions that might be an obstacle to Christian living are given.

DISCUSSION QUESTIONS

1. Would you describe the important groups of your current life (e.g., family, parish, etc.) as communities or lifestyle enclaves? Could you give examples of how your participation in such groups affects the way you hear the Word of God proclaimed?

2. Has the proclamation of the Word of God challenged recently some cultural values which you had always taken for granted (e.g., on questions of the care of the poor in America, on nuclear armaments, on the American economy)? Do you resent or question this type of proclamation?

3. Name three decisive "witnesses" to the Word of God in your own life. Did they challenge more than your personal values and vision?

FOR FURTHER READING

Gregory Baum, *Religion and Alienation: A Theological Reading of Sociology*. New York: Paulist, 1975. This is a challenging reading of our cultural situation from a writer who has formidable theological and sociological insight.

Robert N. Bellah, Richard Madsen, William M. Sullivan, Ann Swidler, and Steven M. Tipton, *Habits of the Heart: Individualism and Commitment in American Life*. Berkeley: University of California, 1985. An interdisciplinary group of scholars has achieved an important and readable synthesis of one of the major obstacles to hearing the Word within the American culture—a fierce individualism that affects our definitions of commitment, communion, and Church.

Regis A. Duffy, *On Becoming a Catholic: The Challenge of Christian Initiation*. San Francisco: Harper & Row, 1984. In this book, the catechumenal process with its persistent emphasis on the Word of God as ''Word from the Cross'' is offered as a model for renewal of Christian community within a commitment context.

EVANGELIZATION: KEY TO A
NEW MOMENT IN U.S. CATHOLICISM

Catherine Pinkerton, C.S.J.

Once again the Catholic Church stands at a point of decision, a time of testing. This is particularly true of the Church in the United States. Ours is a period in history pregnant with the possibility for a new identity for U.S. Catholics, a time when we can emerge as a community of strong moral consciousness in a first world power or fail to realize the prophetic role to which our baptismal commitment calls us.

There is strong evidence of this testing in the questions we ask about ourselves: Why are the gifts of the laity so little recognized within the Church? Why is it so difficult for the institutional Church to address the role of women? Why is the justice agenda not fully embraced by the Catholic community? What right do the American bishops have to speak out on issues such as war and peace and the U.S. economy? Why haven't there been greater ecumenical endeavors? Will we ever see the implementation of shared responsibility at all levels within the Church? What does it mean to be a Catholic?

Questions like these would not have been dreamed about in the pre-conciliar Church. They are indicative of a high degree of pluralism among us, of tensions, confusion, frustrations, the after-shock of Vatican II. Fundamentally, they are a search for a new Catholic identity.

Given the unprecedented challenges facing the Church in the last two decades of the twentieth century, these and even deeper questions become an agenda for those whose ministry is evangelization. They recognize that this is a time of crucial transition. Much more is required than thinking and acting as usual.

I will explore the following questions as a means of focusing on evangelization as the key to a new era in U.S. Catholicism:

1. What movements and events have contributed to the confusion about what it means to be a Catholic in the United States, and what are concrete indications of this confusion?

2. How is an authentic understanding of the nature and process of evangelization key to the development of a valid identity for U.S. Catholics?

CLARIFYING THE CONFUSION:
FROM IMMIGRANT TO MAINSTREAM

Our democratic traditions as U.S. citizens, our religious heritage as Catholics who have experienced the Church since Vatican II and the synods, the movement of the United States into a first world power position, the rapid and continual changes in the global world reality—all are threads woven into our identity as Catholic Christians in the United States. But it is an identity which few Catholics can readily articulate.

In his very fine work, *The Renewal of American Catholicism,* published in 1972, Dr. David O'Brien provides a comprehensive analysis of the factors which contributed to the American Catholic consciousness as it approached and lived through the years of Vatican II. This broad-stroked analysis draws from his book.[1]

The immigrants of the 1840's through the beginning of the twentieth century, until World War II, represented a wave of the European poor, specifically the Irish, Germans, and Italians. A "ghetto mentality" existed among them. They were minorities, most often living in ethnic clusters, following a religion of strong authority patterns and practices very different from those of their neighbors. They were culturally Catholic and faced the dilemma of endeavoring to become citizens of a society which saw their Catholicism as incompatible with the American way of life. They were perceived as paying allegiance to a foreign ruler and adhering to fixed moral codes which, if neglected, would issue in dire results. These immigrants were conscious, however, of the unity and universality of their faith. They accepted the discipline, authority and order it required. They lived the dichotomy of striving to be part of a nation dedicated to personal liberty, independent self-government and the goal of achieving some measure of affluence and success. This was the case for one hundred years.

The onset of Vatican II had a powerful impact on the consciousness of U.S. Catholics. It was a dynamic that forced the American Catholic into new choices. The conciliar teachings challenged some of the elements of their faith which had contributed to cultural Catholicism and separated them from their Protestant neighbors. They were called to integrate the Council's teachings on the freedom of the people of God, the primacy of the individual conscience, and the stress on the ethic of love and justice rather than on a fixed moral code. What did it mean to take responsibility for the life and direction of the Church through new structures such as parish councils and diocesan pastoral councils? They had for decades relied on their clerical leaders for personal and communal decisions. Who actually was in authority? They became intensely aware that what they had known as Catholicism had changed radically in a very short period of time.

It will take Church historians many decades to analyze the radical effects of Vatican II on the U.S. Catholic. The breaking through of the ghetto mentality revealed contradictions, divisions, and paradoxes that had been dormant for many decades. Consequently, different groups placed themselves at divergent points along the continuum of renewal. For some, all change was a departure from the faith. For others, change required too much gradualism or failed to meet their expectations. Some were ready for renewal and realistically embraced it with enthusiasm, knowing that it would never be fully implemented in their lifetime. Certainly, the processes were uneven from parish to parish, from diocese to diocese.

The United States bishops raised this same issue in their report to the Vatican synod's secretariat prior to the special synod on the effects of Vatican II:

> In many respects, the Second Vatican Council has been the greatest gift of the Holy Spirit to the Church in the twentieth century. The council's insights nevertheless came upon the Church quickly and often without adequate preparation. We need now, not to reject the council's legacy, but to understand it better. . . . The council still stands as the best necessary foundation for Catholic renewal in the closing years of the twentieth century.[2]

True, Catholics were unprepared for the implications of the Church's new understanding of herself after Vatican II, an understanding which actually began a process of redefining who they were as Catholics. They were also called to become inserted into and to exercise responsibility within a historical and cultural reality of great complexity. Their Church called them to fashion with her a world of justice and peace.

The final document of Vatican II, "The Church in the Modern World," stated:

> A new humanism is emerging in the world in which man and woman are primarily defined by their responsibility toward their brothers and sisters and toward history.[3]

And within less than a decade after the closing of the council, the 1971 Synod on Justice in the World proclaimed:

> Action on behalf of justice and participation in the transformation of the world fully appear to us as a constitutive dimension of the preaching of the Gospel, or, in other words, of the Church's mission for the redemption of the human race and its liberation from every oppressive situation.[4]

> At the very heart of this world, the Church is to be the locus of conversion . . . the place where the reality of the world is revealed,

where its injustice is laid bare . . . where all are summoned to conversion from this sinful world, not by fleeing the world, but by participation in its transformation.[5]

The very knowledge of that call is far from the consciousness of most
Catholics. Why?

CLARIFYING THE CONFUSION: CULTURAL SHIFTS

It is critical to examine the cultural forces which have been shaping the
consciousness of the post-conciliar Catholic and which have made awareness
of the social mission less than clear—a further element in confusion of Catholic
identity.

The historical reality was and is one of unbelievable change. We live at
an in-between time in history. Constance Fitzgerald, O.C.D., a philosopher,
depicts our historical period as one of impasse, not unlike the dark night of the
soul. For those who have described such a phase in their spiritual journey, it
is a time when God seems so very far away, and at times cannot even be
named, much less called upon. It is a stark moment when who one is or what
one is lies beyond charting. It holds the fear that every effort, every vision and
idea seems fraught with unbelievable limitations, driving one farther and farther into separation from reality and relationships. Those who are students of
the times have little difficulty applying that simplistic description to what is
unfolding in our world. We are, in truth, in that evolutionary dark night and
state of impasse as a nation, as a Church and as a world. As with all moments
of quantum leaps and profound change, we feel disoriented, caught, direc-
tionless. However, ours is also a time of breakthrough, an era of contemplation. We have need to step back, to reflect on the meaning of what is
transpiring around and within us, believing that we are called not to be formed
by the events around us, but rather to transform them, shaping ourselves and
our world toward a preferable future.

In actuality, we are passing between two eras of history, from the industrial revolution to what is termed by futurists as a time of social revolution.
The industrial revolution was not an economic phenomenon alone; it was a way
of thinking and of acting. Science was the modern religion. It promised to save
humankind from natural and religious limits. There was a predictability about
reality. Everything was thought to follow strict principles and laws. The world-
view was orderly. Even humans were thought to behave according to set rules,
each in a similar way. During the industrial revolution, persons became ob-
jectified for consumer and economic reasons. Large corporations emerged;
power and resources became concentrated in the hands of a few. Religion became privatized.

The social revolution, the third wave of history, represents a paradigm shift. It is no longer a matter of predictability. Physical scientists recognize that isolating aspects of the universe is impossible. The human sciences have taught us that persons are infinitely diverse, that they each react differently to given situations. In an open system, there are variables which are not isolated and not predictable. It is in the interrelationship of the parts that reality becomes understandable. There are very few absolutes, "either-or" solutions to problems, but rather "both-and."

Such is the cultural shift into which the "conciliar Catholic" was and continues to be inserted. There is deep societal confusion in this cultural war between the second and third waves of history. The values of which we were once so certain now conflict with new values, both positive and negative. The structures that defined our identity as humans and provided our security are either in a state of disintegration or flux. Significant changes have taken place in defining the family, the neighborhood, the community. There is confusion in understanding the varying relationships between and among individuals or weighing the interpretation of commitment. Self-determination and self-actualization have grasped the human imagination.

Added to the confusion is the fact that we live through our advanced technology in the backyards of the world. The TV screen can frame the global reality instant by instant. What happens in South Africa is back-to-back with the latest neighborhood scandal on the evening news. Violence and terrorism punctuate our every waking moment. We are caught in dramatic dilemmas and contradictions. While on the one hand we call for and work for peace, we prepare for the final conflagration on the other. All of these are evidences of powerful shifts, results of open systems, new consciousness.

How does one respond amid such complexity? Whom does one believe or trust? What are sources of security when those elements and institutions which provided identity and stability are being redefined and in some cases being dissolved? One very real danger is that one may fail to see the positive aspects of the third wave and endeavor to stem its development. There are already movements in that direction. Another alternative may be the choice to live in a tenuous isolation from it, hoping for an eventual return to what one conceives as normality. Such attitudes are not Gospel ones. Ours is the task to find God in the midst of this fragmented but wonderful world being born again through pain and conflict.

CLARIFYING THE CONFUSION:
CHANGES IN THE CHURCH

The search for a Catholic identity is further intensified when fifty-two million Catholics recognize the magnitude of the changes within the fabric of the institutional Church. They experience fewer priests and religious, decreasing numbers of practicing Catholics, more inter-denominational marriages. A recent analysis of the U.S. Catholic population published by The Paulist National Catholic Evangelization Association in Washington, D.C. indicated that one-third of U.S. citizens are unchurched. Of these, thirteen percent were once Roman Catholic. Of that thirteen percent, sixty percent would not consider returning to active practice. However, numbers and personnel alone are not the only factors. Constant unrest centers around topics of celibacy, women priests, birth control, divorce, authority questions. The certainty so much a part of their lives in pre-conciliar days is fragmented.

Yet, there is evidence of great vitality, even of rebirth within the Church. Many people are preparing for ministry in areas of the Church's life. Everywhere, renewal programs draw numbers of people thirsting for a sense of community, a deepening of spirituality, some sense of meaning amid the complexities of contemporary society. What is the quality of faith for which these people yearn? Is the community which they seek a kind of refuge from the harsh realities of life around them? Will the ''renewed'' communities become new ghettos of comfort, of ''bourgeois'' mentality? Why have some parish communities displayed reluctance to admit people who are ''different''? Is this exclusivity a symptom or an accident?

These ''different'' people are represented by the following:

1. Sixteen million Hispanics whose roots are Catholic and who should comprise one-third of the U.S. Catholic population. Many of them attest to a less-than-welcoming attitude in parishes.
2. Twenty-two million blacks, eighty percent of whom live in urban areas. The problem of racism existing within the Church was clearly evidenced in the plea of Bishop Joseph Francis of Newark to the U.S. bishops in 1983. He asked that they devote the same kind of study and follow-up to their pastoral on racism, *Brothers and Sisters With Us,* as they did to the pastoral on war and peace.
3. The Central American immigrants and refugees, the Haitians and Cambodians as well as the numbers of Asian-Americans who seek for their families not only refuge but hope and freedom of spirit.

CLARIFYING THE CONFUSION:
THE U.S. REALITY

Based on its heritage of commitment to liberty, equality, its dedication to human rights, the United States should stand as a beacon of hope to the world. We are essentially a free and open society. We have a marvelous form of government. We are a people of great benevolence. Until recently, our technological and scientific capabilities were unparalleled in the world. It was the fact that America held out to its people the best hope for humanity that led church leadership to call Catholics to love and to participate in national life. To be a good Catholic was consonant with being a good American. Freed from the fetters of the ghetto mentality, Catholics soon overcame the social, political and economic barriers which had kept them from being mainstream. By reason of hard work, education, and determination, they stand today squarely in the middle class representing a segment of affluence.

The growing questions are: Have we become so much a part of the bigness, the consumerism, the competition that represents the quest for the American dream that we have lost the ability to critique the direction, practices and policies of our nation which are in conflict with the Gospel and humanity's best future? Have we become dragged into the sinfulness that webs itself through so much of our social fabric, finding its way into our families, our communities, our business and corporate offices? How do we respond to our nation's preoccupation with sophisticated systems of defense and the massive expenditures, to the Western horror of Communism while ignoring the consequent fear and poverty falling upon humankind as a result? How do we reconcile our comfort with the hunger, ignorance, thirst for justice and political voice of the world's poor? Do we see religion divorced from the ethical and social demands of the Gospel?

If the Catholic community understood its role as a strong thread in the moral consciousness of this nation, it could be a powerful force in bringing greater consonance between the principles upon which this republic was founded and some of its present policies and directions. That Church leadership clearly realizes this potential is evidenced by their recent challenges to the Catholic people.

The U.S. bishops have moved to a near-prophetic stance in their pastorals on war/peace, the U.S. economy, racism, the Hispanics, and in their statements on Central America, South Africa, the Philippines, and capital punishment. Understood correctly, these pronouncements are a critique of the dominant consciousness in our national life. They call for a change not just of legislation or policy or direction; they call for a change of mentality, a change of hearts and minds. They truly represent a challenge to our nation to embrace the agenda of justice and peace. To U.S. Catholics the bishops are signifying that the Church has a major role to play as agent in society.

The reactions and responses to the statements of the bishops are mixed in nature, again reflecting the pluralism among American Catholics and their confusion about the role of the Church in the life of the State. Inherent in the efforts of the bishops, however, is a clear understanding that a coherence is absolutely necessary at this point in U.S. Catholic Church faith life. The bishops are not taking to themselves a political role. Its history cautions the Church about ever again undertaking a purely political task, given its involvement and dominance in given eras of history. Nevertheless, it is challenged to speak to this society and to the global reality taking place. The Church is likewise challenged to stimulate the moral consciousness of its people, pointing the way toward their responsibility as Church for addressing the issues which affect the human community at every level of its life.

For the message to have credibility, however, the Church must regulate the consistency between its own internal life and its proclamations to society. The clarity of its role in helping to fashion a Gospel world reality will stand or fall on how well its own structures, systems, policies and laws are centered in and reflective of the Gospel message. The Church at every level of its life from pew to episcopacy must be a credible witness to the Gospel it proclaims, recognizing and articulating its own need for conversion and reformability.

It is not enough, therefore, that the leadership of the Church promulgate pastorals and statements on significant social issues. They are to be commended for their prophetic leadership and their efforts to teach in this manner. The gap that must be closed is that which exists between them and the wide spectrum of the Catholic membership. How can Catholics be brought to see these positions on social issues as mandates for a change of attitude? As a call to conversion? More often than not, persons in the Church or on its margins who address such issues are considered outside the mainstream, even a cause of some embarrassment.

THE TASK OF EVANGELIZATION

My thesis is that the dynamic which has kept us from adequately addressing the justice agenda is deeper than fear. Our failure to respond as a Catholic community stems from a lack of authenticity, a loss of true Gospel identity. The reasons for that loss were briefly, rather than comprehensively, analyzed. Where do we go from here?

This brings me to what I see as the task of evangelization. No ministry in the Church is as critical as that of evangelization properly understood. Paul VI stated:

Evangelization is a question not only of preaching the Gospel in ever wider geographic areas or to ever greater numbers of people, but also of affecting, and as it were upsetting, through the power of the Gospel, humankind's criteria of judgment, determining values, points of interest, lines of thought, sources of inspiration and models of life, which are in contrast with the Word of God and the plan of salvation (EN no. 19).

Such "upsetting" through the power of the Gospel, criteria of judgment, determining values, points of interest, lines of thought, sources of inspiration and models of life requires a change of consciousness and therefore a process of conversion. Such consciousness would lead to the development of an integrated spirituality which links personal faith and personal conversion with societal and global transformation. Traditional spirituality falls short in disclosing the prophetic dimension of the Gospel. It has focused almost exclusively on the personal relationship with God, neglecting the social as integral to that relationship. What is required is a change of consciousness whereby one comes to see that there are no neutral areas of life. Every action one performs, every relationship into which one enters, every choice one makes either realizes the Gospel or fails to do so. The truly maturing Christian is able to face the contradiction between the ideal and real in society as symbolic of the ideal and concrete within the self. Given this orientation, the maturing person can keep on hoping in spite of the apparent movement of history in the wrong direction and still see the efforts toward justice and peace as fidelity to the God who is forever faithful. Such a spirituality is not a matter of learning about God but of actually experiencing God at the center of everything, the God who is revelatory in history and who calls us to co-create that history by speaking and living the radicalness of the good news.

The task, then, of evangelization and conscientization go hand-in-hand. Too much fragmentation has characterized the past—evangelization and social justice, spirituality and politics, contemplation and action, ministry and prophetic witness. Only in the unity and integration of prayer, community, and ministry focused on the development of a moral consciousness on all human issues can we become authentic Catholic Christians at this time. Evangelizers are called to be catalysts of this new consciousness within the evangelizing community. They can bring those charged with various aspects of the formation of the community (e.g., liturgy, preaching, catechesis, counseling, pastoral services of every name) to focus on the reidentification of the Catholic community as a community of conscience. These communities will be marked, I believe, by emphasis on the development of an integrated spirituality in which the justice dimension will be woven into the fabric of renewal rather than as an adjunct to such processes. Such a dynamic would include:

1. Studying with parishioners the long and rich heritage of Catholic social teaching, the recent pastorals and statements of the U.S. bishops as key to a comprehensive understanding of what it means to proclaim and live the Gospel at this historical moment and in this national and global reality.
2. Strengthening this knowledge by developing the skills of social analysis which would empower people to address structural and systematic

injustice in their ecclesial and civil communities. This should be seen not as an invitation to become involved in the transformation of the world as a humane task, but rather as the vehicle of one's own conversion and faith development.

3. Providing experiences in theological reflection within the community so that every aspect of daily life would be evaluated in the light of the Gospel.

If, then, evangelization and conscientization take hold at every level of the Church's life, we will not fear to face the issues. We will be communities of conscience in our chanceries, our parishes, our religious congregations, our various entities. Freed finally of our "ghetto mentality" and our "bourgeois attitudes," we may become prophetic communities endeavoring to live the radicalness of the Gospel message. As communities of inclusion, we shall welcome all as brothers and sisters, knowing that our wholeness comes from the richness of the integration and giftedness of differences. We shall not only be led to the margins of society; we shall be forced there. As we learn what it means to preach the good news to the poor, we will also come to recognize the depths of our own poverty moment by moment. God, finding us empty, can fill us with love and life. However, we may lose the prestige and the acceptance of many in the mainstream of society. Why? Those who criticize the dominant consciousness and lament their participation in its formation forfeit their membership and relinquish the privileges of belonging. Our right to critique that culture with which we no longer seem to identify will undoubtedly be questioned. Perhaps for the first time we shall know a sense of powerlessness. In all, we may run the risk of becoming a Beatitude people charged with the energy and abandon of the Gospel—not afraid to face the issues.

NOTES

1. David J. O'Brien, *The Renewal of American Catholicism* (New York: Paulist Press, 1972), pp. 1–25.

2. James W. Malone, "Vatican II and the Post-Conciliar Church," *Origins,* September 26, 1985.

3. Constitution on the Church in the Modern World, no. 55.

4. Justice in the World, no. 6.

5. *Ibid.,* no. 38.

DISCUSSION QUESTIONS

1. Out of what interpretation of Gospel mission do you evangelize? Out of what world-view?

2. What does it mean to be a disciple in today's Church? How do you present this concept of discipleship to the catechumen?

3. What would be your definition of an authentic spirituality for our times?

4. As you think about the parish communities into which new members are initiated, what elements are in need of conversion and authentic renewal?

5. What changes do you envision before the U.S. Catholic Community takes seriously the call to evangelization as transformation of the ecclesial and world reality?

FOR FURTHER READING

Walter Brueggemann, *The Prophetic Imagination* (Philadelphia: Fortress Press, 1978).

Brueggeman holds that at this period of history prophecy should be given serious consideration as an element in ministry. He explores the task of prophetic ministry as nurturing, nourishing and evoking a consciousness and perception alternative to that of the dominant culture around us. This work offers great challenge to those who evangelize in the U.S. Church.

Jose Comblin, *The Meaning of Mission* (Maryknoll: Orbis Books, 1984).

Proceeding from his belief that the theology of Gospel mission has not yet been developed and spelled out satisfactorily, Comblin develops his thesis that we are on the threshold of a new way of living the Christian life. This dynamic will revitalize the older churches and lead to the establishment of new churches.

Vincent Cosmao, *Changing the World* (Maryknoll: Orbis Books, 1984).

Cosmao offers the reader a new and challenging rereading of the Gospel in the light of today's problems. From this rereading and social analysis, he develops a comprehensive agenda for the churches of Judaeo-Christian tradition.

Johannes Metz, *The Emergent Church* (New York: Crossroad, 1981).

Metz examines the "bourgeois mentality" of the German Church and the contradictions between that mentality and the messianic reading of the Bible. His analysis is highly applicable to the American Church and is an excellent corollary to Brueggemann's *The Prophetic Imagination*.

David J. O'Brien, *The Renewal of American Catholicism* (New York: Paulist Press, 1972).

Though written in the early post-conciliar period, O'Brien's responses to the question "What does it mean to be an American Catholic?" are ones which still deserve serious consideration. O'Brien traces the "coming-of-age" of American Catholicism and sees its renewal as interrelated with social and political action.

Michael Walsh and Brian Davies, *Proclaiming Justice and Peace: Documents from John XXIII to John Paul II* (Mystic, Conn.: Twenty-Third Publications, 1984).

The recent teachings of the Church on justice and the role of the Christian in the modern world offer insights and challenges which the evangelist will find formative of the individual seeking membership in the Church. These documents "sing" of a new vision for U.S. Catholicism.

SHARED PRAXIS: AN "ORDINARY" APPROACH TO EVANGELIZATION

Thomas H. Groome

My essay is a reflection on the issue of method for evangelization. *Evangelii Nuntiandi* certainly makes it clear that evangelization is a perennial task of the whole people of God, a constitutive part of the Church's mission in which all baptized Christians are to participate. The preceding essays in this volume have reiterated and expanded upon that mandate. That as Christians we are to evangelize is beyond doubt. But how will we go about it? With the challenge well defined, it is appropriate now to ask such a "how to" question with a certain urgency and with an eye to the historical reality of pastoral practice.

I will suggest one "approach," not so much a method as a style for doing evangelization. I call it an "ordinary" approach, first, because it is a rather everyday way of structuring such human interaction, and, second, because I envision it being used in an ordinary moment of interchange between a Christian evangelizer and a curious inquirer. Extraordinary moments of conversion, the proverbial Damascus Road experience, may well require another approach entirely and I have had scant experience with such moments.

Before offering my "ordinary" response to the "how to" question, however, I must first summarize what I understand to be the purpose of Christian evangelization. I do so, not to harrow ground that has already been well plowed both in *Evangelii Nuntiandi* and in the preceding essays, but because my suggestion of a "how to" arises directly from my understanding of the "what for" of evangelization. I'm convinced that we must always keep clearly before us what we are evangelizing "for" if we are to devise adequate and appropriate ways of proceeding. So—what is the purpose of Christian evangelization?

FOR "LIBERATING SALVATION"

I think it is fair to say that traditionally we considered the ultimate purpose of evangelization to be the "saving of souls." We brought the good news to those who had not yet heard it or who having heard it had rejected or fallen away from it, in order to aid their eternal salvation. That salvation, however, was understood exclusively in a spiritual and other worldly sense.

One of the richest gifts that comes to us from *Evangelii Nuntiandi* is an expanded understanding of salvation. Without losing the spiritual and extra-historical dimensions of salvation in its fullness, *Evangelii Nuntiandi* stretches the notion to a holistic understanding that attends as well to the intra-historical liberation of all people, on personal, interpersonal and social levels. The document is careful not to reduce salvation to "a simply temporal project" or "to material well-being" (EN 32). Liberating evangelization must always lead people towards "the divine absolute" (EN 33) and include "the prophetic proclamation of a hereafter, [humankind's] profound and definitive calling" (EN 28). But while reiterating such traditional affirmations about our purpose in evangelizing, the document insists that salvation is also to begin within history, with a liberation "from everything that oppresses [humankind]" (EN 9). It adds that the Christian community in announcing the good news has the duty to proclaim liberation from all that prevents our full humanity . . . "and the duty of assisting at the birth of this liberation, of giving witness to it, of insuring that it is complete" (EN 30).

The very language pattern in which the document often interchanges the words salvation and liberation or talks of "liberating salvation" points compellingly to its broadened and holistic understanding of salvation. It is this expansion that brings the document to offer its own most pithy statement of the purpose of evangelization.

> For the Church, evangelization means bringing the good news into all the strata of humanity, and through its influence transforming humanity from within and making it new. . . . The purpose of evangelization is therefore precisely this interior change, and if it had to be expressed in one sentence the best way of stating it would be to say that the Church evangelizes when she seeks to convert . . . both the personal and collective consciences of people, the activities in which they engage, and the lives and concrete milieu which are theirs (EN 18).

Note that the good news is to enter into all strata of society, to transform humanity from within, to convert the personal and social consciences of people and to transform the historical contexts in which we live. This is why proclaiming the good news calls us to actively engage in "promoting in justice and in peace the true, authentic advancement of [humankind]" (EN 31). Nothing less will be the good news of God's reign (EN 8 and 34), that symbol which calls us to do God's will on earth as it is done in heaven. The reign of God in Jesus, and conversion thereto, demands a radical and on-going commitment to the transformation of ourselves and our social structures toward God's vision of peace and justice, love and wholeness for all humankind.

Evangelii Nuntiandi insists that the content of evangelization must always "be profoundly dependent on Gospel teaching and faithful to the magisterium" (EN 43). Yet, its meaning and purpose must always be indigenized and adapted within each cultural and social context (EN 40). This brings us to the pressing question, also suggested by the subtitle of this volume of essays: What are we evangelizing "for" *in the United States of America?* Surely our sense of purpose takes a distinctive twist when we remember that we are to evangelize for liberating salvation in the richest and most powerful nation on the face of God's earth. Ours is a nation founded on the kingdom principles of "liberty and justice for all." That we enjoy a goodly measure of both liberty and justice cannot be denied. But there is also a deep and pervasive underside to our American reality which is not of God's reign. The rampant consumerism of our society that absorbs forty percent of the earth's resources with only six percent of its population; the economism (as Pope John Paul II calls it in *Laborem Exercens*) we so readily practice that makes profit the supreme law; the racism that continues to divide us and discriminate against anyone other than the white majority; the sexism and patriarchy that denies women their equal rights and diminishes the humanity of men as well; the often myopic foreign policy of our government that supports racist and totalitarian regimes as long as they promise to alleviate our "red scare"; our demonic militarism that has placed the nuclear sword of Damacles over the heads of humanity; the "abortionism" in our society that has led to the wanton destruction of millions of unborn lives—all of this and more presents the Christian evangelizer in America with pressing social responsibilities.

Our Catholic bishops have issued their pastorals on racism and peace, and are preparing statements on the economy and on sexism precisely because they realize that as American Christians, citizens of the most influential nation in the world, we must face our social and political responsibilities with special urgency. As members of a universal Christian community we must remember that the underside of our American society has dreadful consequences far beyond our own borders. Our sinful social structures help to maintain countless millions of people in the third and fourth worlds in poverty and oppression. The struggles for liberation in those worlds will bear little fruit without a revolution of values in our own. Evangelization of people for Christian faith in this country, then, cannot be reduced to an individualized process of bringing people to accept Jesus as the Savior of their souls. It calls us to evangelize ourselves and others toward a radical conversion, a transformation of our own hearts and lives that will express itself in action for social and political transformation of our nation according to the values of God's reign. With that sense of purpose in mind, we are now ready to reflect on how we might go about such evangelization.

SOME PARAMETERS FOR OUR PROCESS

Evangelizing people to become disciples of Jesus can never settle for bringing them to the "right idea" of discipleship but must be formative for following his "way" in a lifestyle of right action. That is a lifelong conversion process that calls us constantly to critically discern the meaning of the Gospels in our historical context and to commit ourselves to living their truth on all levels of our existence. That kind of conversion is very similar to what Paulo Freire means by "conscientization," the kind of critical consciousness that acts to change one's self and one's reality. Evangelization in Christian faith requires a process that will help people to critically reflect upon their own lives and structures (political, economic and cultural). This reflection must be done in the light of a personally appropriated and critical understanding of the Gospel for the sake of action toward self and social transformation. Christian evangelization must use a process that will, by God's grace, bring people into what we might call a "kingdom consciousness"—that is, a critical reading of reality in light of a faithful reading of the Gospels, and the decision to change one's life and the social reality of America toward the coming of God's reign. A process that does not evangelize for such kingdom consciousness and action (what Gutierrez calls "conscientizing evangelization"[1]) is unlikely to promote the kind of salvation/liberation of which *Evangelii Nuntiandi* speaks.

The Church is capable of such evangelization insofar as we are a community that clearly and effectively signifies and embodies a reign of God consciousness in the world. Vatican II describes the Church as "the universal sacrament of salvation"[2] and *Evangelii Nuntiandi,* footnoting that description from Vatican II, calls the Church "the visible sacrament of salvation" (EN 23). But as we call the Church a sacrament of salvation we must remember our time-honored and traditional description of a sacrament: an effective sign that causes to happen what it signifies. To be a sacrament, then, of salvation/liberation requires that the Church embody within itself the values of God's reign and actively engage in our society on behalf of those values. To be such an efficacious sign, we, as a Christian community, must be ever renewing ourselves, ever attempting to eradicate from our midst all forms of social sin; patriarchy, sexism, triumphalism, clericalism, racism, consumerism, ageism, abortionism, and every other form of structural oppression. Such ecclesial renewal is essential if we are to be credible partners in the struggle against all forms of social sinfulness in the society and world.

> As a sacramental community, the Church should signify in its own internal structure the salvation whose fulfillment it announces. . . .
> As a sign of the liberation of [humankind] and history, the Church

itself in its concrete existence ought to be a place of liberation. . . .
If we conceive of the Church as a sacrament of the salvation of the
world, then it has all the more obligation to manifest in its visible
structures the message that it bears.[3]

For us as a Church, then, the very process of evangelization requires that
we put our own house in order. Nothing will more readily attract people to
investigate a life of Christian faith than if the Church lives what it preaches.
And nothing is more likely to turn people away from Jesus and the Gospel than
the Church's obvious failure to be an effective sign of the values of God's
reign. Let us be clear that our efforts to renew the Church, the challenge to
recognize and honor the rights and duties of all the baptized, the struggle for
women's full participation within it, our attempts to make ourselves into an
inclusive community of love, peace, justice, and reconciliation—all such efforts at ecclesial reform are a constitutive part of our process of evangelization.
Without such public praxis—because a sacrament must be seen to be effective—who will ever believe that the salvation we proclaim means "liberation
from everything that oppresses [humankind]" (EN 9).

Having said all of that, however, it would be naive to claim that the
Church must first put its own house in perfect order before it attempts to evangelize. If we wait that long, we may never get to the task at all. We must remember that the act of evangelizing is always a "two way street." In
evangelizing we also become evangelized. Getting on with the task of evangelization may well be among the most effective ways of renewing our faith
community. Surely that lesson has been learned from our parishes that have
attempted to implement the RCIA. The efforts to recruit and form new members in Christian living has been a powerful source of reform for the parishes
themselves. And so, we return to the more methodological question of how to
go about evangelizing in a specific historical moment when we attempt to bring
God's good news in Jesus to someone who has not yet heard it, or having heard
it has not accepted its challenge, or who had once accepted it but whose faith
has now become dormant.

SOME HINTS FROM THE PRAXIS OF JESUS

There is a certain style or approach to evangelization that we can detect
in the praxis of the historical Jesus. It is evident in particular Gospel incidents
but it is even more noticeable if we stand back from particular examples to get
the overall impression of how he went about it. I will suggest five characteristics of his approach to evangelization that provide hints as to what our style
should be.

1. To begin with, and to note the obvious, Jesus took the initiative of going into the towns, villages and marketplaces of life to proclaim his message. Active recruiting was a hallmark of his style of evangelizing. But it was his own living witness, his own embodied truth, that most attracted people to investigate his word. Having aroused interest, he could then say "See for yourself" and invite scrutiny of the praxis of his own life (see Lk 7:18–23 and Mt 11:2–6).

Both as a community and as individual Christians we too must take that same kind of initiative and outreach to unchurched people or to dormant Christians. In our neighborhoods, businesses, leisure and work places, we will constantly find opportunities to invite people to look at the "way" of Jesus as a model for making meaning out of their lives. We must sear into our consciousness the responsibility we have by our baptism to take those opportunities. Our outreach can obviously be done by formal programs sponsored by a local parish or church agency, but it can also be as low-key as a well-placed few words at the right time, even in a casual conversation. Having attracted the interest of a would-be catechumen, however, our lives must then be ready for scrutiny as to how well we embody "the way" ourselves. Upon such scrutiny a person's continued interest in being a disciple of Jesus is likely to rise or fall.

2. Returning to the praxis of Jesus again, we can see that having attracted attention, his style of evangelization was then to invite people to turn toward their own reality, their own lives, and to reflect upon them. This style is most obviously evident in his use of parables. As stories raised up out of the everyday reality of his hearers, Jesus posed the parables as icons through which people could look to see their own selves, values, lifestyles, issues, etc. In contemporary language, the parables were Jesus' way of turning people toward their own present praxis in the world.

He never used the parables, however, to simply confirm his hearers in their present praxis and ways of looking at life. Instead, he constantly gave unexpected twists to his stories that tended to turn the worldview of his hearers upside down, to call them and their praxis into question. None of his hearers would have expected the Samaritan to be neighbor to the man beset by robbers; none would expect the father to welcome home the prodigal after he had jeopardized his birthright. Such subversive twists were his way of inviting people to critically reflect upon their lives, to question the very ground on which they stood, to come to a whole new consciousness and way of looking at life. In short, he used the parables as a conscientization process.

The style of our evangelizing too must always invite people to look closely at their own lives, situations, and praxis in the world. This requires that we be cognizant of the context and issues of the people we would evangelize. *Evangelii Nuntiandi* wisely advises:

> Evangelization loses much of its force and effectiveness if it does
> not take into consideration the actual people to whom it is addressed,
> if it does not use their language, their signs and symbols, if it does
> not answer the questions they ask, and if it does not have an impact
> on their concrete life (EN 63).

But while beginning with the reality of people's own praxis, then we must pose
the kinds of questions that cause them to reflect critically upon their lives. We
must invite them to "decode" (Freire's term) their own reality, to unmask their
forgotten assumptions, to question their taken-for-granted views, to discern the
likely and intended consequences of their present lives. Bringing people to critically reflect upon their own reality ought to be a constitutive part of the process if it is to be a "conscientizing evangelization." In such critical reflection
on present praxis lies the possibility for coming to a kingdom consciousness.

3. In the praxis of Jesus we see that while he invited people to look critically at their own reality, he also had a new word for them, the good news
that God's reign is at hand (Mk 1:14). This is to notice that his evangelizing
included definite moments of clear and confronting instruction in which "he
taught them with authority" (Mt 7:27). His instruction was in continuity with
the faith of his Hebrew ancestors. He insisted that he had not come to abolish
the law and the prophets but "to make their teachings come true" (Mt 5:17).
But he also brought new dimensions and depth to the old story, new alternatives to confront old ways. He could boldly proclaim, "You have heard it said
. . . but I say."

As we evangelize, we must also be informed and ready to share the "faith
handed down," to make accessible the rich traditions of Scripture, teachings
and practices that represent the faith of our Christian community. At times that
instruction will be a priestly word of consolation, at other times a prophetic
word of confrontation, or again a political word of conscientization. Whatever
its flavor, our instruction should never be made to sound like stale rumors. It
must always be good news that brings the promise of new life.

4. In the evangelizing praxis of Jesus we notice a deep respect for the
freedom of his listeners. Notice that his call to discipleship in the Gospels is
always in the vocative case, an invitation to choose for one's self rather than
a command to submit to his authority. He blessed the people who had the eyes
to see and the ears to hear the truth in him (Mt 13:11). But he clearly wanted
people to see and hear for themselves, to come to their own knowing rather
than to what the preacher already knew. His listeners were free to turn away
as with the rich young man in Luke 18 or the disciples in John 6 ("Would you
also go away?"). The two disciples who encountered the risen One on the road
to Emmaus are invited to reflect on their own stories and visions, and are in-
structed in the story and vision of the community. But never are they told what

to see. The Stranger waited for them to come to see for themselves—in the breaking of the bread.

That same respect for the freedom of those we would evangelize must also characterize our style of evangelization. Vatican II, in its *Declaration on Religious Freedom,* said:

> In spreading religious faith and in introducing religious practices, everyone ought at all times to refrain from any manner of action that might seem to carry a hint of coercion or a kind of persuasion that would be dishonorable or unworthy. . . .[4]

Our task is, by God's grace, to sponsor people to see for themselves the truth and meaning of Christian faith for their lives. They are to freely appropriate it and make it their own rather than simply accepting what we tell them or submitting blindly under the weight of any authority.

5. Finally, in the evangelizing praxis of Jesus, while he respected their freedom to choose, there is no doubt that he called people to decision, to a response of changing their lives. Nowhere do we get the impression that he was proposing a philosophical construct for the intellectual titillation of his hearers. Never did he say, as a Greek philosopher of his time might have said, "This is my idea." But he did say "This is my body . . . this is my blood" and called people to decision and discipleship as followers of his way of life. The faith response he invited can never be reduced to intellectual agreement with philosophical ideas. He invited people to decision for a truth that is lived, for a knowledge that is done. "If you live according to my teaching, you are truly my disciples; then you will know the truth, and the truth will set you free" (Jn 8:31–32). Again, we hear the note of freedom there, but that liberating salvation comes from choosing to live his "way," and not merely from an intellectual assent to the teachings of the Gospel.

Our evangelizing, likewise, is to invite people to concrete decision, to the practical consequences of living the Christian faith. Those consequences are to be lived on personal, interpersonal and social levels, in political as well as ecclesial contexts. They must engage the whole person—head, heart, and lifestyle—as he or she comes to live a reign of God consciousness in the world.

SHARED PRAXIS AND EVANGELIZATION

I have written about shared praxis as an approach to religious education in some detail elsewhere, and the reader may wish to refer there for a more detailed description of the approach.[5] Here, however, I want to reflect briefly on the process of shared praxis in the context of evangelization. Shared praxis has much potential as a style of evangelizing, especially when one has a similar sense of purpose as outlined in the opening part of this essay. As an intentional process it is very much in keeping with the style of evangelizing that we detected in the praxis of the historical Jesus.

When shared praxis is used as an intentional process, I understand the most complete expression of it to entail a focusing activity and five closely related movements. The movements will often overlap or be combined; they are to flow together as an orchestrated whole rather than being disjointed; they can be spread over a variety of time frames and may often occur or reoccur out of sequence. Yet, the movements, while they form a whole in practice, can be separated and recognized as distinct for the sake of analysis.

Here I will give the movements names that might be more explanatory for the task of evangelization. I am imagining the process being used in the classic evangelizing situation, the initial outreach with potential Christians; we will call them "inquirers." The use of the process in a more in-depth catechumenal program like the RCIA movement is already quite widespread and familiar. (It could, of course, also be used in a Christian family or community where "all the members evangelize and are evangelized"—EN 71.)

OUTREACH ACTIVITY

The outreach activity is any attempt to generate interest in would-be inquirers about the Christian faith as a way of making meaning out of life. It attempts to turn people toward the ultimate issues of their own lives and the possibilities there may be for them in the Christian faith. An outreach activity could be as obvious as an announcement in a local newspaper or church bulletin that a new catechumenate program is about to begin in a parish. It could be as subtle as a passing word to a friend that invites one to think about his or her own relationship with God with a hint that the way of Jesus might be a model for living that relationship.

MOVEMENT ONE: LOOKING AT ONE'S OWN LIFE IN FAITH

The first movement invites the inquirers to talk descriptively about their lives and especially about how they handle the foundational and generative themes therein—in other words, about how they live in relation to ultimate questions. I am convinced that turning people toward their own ultimacy is an effective way of helping them to find the presence of God in their lives (see Rahner's notion of the "supernatural existential"[6]). This movement might include some actual "God-talk" or it might be a description of their faith, more broadly defined, as their way of making meaning out of life. Thus, an evangelizer might ask "What do you do with the whole question of God in your life?'' or, less overtly, ''When you listen to the heart of yourself, what do you find going on there?''

The evangelizer will play the role of good listener. If he or she raises questions, they should be the kind that help the inquirers to express their own sense of life's purpose, the issues that console or worry them, their hopes and fears, joys and sorrows. The important task here is to bring the inquirers to a conscious expression of their own lives in the world, and the way they have of making meaning out of them, i.e., their own praxis of faith.

MOVEMENT TWO: CRITICAL REFLECTION UPON ONE'S OWN LIFE IN FAITH

If the first movement is describing one's praxis in faith, the second is critical reflection upon what one has expressed. Here the inquirers are invited to stand back from what they said in the first movement and to begin a process of critical reflection that questions their present praxis of faith. In addition to being a good listener, the task of the evangelizer is to raise the kinds of questions that enable inquirers to unmask their forgotten assumptions, to question arrangements that they may be taking for granted, to uncover the familial, social and cultural sources of how they presently make meaning out of life, to imagine their best hopes and dreams for themselves and for those they love.

Depending on the trust level between the evangelizer and the inquirers, the context, the time available, what happened in movement one, etc., the questions here might be such as: What or who has been most influential in shaping your deepest attitudes toward . . . (God, yourself, your sense of purpose, or whatever the ultimate issue may be)? What assumptions are you making when you do or say (such and such)? In what ways are you satisfied with how you handle those ultimate questions? In what ways are you dissatisfied? Is there anything you would like to change about . . . (whatever they said of their present praxis in faith)?

This second movement will often entail biographical reflection but it will include social analysis as well. It can engage people's reason, memory or imagination about themselves in the world. Therein lie the seeds for critical consciousness that can lead to action for transformation. Movements one and two together amount to the inquirers sharing their own stories and visions of life and faith.

MOVEMENT THREE: THE CHRISTIAN STORY AND VISION

The third movement is when the evangelizer deliberately makes present the heart of the Christian faith to the inquirers, especially that of Christianity which responds to the life questions and ultimate issues the inquirers have already raised. Snippets of this story and vision may well have been shared already in the dialogue of the opening movements, but now, in the terminology of the early Christians, this is a moment for deliberately proclaiming the *kerygma* of Christian faith, i.e., a brief summary of its truths, promises and possibilities. (Presumably the didache will come later in a catechumenal program.) The important point is for the evangelizer to bear witness to the good news of Jesus in a way that is likely to be relevant to the life questions of inquirers, to establish points of correlation and resonance between the stories of the inquirers and the story of the Christian community. An example may help to clarify what I mean.

Some time ago I was in a situation where a woman poured out as sad a life story as I have ever heard. In the course of her account she mentioned that she had long ago given up the practice of her Christian faith. The tragedies that had come her way were enough to crush the hopes of any person. She noted that she felt totally abandoned by her family and friends years ago, but had now reached the lowest ebb of all and had concluded that even God had totally abandoned her.

Part of my response to her feeling abandoned by God was to tell her the story of Jesus feeling abandoned on the cross, and of his cry "My God, my God, why you have abandoned me?" We talked about that story for a long time, and at the end of our conversation, she admitted that for the first time in many years, to use her own words, "that character Jesus has begun to interest me again." I was confident that I had been graced to raise up a part of the story that deeply touched the faith praxis of her own life.

MOVEMENT FOUR: MAKING THE STORY ONE'S OWN

The purpose here is for the inquirers to come to see for themselves what they can now see, to appropriate the good news made present in the third movement to their situations, to make it their own in the context of their lives. So often this movement is one of waiting for the evangelizer, one of gentle presence, giving time for the inquirers to do with it all what they will, as the Spirit moves them. The evangelizer must encourage their most honest thoughts, feelings, reactions, insights, and questions. Only thus can they come to make the story their own.

This movement must be totally free of any note of coercion or argument for them to agree with the evangelizer. In that process of "seeing for oneself" lies the possibility of a critical and kingdom consciousness but one that must always be free of manipulation of any kind. The journey of any human being to God is a sacred and unique one. God's grace draws people to himself in a myriad of different ways. The *kairos* time and unique form of that allurement should always be respected.

MOVEMENT FIVE: INVITING DECISION
FOR LIVED CHRISTIAN FAITH

The right time to invite the inquirers to decision must be carefully discerned. It will vary from person to person, and can only be decided in the context of each encounter. That there should be such an invitation to decision at some point, however, seems beyond question. It can be direct or indirect, subtle or quite overt, an opportunity for a major life decision or simply a choosing to take the next small step. As Jesus invited his hearers to decision, so too the evangelizer today must be the catalyst that puts the question to inquirers, in one way or another, "What do you want to do about all this?"

The inquirers will need the continuing support of the evangelizer in their time of decision. Like any fragile plant, they will need a great deal of nurture. People who were once members but left the community may need to reenter gradually and with positive initial experiences. (When one of my undergraduates who has been away from the practice of their faith expresses an interest in "going to Mass sometime" I am always careful to recommend what I think will be a good liturgy.)

The evangelizer needs to remember that the kind of decision invited at this fifth movement must contain within it an honest indication of what it means to live a life of Christian faith in the world. The inquirers should never be given the impression that they are being invited to join a salvation club for their souls in a privatized and other-worldly sense of salvation. They are being invited to begin the process of transforming themselves on every level of their existence within a community that is itself in need of transformation and to contribute to the transformation of our society toward the reign of God.

The critique of their own reality (Movement 2) and the critical appropriation of the story and vision of Christian faith (Movements 3 and 4) can be the beginnings of a kingdom consciousness. But that consciousness must be acted upon for transformation on personal, interpersonal and social levels. Christian conversion will invite them to change their politics as much as their prayers, to struggle for peace and justice as much as to enter or renew a Church affiliation. If we stop short of inviting people to that kind of decision, we have not evangelized for the kind of Christian faith that leads to "liberating salvation." And that must always be the purpose of whatever process we use.

NOTES

1. Gustavo Gutierrez, *A Theology of Liberation* (Maryknoll: Orbis, 1973), p. 116.

2. "Dogmatic Constitution on the Church," *The Documents of Vatican II*, Walter M. Abbott, ed. (New York: America Press), p. 79.

3. Gutierrez, *Liberation,* p. 261.

4. Abbott, *Documents,* p. 682.

5. See Thomas H. Groome, *Christian Religious Education: Sharing Our Story and Vision* (San Francisco: Harper and Row, 1980), especially Chapters 9 and 10. For a briefer description in less technical language see the back pages of the Teacher's Guide for any grade of the *God With Us,* Grades K to 8, religion curriculum (New York: W.H. Sadlier, 1983, 1984, and 1985).

6. Rahner's notion of the "supernatural existential" is the idea that embedded at the heart of human existence is an apriori mediation of God's grace that gives the human person a permanent capacity for the divine. It means that by nature we are lured to the transcendent, to self-consciously and freely reach out toward relationship with God. For a more detailed treatment, see Karl Rahner, *Foundations of Christian Faith* (New York: Seabury Press, 1978), especially the opening chapters.

DISCUSSION QUESTIONS

1. How do you describe what you consider to be the purpose of evangelization?

2. How do you imagine that purpose shaping your own approach to evangelizing?

3. Can you think of some special circumstances that make evangelization in America a unique challenge?

4. What can you learn from the praxis of Jesus about how you might evangelize today?

5. Can you imagine a circumstance in which you might use a shared praxis approach to evangelization? How would you begin?

FOR FURTHER READING

Paulo Freire, *Pedagogy of the Oppressed* (New York: Seabury, 1970).
    A classic work for anyone interested in a praxis approach to any form of ministry but especially education and evangelization.
Gustavo Gutierrez, *The Power of the Poor in History* (Maryknoll: Orbis, 1983).
    Has some excellent sections on what it means to evangelize for "liberating salvation."
John Walsh, *Evangelization and Justice* (Maryknoll: Orbis, 1982).

A helpful guide to what it means to sponsor people toward maturity of faith, while connecting the themes of evangelization and justice.

Sara Little, *To Set One's Heart* (Atlanta: John Knox Press, 1982).

Offers five models for teaching in the context of Church education but also suggestive approaches for evangelization.

USING SOCIOLOGY FOR
EFFECTIVE EVANGELIZATION

Dean R. Hoge

In *Evangelii Nuntiandi,* Pope Paul VI set forth the theological grounding and goal of evangelization. When taking up the topic of methods in Chapter Four, the Pope stressed that methods of evangelizing must vary from situation to situation:

> The question of "how to evangelize" is permanently relevant, because the methods of evangelizing vary according to the different circumstances of time, place, and culture, and because they thereby present a certain challenge to our capacity for discovery and adaptation (#40).

The contribution of sociology is mainly at this point. Sociology as an empirical science has nothing to say about the theological grounding or goal of evangelization, but it has quite a lot to say about methods and strategies. This is because various Christian churches in America have tried out numerous evangelization methods and have commissioned social scientists to evaluate the methods and gather other pertinent data. The research is directly useful to Catholic evangelization, but it is not widely known and appreciated.

By far the most research on evangelization in America has been done by Protestants. This is due to several factors, including the greater emphasis on evangelization among Protestants, the greater pragmatism of Protestant leaders, and a lack of faith in social science among some Catholics. The Protestant research is very relevant to American Catholicism, as we shall see. The purpose of this chapter is to spell out some reliable findings of the research, Protestant and Catholic, which can help church leaders carry out effective evangelization. First I will describe the existing research, then I will discuss three topics: (1) the process of evangelization, (2) persons and groups most receptive to evangelization, and (3) institutional factors aiding evangelization.

OVERVIEW OF EVANGELIZATION RESEARCH

Reliable sociological research can be done on evangelization as much as on any other human social action. But we must be clear about conceptualizing and measuring outcomes. Whereas *Evangelii Nuntiandi* is not very concrete about the desired outcomes of evangelization, sociological research requires some observable or inferable measure of outcomes. In most of the research the outcome is conversion to the church or joining the local congregation. Protestant researchers have often asked why new members have joined one particular Baptist or Methodist or Lutheran church rather than one of the others nearby. Sociological researchers cannot study the inner workings of the Spirit or movements of the heart except as they become observable in attitudes or behavior. And research has little to say about other outcomes of evangelization such as intensification of faith among existing church members, touching large numbers of people through mass media, or social witness for human liberation.

Research on evangelization goes back at least to the 1920's, when Protestant denominations and local councils of churches sponsored dozens of studies. Most were city-wide canvasses sponsored jointly by coalitions of churches, interview studies of persons joining individual congregations, or interview studies of residents of new neighborhoods. Countless city maps were drawn pinpointing locations of Protestant churches, charting neighborhood changes, and rating census tracts on their potential for evangelization efforts.[1] The basic finding was that the evangelizing success or failure of particular missions or churches could be fairly well predicted from neighborhood data on ethnicity, income, family status, and home ownership.

A second type of research assessed the impact of Billy-Graham-type evangelistic campaigns. Several studies were done, using the names of people who came forward at the end of the sermon to give their lives to Christ, or using before-after studies of particular groups who attended the meetings.[2] The findings of these studies can be summarized easily: there is no demonstrated effect of such evangelistic campaigns on unchurched persons. Most of the people who come forward at the altar calls either are strongly committed church members already (who are making a personal reaffirmation of faith) or they have only transient church involvement in the months following.

A third body of research has been done by sociologists and anthropologists studying recruitment to various religious groups. Groundbreaking studies have been done in the past twenty years on recruitment to Pentecostal churches, the Moonies, and several sects and cults.[3] These studies furnish us with the most penetrating information on the processes of religious change.

Research on Catholic evangelization has been less extensive. Joseph Fichter studied converts to Catholic parishes in New Orleans in the 1950's, where he found that seventy-five percent of all the converts came through interfaith marriage.[4] Several studies have been made of recruitment to the Catholic charismatic renewal.[5] And in 1979–80 the writer carried out an interview study of adult converts, sponsored by the Bishops' Committee on Evangelization.[6] It found that an estimated eighty-three percent of all adult converts came through interfaith marriage. One must conclude that evangelization to Catholic parishes has two general forms—conversion as a result of interfaith marriage and conversion as the result of personal religious seeking. We will describe each.

THE PROCESS OF EVANGELIZATION

Most converts to the American Catholic Church come through interfaith marriage. Some people question whether this should be considered evangelization, since the process takes place "naturally," without any evangelization efforts by the Church. This view is only partly correct, since the decision-making accompanying most interfaith marriages is not automatic or "natural" and may have different kinds of outcomes over a five or ten year period.

Researchers have found that interfaith marriage is increasing in the United States, and it will inevitably increase even more. At present about forty or fifty percent of all marriages involving Catholics are interfaith.[7] In the 1950's Fichter estimated the figure at thirty percent for the New Orleans area.[8] The major predictor of which spouse, if any, converts to the other's faith at marriage or soon after is the relative strength of the two persons' church commitment and the church commitment of their respective families. Statistically, the spouse with the weaker church commitment is usually the one to convert, if any, and this is even more true if the church commitment of that spouse's family is also weak. Other factors also have an effect, including the experience of the non-Catholic spouse in the convert class (or the new Rite of Christian Initiation of Adults), the quality of relationships with clergy and fellow laity in the two spouses' churches, and so on. According to the best estimates, the Catholic Church in America loses about as many members through interfaith marriage as it gains.

Turning to evangelization apart from interfaith marriage, we are best guided by impressive research by Lofland and his associates, and by Gerlach and Hine.[9] Their theories have been subsequently shown to apply to many religious groups including Catholics. A simplified version of the Lofland model, adapted to the Catholic Church, is shown in Figure 1. The model has the form of a funnel or a flow chart. At the top are all non-Catholics in America, and at the bottom are a few who have become committed Catholics. Three conditions, or decision points, determine whether any individual person will become a committed Catholic or not. The three decision points have a definite sequence in most cases, so the model describes the vast majority of conversions.

Condition #1 near the top of the model is merely that the potential convert have a Christian world view. Research shows that few persons not having this world view become members of Christian churches, and conversion from a

FIGURE 1
THREE SUCCESSIVE CONDITIONS
FOR BECOMING A CATHOLIC CONVERT

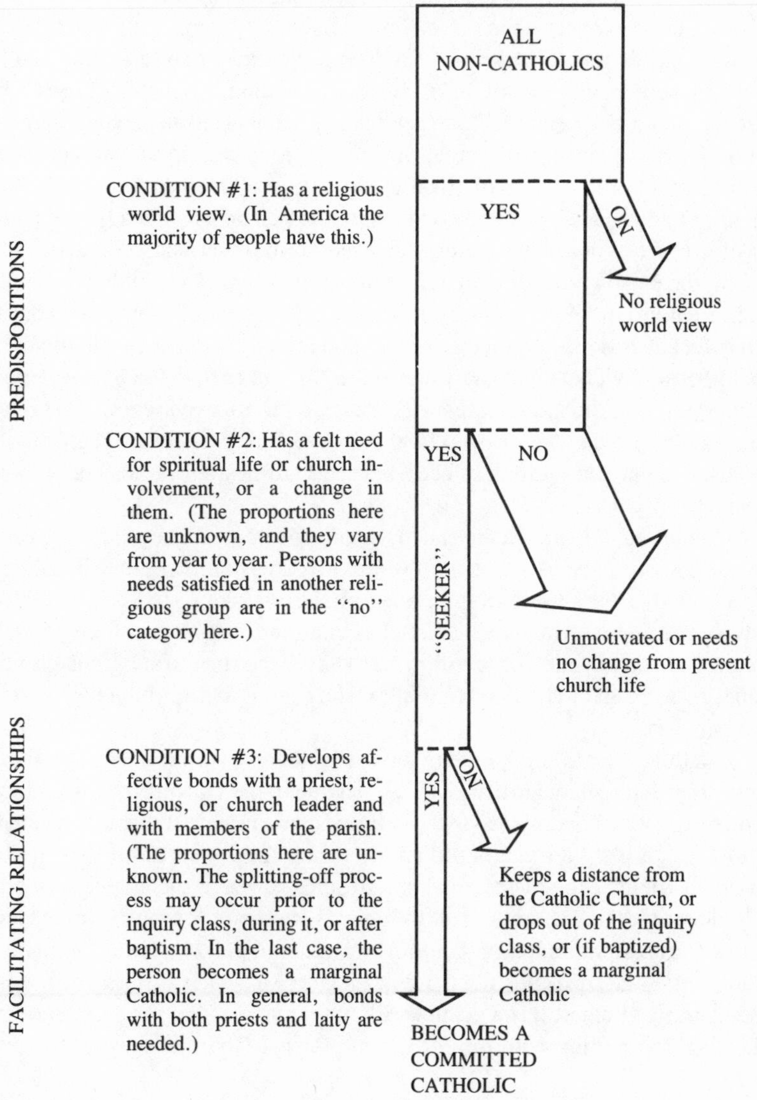

ALL
NON-CATHOLICS

PREDISPOSITIONS

CONDITION #1: Has a religious world view. (In America the majority of people have this.)

YES

ON

No religious world view

CONDITION #2: Has a felt need for spiritual life or church involvement, or a change in them. (The proportions here are unknown, and they vary from year to year. Persons with needs satisfied in another religious group are in the "no" category here.)

YES   NO

"SEEKER"

Unmotivated or needs no change from present church life

FACILITATING RELATIONSHIPS

CONDITION #3: Develops affective bonds with a priest, religious, or church leader and with members of the parish. (The proportions here are unknown. The splitting-off process may occur prior to the inquiry class, during it, or after baptism. In the last case, the person becomes a marginal Catholic. In general, bonds with both priests and laity are needed.)

YES   ON

Keeps a distance from the Catholic Church, or drops out of the inquiry class, or (if baptized) becomes a marginal Catholic

BECOMES A
COMMITTED
CATHOLIC

[From Dean R. Hoge, *Converts, Dropouts, Returnees* (Washington, D.C.: USCC Publications, 1981) p.17.]

163

totally secular world view is very rare. In the United States today the vast majority of people have some version or variation of a biblical world view, and this makes the United States a more receptive missionary territory than, for example, an Islamic nation or one with a predominantly animistic world view. Therefore the widest arrow leading from condition #1 is Yes.

Condition #2 is that the person have a felt need for spiritual life or church involvement, or for a change in them. The person may have a feeling that he or she lacks personal meaning, or needs affirmation, or feels oppressed by guilt, or is at a dead end in life. Such feelings may occur in situations of life change such as marriage, divorce, movement from one city to another, sickness, marital crisis, or loss of a loved one. At such times the most basic and urgent religious questions come to the fore. The person may already be a member of a church, but if the feelings of need are not met and satisfied in that church, the person will begin to search for other options and will become open to different groups. Very often members of a church will be open to a change if they feel a barrier between themselves and their own clergy or fellow members. Most individuals in society are in the No, rather than the Yes, category in condition #2, though feelings will change with life experiences, and it has been rightly said that the mission field is forever being renewed. People in the No category have traditionally been labeled hard-hearted or not ready to receive the Gospel.

Conditions #1 and #2 are called "predispositions." They may be present for months or years. A person with both predispositions present is called a "seeker," that is, he or she is in need of spiritual help and is more or less actively seeking it. American society has thousands, maybe millions of seekers; they are candidates for recruitment to any of a range of religious groups. Some are dormant or alienated Catholics who cannot find spiritual help in their own parishes.

Condition #3 is unlike the others. It is not an internal state but rather a question of interpersonal relationships. The potential convert must develop a positive affective bond with a priest, religious, or church leader and with members of the parish. Personal bonds are necessary for any recruitment to occur. No one is brought to any religious group solely through theological teaching or Bible study. (Understanding of this point is one source of success of the new Rite of Christian Initiation of Adults.) An affective bond includes familiarity, authenticity, and trust. It is not a pseudo-relationship such as might be used in salesmanship. Rather, it is a genuine reaching-out from one person to another, affirming and joining with him or her in praising God and seeking to know God's will.

The person with whom the seeker develops an affective bond is called a "facilitating person" by the theorists. Facilitating persons are usually someone the potential convert knows beforehand. The most effective facilitating persons are relatives, neighbors, close friends, and fellow workers. New relationships such as might be established in evangelization meetings or house-to-house calling are not strong enough to serve for facilitating converts, though they may develop into enough strength and affirmation in the course of time.

One theorist stresses that evangelization is matchmaking. The person is not converted to religion in general or to the Catholic Church in general but to a particular group at a particular location with a particular leader. Like matchmaking, the process takes time and involves a process of courtship and testing, since it depends on the development of strong bonds of trust and affirmation.

The most potent facilitating persons are priests, sisters, or parish leaders, since they embody a great amount of what the parish is. Bonds with priests are the most powerful of all. But bonds with fellow lay members are needed if the person is to maintain commitment over a period of time; if they are lacking, the person will not feel at home in parish life and will often drift into being a marginal Catholic.

The model does not emphasize preaching and teaching until rather late in the process. This point is emphasized in a Mormon evangelization handbook which describes the most common processes in evangelization and recommends that teaching Mormon doctrines to potential converts should be delayed until personal bonds are established with at least one family in the congregation. The manual says that the most promising persons to be recruited are married couples concerned about family life, and the most effective evangelizers for them are Mormon couples in similar circumstances.[10]

This theory of evangelization has only a limited place for mass media or various forms of advertising. They are useful only as help to the crucial bond-building process. The most effective use of evangelization crusades is as occasions for awakening weak ties to other persons. For example, during an evangelization program a committed church member can go to a neighbor or workmate and say, "Katy, our church is having a terrific program on _____ which I think is worthwhile, and you will too. Would you like to come with me on Sunday night?"

PERSONS AND GROUPS MOST RECEPTIVE TO EVANGELIZATION

As the model of the evangelization process indicates, not all people are equally receptive to evangelization. Most people do not possess condition #2—having a felt need for spiritual life or church involvement, or for a change in them. But researchers have discerned some definite patterns in receptivity of persons and groups. One finding has been that people have a greater felt need for a change in spiritual life or church life after other changes in their lives. Religious change is often a result of other life change. In American middle class culture most life decisions revolve around work and family life, and religious life is especially associated with the family. Therefore changes in family life are predictive of openness to change in spiritual life—either toward greater or less involvement, or possibly for recruitment to another group. From this it follows that people new in town are more receptive to evangelizers than are unchurched people who have been in town for a longer time. It is because movement produces openness, and after six months or a year, relationships in a new setting tend to solidify.

Another finding has been that young adults are more receptive than older adults. In our interviews with new converts in 1979–80, we found that even among the converts not in an interfaith marriage, young adults predominated. The median age was thirty-four. A principal explanation is that in American society more life changes occur for young adults than older adults. For example, residential mobility studies have found more moves per decade, on the average, for people in their twenties than in their thirties, more for people in their thirties than in their forties, and so on.

The most receptive group is young adults taking on stable adult roles. When young people marry and have children, settle into careers, buy a home or at least psychologically buy into a community, and begin thinking about family life, they are often interested in immersing themselves in a church community and deepening their understanding of faith and tradition.

It is possible to design evangelization efforts based on the overall receptivity of various groups. In America there are three main target groups for evangelization—inactive Catholics, inactive Protestants and Jews, and persons without any religion. Active Protestants and Jews are by and large not available, since they are committed to their own groups. Of the three target groups, the one with greatest yield per unit of effort is inactive Catholics. This is the experience of evangelizers, and it follows from the process model outlined above. It is because the predispositions for evangelization are more present among inactive Catholics than anyone else. The target group with least yield per unit of effort is persons without any religion. They often lack a world view similar to Catholicism, and their other attitudes tend to be liberal and relativistic.[11] Also their social networks include relatively few committed Catholics; hence facilitating persons are rarer.

Since inactive and alienated Catholics are a prime target for evangelization, some research has been done on them. A 1978 Gallup survey was commissioned to study unchurched Americans, and it used a minimal definition of "active"—namely, that a person is an active churchgoer if he or she attended church at least twice in the last year, not counting Christmas, Easter, weddings, and funerals. By this measure twenty-four percent of all Catholics are inactive, about fifteen million in all. Inactive Catholics are disproportionately male, young, living in the western states, in broken families, and married to non-Catholics. They are less educated than active Catholics and less inclined to join other organizations (besides religious organizations). They are less happy in general than active Catholics, and they are less satisfied with their family lives. They are more tolerant of variations in personal behavior, including use of marijuana, premarital and extramarital sex, abortion, and use of pornography.[12]

Inactive Catholics are not disinterested in the Church. Eighty-seven percent would like a child of theirs to receive religious instruction. Their religious beliefs are not greatly different from active Catholics; for example, seventy-six percent of them believe in the resurrection of Christ, compared with ninety-three percent of active Catholics.

Why are they inactive? We interviewed about two hundred in 1979–80 to try to find out. The reasons given us were numerous and difficult to interpret, but we found out that a massive dropping out from church occurs among teenagers and persons in their twenties. It takes place partly as a by-product of tensions in their families, partly because the youth object to Catholic moral teachings or are living in conflict with them, and partly because they have developed no internalized faith and thus find the Mass boring.

Many inactive Catholics can be reattracted to active church life later, through new facilitating persons. People who had bad experiences with priests or nuns in the past will often respond to different priests or nuns in different places, who authentically reach out to them. People who had unpleasant experiences in their parishes as youth will often be open to reuniting with a different style of parish at a different place.

I would like to tell of a very interesting research experiment we did in 1979. We bought two advertisements in Washington, D.C. newspapers saying that a research team at Catholic University wanted to talk with inactive Catholics. The ad said that no effort would be made to change anyone's views; we wanted only to listen. In the first two days we had about one hundred calls, and later about forty more came in. We interviewed some people in group settings and others by phone. Though the people were diverse, we found that they had one predominant kind of life story: they had been reared in a strong Catholic upbringing, usually including Catholic school, and they affirmed this experience. Then later there was an incident or development which thrust them out of the Church. It was upsetting, and years later it was still bothering them. The incidents varied, but many had to do with birth control, divorce, marriage to a non-Catholic, annulment, or teachings about sex. A few had to do with Catholic schooling for children, conflicts with priests, or disillusionment with the Church for one reason or other.

Now these people were in a third phase of their religious life. After their initial alienation from the Church, they were trying to reach out again. When they saw our ad they phoned us with the vague hope that we might facilitate some form of detente with the Church. At least we might listen to them and affirm that they were not such bad people after all. When we interviewed them we soon saw that they were not much interested in being part of a research project. Rather, they wanted to speak to priests, and they wanted love and reconciliation. We referred a number of them to a priest who was actively ministering to alienated Catholics.[13]

The lesson we learned was that a large number of alienated Catholics are ready to begin fresh conversations with the Church, and if the situation feels right they are ready to confess, take the sacraments again, and become active. The barriers which are keeping them away are burdens, and if they can be thrown off the people experience joy and new life.

INSTITUTIONAL FACTORS AIDING EVANGELIZATION

Finally, let me note some implications of evangelization research regarding institutional factors. I shall mention five.

First, parishes in certain social settings can be expected to have greater success in evangelizing. The most favorable setting is in a neighborhood with young families of above average education, and with a fairly high rate of moving in and out. Neighborhoods with population movement present more opportunities for evangelizing.

Second, certain styles of parish will have greater success in evangelizing. Based on information from our interviews in 1979–80, we know that parishes with a greater sense of ownership by the lay people will do better, since their lay people will be more effective as facilitating persons. A participatory leadership style encourages this sense of ownership. The more people love their parish and its members, the more effective evangelizers they will be.

Third, we have noted that priests and women religious are especially effective as facilitating persons since they are perceived as representing the essence of the parish. Pastors should become visible in the broader community, insofar as this is possible, in roles which embody the Gospel and the nature of the parish. Public service and advocacy roles are examples.

Fourth, parishes should be encouraged to develop their own identities, symbols, and styles. If lay people talk of their parishes as having a specialness, evangelization is aided. They will say, ''We're the parish who *does* this or that, or who *is* this or that,'' or ''We're a special parish.'' Rapid changes in parish staffing inhibit the development of such special parish identities and should be avoided, especially if positive identities are developing. Also rapid changes in staffing hinder the development of strong human bonds in the parish.

Fifth, church-shopping among Catholic parishes aids the matchmaking process and enhances the chances that potential converts will develop facilitating relationships in at least one parish.

But institutional policies are not the main thing. Evangelization is spiritual and interpersonal, not institutional. It occurs where genuine human bonds develop between committed Catholics and outsiders and where the bonds are nurtured in a setting of praise, love, and service.

NOTES

1. For an introduction to this work see H. Paul Douglass and Edmund de S. Brunner, *The Protestant Church as a Social Institution* (New York: Harper and Row, 1935) and Murray H. Leiffer, *The Effective City Church,* 2nd ed. (Nashville: Abingdon Press, 1961.)

2. See Kurt Lang and Gladys Engel Lang, "Decisions for Christ: Billy Graham in New York City," in Maurice R. Stein (ed.), *Identity and Anxiety* (Glencoe, Ill.: Free Press, 1960), pp. 415–27, and Weldon T. Johnson, "The Religious Crusade: Revival or Ritual?" *American Journal of Sociology* 76:873–90 (1971).

3. See John Lofland and Rodney Stark, "Becoming a World-Saver: A Theory of Conversion to a Deviant Perspective," *American Sociological Review* 30:862–75 (1965); John Lofland, "Becoming a World-Saver Revisited," *American Behavioral Scientist* 20:805–18 (1977); Luther P. Gerlach and Virginia H. Hine, *People, Power, Change: Movements of Social Transformation* (Indianapolis: Bobbs-Merrill, 1970); David A. Snow, Louis A. Zurcher, Jr., and Sheldon Ekland-Olson, "Social Networks and Social Movements: A Microstructural Approach to Differential Recruitment," *American Sociological Review* 45:787–801 (1980).

4. Joseph H. Fichter, *Social Relations in the Urban Parish* (Chicago: University of Chicago Press, 1954), p. 76.

5. See Michael I. Harrison, "Sources of Recruitment to Catholic Pentecostalism," *Journal for the Scientific Study of Religion* 13:49–64 (1974); Kenneth H. McGuire, "People, Prayer, and Promise: An Anthropological Analysis of a Catholic Charismatic Covenant Community," Ph.D. dissertation, Ohio State University, 1976; Max Heirich, "Change of Heart: A Test of Some Widely Held Theories About Religious Conversion," *American Journal of Sociology* 83:653–80 (1977); Meredith B. McGuire, *Pentecostal Catholics* (Philadelphia: Temple University Press, 1982).

6. Dean R. Hoge, with Kenneth McGuire and Bernard F. Stratman, *Converts, Dropouts, Returnees: A Study of Religious Change Among Catholics* (Washington, D.C.: U.S. Catholic Conference, 1981).

7. These figures are estimates, since no exact information exists. See Dean R. Hoge and Kathleen M. Ferry, *Empirical Research on Interfaith Marriage in America* (Washington, D.C.: U.S. Catholic Conference, 1981).

8. Fichter, *op. cit.,* p. 76.

9. See note 3.

10. The Mormon manual is discussed in Rodney Stark and Williams Sims Bainbridge, "Networks of Faith: Interpersonal Bonds and Recruitment to Cults and Sects," *American Journal of Sociology* 85:1376–95 (1980).

11. Data on characteristics and attitudes of the target groups are given by David A. Roozen in *The Churched and the Unchurched in America: A Comparative Profile* (Washington, D.C.: Glenmary Research Center, 1978). For other data on inactive Catholics see the Gallup Organization report *The Unchurched American* (Princeton, N.J.: Gallup, 1978).

12. Roozen, *op. cit.*

13. Dean R. Hoge, Kenneth McGuire, and Bernard F. Stratman, "Using the Newspaper to Contact Inactive Catholics," Xerox report (Washington, D.C.: Office of Evangelization, 1979).

DISCUSSION QUESTIONS

1. Why have Catholics in the past stressed evangelization less than American Protestants?

2. Can evangelization skills and methods be taught to committed church members, or are they something which is either naturally present or absent?

3. Which roles and activities in a priest's life are most crucial for aiding evangelization? Is the priest's person or office more important?

4. Will the current shortage of priests be a hindrance to evangelization in America? What steps might be taken to avoid any hindrance?

5. The evangelization process model stresses "facilitating persons." Who is able to fulfill this role, and for which persons?

FOR FURTHER READING

Dean R. Hoge, with Kenneth McGuire and Bernard F. Stratman, *Converts, Dropouts, Returnees: A Study of Religious Change Among Catholics* (Washington, D.C.: U.S. Catholic Conference, 1981). This easy-to-read report tells of the results of an interview study with converts, Church dropouts, and people who returned to Church life. It includes thirteen illustrative life stories.

Gallup Organization, *The Unchurched American* (Princeton, N.J.: Gallup Organization, 1978). This survey report provides the most useful data available on churched and unchurched people in America—including churched and unchurched Catholics. It is composed mostly of data tables, with a short interpretative essay.

A CATHOLIC VISION
FOR THE SOUTH
Bernard Quinn

When Matthew Ricci, S.J. came to China in 1583 he faced a blank wall. Almost nothing was known about the Chinese and their way of life. At his death in 1610, the Christians in China numbered about twenty-five hundred, including many persons influential in the national life. Christianity had been presented as an acceptable religion both intellectually and spiritually, and missioners were thought of as learned and holy men.[1]

Ricci's approach had three dimensions. First, he took the Chinese culture seriously: he studied it. Second, in presenting the Catholic faith he not only condemned the evil he found in China, but he lifted up the good. And third, he had a vision: a China fully Chinese and fully Catholic.

In the Chinese culture and religion Ricci found much to condemn. He had little patience for the Buddhism and Taoism of the time, which had degenerated into idol worship, superstition and exploitation. He made no secret of his views, thus exposing himself to the wrath and resentment of the parties involved.

Ricci spent long hours at home in his pavilion poring over the literature of Chinese philosophy and history. He discovered a tradition-directed society, where the reverence for ancestors was strong and education was a process of imbibing the traditions handed down. From this he knew he would have to present Christianity as a fulfillment rather than as a novelty. He was pleased to discover, therefore, that the Confucian philosophy of harmonious relationships, virtue and cosmic unity could serve as an excellent base. He was able to present Christianity as the fulfillment of the highest aspirations of the Confucian ethic. The Chinese were delighted to learn from Ricci that harmonious human relationships could somehow become caught up into the very life of God.

Ricci took the Chinese culture seriously enough to be willing to adapt his missionary style. Instead of saying, "All missioners preach; therefore I must preach," he asked, "In Chinese society how do ideas and values actually get communicated?" He found that only political radicals made use of open preaching, but that books were considered sacred and influential in Chinese life. For this reason he devoted considerable time to writing. His book on friendship became a Chinese classic. In the same way, after first adopting the style and dress of the religious holy man (bonze), he later adopted the dress and manner of a learned "graduate," which gave him a more influential role in Chinese life.

Perhaps the most significant characteristic of Ricci, however, was his Catholic vision. A vision is a mental image produced by the imagination. Ricci's image of the future embraced a Chinese expression of Catholicism which was at the same time true to the genius of the people and fully incorporated into the unity and universality of the Catholic Church. He was not interested in importing European forms or customs into China. He was not interested in syncretism—a religion half-Christian and half-pagan. He was not interested in departing from the teaching or discipline of the Roman Church. His dream for the future was a China fully Chinese and fully Catholic.

Partly because of the work of Father Pasquale D'Elia, S.J. in editing the Ricci *fontes*[2] during the early decades of the twentieth century, Ricci's ideas on culture entered into the missionary thinking of Vatican Council II.[3] Since the council there has been much interest in "inculturation," especially in the third world. Now it is time to ask if those of us committed to evangelization in our own country can begin to think in the same way. I suspect that if Ricci had been assigned to evangelize Italy, his native land, he would have taken the same basic approach that he did in China. He would not have thought that he knew all about the Italians from the perspective of evangelization, just because Italy is where he was born and raised. I also suspect that he would have studied the culture just as thoroughly as he studied the Chinese culture, and would have struggled toward some vision of what, in the particular circumstances of the Italy of his time, Catholic evangelization should rightly bring.

As evangelizers, can we too have a Catholic vision for the south?[4] Can we dream of a south that is fully southern and at the same time, with all the necessary qualifications, fully Catholic?

SHOULD CATHOLICS DEVELOP A VISION FOR THE SOUTH?

What right has the Catholic Church to have a religious vision for the south? Isn't it presumptuous to develop hopes and dreams for a region where 62.8 percent of the people are active members of other Christian churches, and only 2.9 percent of the people are Catholics?[5] Does such an attempt somehow imply arrogance and a lack of respect for the south, its churches and its religion? After all, Ricci was dealing with a non-Christian land. The south is heavily Christian. From the religious point of view, China and the American south can in no way be equated.

It is not for lack of appreciation for southern religion that Catholics desire to develop a special vision. Catholics recognize that the Holy Spirit is present in the other churches and ecclesial communions, "working through them as instruments for the sanctification of their members, using their ministers and their authorities, not withstanding the structural and other defects of these churches and communities."[6] In the words of Vatican II, "These separated churches . . . have by no means been deprived of significance in the mystery of salvation."[7] Whatever vision is developed, therefore, will be expressed in the context of a profound respect for these ecumenical realities, and a humble appreciation for the past, present and future roles of the Protestant churches in creating the region's religious spirit.

On the other hand, the Catholic Church is what it is.[8] "This Church [of Christ]," as Vatican II stated, "constituted and organized in the world as a society, subsists in the Catholic Church, which is governed by the successor of Peter and by the bishops in union with that successor, although many elements of sanctification and of truth can be found outside of her visible structure. These elements, however, as gifts properly belonging to the Church of Christ, possess an inner dynamism toward Catholic unity."[9] What Christ gives his Church through the Holy Spirit is the *fullness* of the elements of grace by which the Church is constituted. Historically that fullness is found in the Catholic Church, but not in the sense that *some elements are not also truly found* in the other churches and ecclesial communities.[10]

Conscious of the fullness which it possesses, therefore, the Catholic Church is entirely at ease in concerning itself with the religious needs of the whole inhabited world.[11] Without the Catholic Church, gathered and constituted in a given place, the fullness of Christ is simply not present. The Church, therefore, does not exclude from its loving care, in faithful and humble service, even those areas like the south, where other Christians are in the majority. But in developing a vision in such areas, it must be conscious of the many elements of sanctification also contained in the other Christian churches, and must keep them strongly in mind. Catholics, therefore, are called upon to combine gratitude for what is already there with consciousness of the fullness that could be. We do not ask "How can we compete?" but "What gifts can we bring?"

WHAT CATHOLICISM CAN BRING TO THE SOUTH: THE CONTENT OF THE CATHOLIC CONTRIBUTION

Discovering "what gifts we can bring" is not as easy as it might sound. Like Ricci, we must be ready to devote the time and effort to answering this question that the magnitude of the task requires.

What we are seeking is nothing less than insight into the *content* of the Catholic contribution to the south, the ultimate basis of a Catholic vision. I would suggest that *four questions,* drawn from an analysis of Ricci's life and work, will help us to define our task:

1. What are the values, beliefs and practices in the religion and other cultural dimensions of the south that need to be *affirmed, strengthened, celebrated?*
2. What are the values, beliefs and practices that need a *different stress* than they now have?
3. What values, beliefs and practices are lacking and need to be *supplied?*
4. What values, beliefs and practices are evil and need to be *condemned?*[12]

Some examples from southern culture will serve to illustrate how these questions apply. I will use the Baptist faith as a point of departure, not because there are no other significant denominations in the south, but because that faith is such an important cultural element.[13]

The seventeenth century Baptist movement in England was essentially a reform within a reform.[14] Baptists were dissatisfied with the half-hearted reforms of Henry and Elizabeth, and carried to its logical conclusion the basic Protestant instinct to remove the "Catholic clutter" between God and man that was the heritage of the Middle Ages. Baptists stressed devotion to the Bible and the individual's direct and personal relationship with God through Jesus Christ. This personal relationship is brought about by the direct action of the Holy Spirit, who elicits a conversion experience in the believer, which in a classic sense is sudden and emotional in nature. Conversion is often the result of a moral crisis, a recognition of sinfulness, and a determination to accept Jesus Christ as personal Savior. In this extremely personal religion there is little room for sacraments in the Catholic sense, or for church authority, religious orders, saints or liturgical practices.

1. Along with Baptists we can *affirm* the importance of a personal relationship with God, relating it to the Catholic mystical and ascetical tradition. We can rejoice in the Baptist zeal for the Bible, even though we locate the Bible differently within the tradition of the Church. We not only affirm but are inspired and encouraged by Baptist zeal for evangelizing the neighbor; here through their good example Baptists call us to greater faithfulness to our own Catholic tradition.

2. From a Catholic perspective, other elements of Baptist practice will call for a different *stress*—the social dimensions of morality, for example, or the gradual and incremental workings of God's grace within our hearts, even sometimes without a self-conscious moment of conversion.

3. Catholics are called upon to *supply* the Eucharist and the other sac-

raments, not as symbols only but as real encounters with Christ. Other missing elements include the communion of saints, the richness of monasticism and other forms of religious life, and the gift of Church authority, which can carry people beyond the horizon of their own culture and experience and free them to meet the universal Christ.

4. Although not specifically in the area of religion, an example of what needs to be *condemned* in the general culture is racism.

It is clear that bringing the fullness of Christ requires us to struggle with *all four* of the questions, not just with one or two. Acceptance, affirmation and praise of the culture is certainly called for; it is part of the gift that we bring. Yet however conscious we are of our own failings, there are times when we are compelled, in imitation of the Lord, to reject and oppose what cannot be tolerated or sustained.

Because we are firm in believing that the fullness of Christ is to be found in the treasury of the Church's storehouse, embedded somewhere, at least, in the universality of Catholic tradition and experience, it is up to us to bring forth from this storehouse things both new and old (Mt 13:52). On the other hand we must be ready to learn from the graces and gifts he has placed in the hearts of others, so that those we serve can lead us on to a greater faithfulness to our own tradition. For example, the zeal that Southern Baptists show in caring for the spiritual welfare of others can inspire us to greater efforts in evangelization. "Bringing gifts," therefore, should constitute a true "exchange."

TOWARD A CATHOLIC VISION FOR THE SOUTH

Suppose, in God's providence and in his own good time, the Catholic Church is able to make the contribution we have been talking about, and the gifts we bring are freely received and welcomed. When these gifts are added to what is already there, what would the south look like? In other words, what is our Catholic "goal" or "vision" for the south?

It is necessary to approach this question in two ways: to consider the Church's vision in general, insofar as it applies to *all* places, and to consider how that vision needs to be particularized in a *given* place.

First the Church's vision in general. Our hope would be that most of the people would come to believe the fullness of Christ's message and to possess within the unity of the Catholic Church the fullness of divine assistance to live according to its implications. Thus we would visualize organic Church unity, whether this comes about through the reconciliation of church bodies or through the reconciliation of individual persons in an ecumenical spirit. Beyond reconciliation, however, we would hope that many would be struggling to live according to the Gospel they profess, not only in their directly religious activities, but in their familial, economic, educational, political and recreational lives as well.

As a result of all this, the fullness of the Christian message would eventually come to provide an ultimate basis, or living core, not only of religious life, but of the familial, economic, educational, political and recreational systems. Thus the fullness of Christ's message would become embedded not only in the hearts of individuals, but in the social systems and culture[15] as well. As Paul VI states in *Evangelii Nuntiandi*, "The Church evangelizes when she seeks to convert, solely through the divine power of the message she proclaims, both the personal and collective consciences of people, the activities in which they engage, and the lives and concrete milieux which are theirs."[16]

If the Church's general vision is to bring the fullness of Christ's message to the hearts of individuals and to all the social systems, what are the characteristics of that vision that apply to a particular region, that is, insofar as one region differs from another? First, the Church desires to incorporate everything that is good in the regional culture into a local expression of the fullness of Christian practice and belief. As Vatican II states, "[The Church] fosters and takes to herself, insofar as they are good, the ability, resources and customs of each people. Taking them to herself she purifies, strengthens, and ennobles them. The Church in this is mindful that she must harvest with that King to whom the nations were given for an inheritance and into whose city they bring gifts and presents."[17]

At the same time the Church tries to bring the people of the region into the closest possible unity, in faith and communion, with the universal Church.[18] What this unity implies, by way of church practice and discipline, by way of theological and philosophical categories in which the faith is expressed, and by way of daily life and custom is not immediately evident, and insight into these matters will require much work. Needless to say, this insight will not be achieved apart from the active guidance or apart from obedience to the Apostolic See, whose particular task "consists exactly in serving this universal unity."[19]

A Catholic vision, therefore, would see a south enjoying unity in diversity—possessing a distinct religious expression, but united in faith and communion with the universal Church. Our hope is for a region fully southern and fully Catholic.

AN APPROACH BASED ON THE VISION

If all this is to become a reality, the Church must move ahead on several distinct but related fronts. First the faith of the Catholic community must be nourished. Second, there must be efforts at reconciliation among Christians, corporately or individually. Third, the unchurched[20] must be evangelized and brought into full unity with the Church. And fourth, there must be direct efforts at Christianizing the temporal order so that the familial, economic, educational, political and recreational systems will embody the Gospel message. Some of these ministries will be carried out by the Church in its own name, acting officially as Church; others will be done by individuals acting in their own names as baptized Christians.

All four ministries—nurture of the Catholic faithful, seeking Christian unity, evangelizing the unchurched, and Christianizing the social order—are related to one another. For example, conversion of heart is a prerequisite for Christianizing the social order.[21] Thus a direct focus on nurture, unity and evangelizing the unchurched is very much in order. In the same way, if the social order is based on truly Christian principles, individuals can more easily live a Christian life. Thus direct efforts to Christianize social systems and cultures is needed. One ministry is no substitute for another; there must be a direct focus on all four, even though not every person in the Church is called to be equally involved in all. So if our interest here is in evangelization, and especially of the unchurched, we need to carry it out in an atmosphere which acknowledges and supports the complementary role of the other dimensions of ministry in making our Catholic vision a reality.

Turning our attention to the unchurched of the south, we find that there are 10.5 million people—more than one-third of the population—who do not actively participate in any religious group.[22] Many of these people come out of evangelical Protestant backgrounds, and all of them have been influenced by the evangelical ethos that plays such an important part in the life and culture of the south. Our hope, as Catholic evangelizers, is to help them approach Christ more fully and to gain unity with the Catholic Church. Through the Church, Christ offers them the key to the meaning of life, an individual and social moral teaching, and helps—both visible and invisible—for participating in the divine life.

What may we say to them, through our words and through the witness of our lives, that will help them come closer? Later on, after the content of our Catholic contribution to the south has been set forth in greater detail, it will be possible to give a more definite shape to our evangelical message. Nevertheless, two principles, drawn from observation of the methods of Matthew Ricci, can be applied. The first principle is, "Not only affirm but supply," and the second is, "Appeal beyond the felt needs."

Not Only Affirm But Supply. In approaching the unchurched it is appropriate, of course, to stress the elements within Catholicism that are also found in the evangelical southern religions. Bible study and devotion to the Bible would be one obvious example. But it is also important to stress the Christian elements that we supply which are *not* already there, such as sacramental realism in the Eucharist. This is not done in any competitive sense, or with a condescending attitude toward evangelical religion, but as an expression of our love. Unless we can communicate to the unchurched that Catholicism contains a fullness of Christ's riches, we are not making our best contribution. We wish to draw people into unity with the Church not only on the basis of elements which Protestants share with us already, but on the basis of Catholic fullness in Christ. Such an approach also offers persons consciously or unconsciously looking beyond evangelical religion the alternative of a true choice.

Appeal Beyond the Felt Needs. In evangelization it is important to take into account the needs that people actually feel, but not to base our presentation of the Christian message exclusively on them. There are real needs, for example the Eucharist, which ought to be awakened by evangelization, even though people might not feel the need at first. The dimensions of the Christian message that correspond to these unfelt needs should not be omitted for fear of rejection, however careful we might be to discern the proper time. Further, a whole hierarchy of values usually enters into an important human decision. It is the evangelizer's responsibility to emphasize certain values over others and to clarify the relationships among them. Certainly the desire for security, spiritual comfort, self-fulfillment, esteem, prestige, emotional experience, and a sense of belonging could all consciously or unconsciously affect a person's decision to join the Church. But evangelization must make clear that all these things are subordinate to the love of God and neighbor, and to the desire to participate in a eucharistic community that offers a share in the divine life.

EVANGELIZATION AND CONTENT

I hope this brief treatment of the two principles will highlight the importance of searching for a clear understanding of the precise *content* of the Catholic contribution to the south, whether the four questions from Ricci be taken as a method of doing this or not. It is my purpose to suggest that this content, once understood, should constitute the primary and indispensable basis of Catholic evangelization. Techniques and methods are important, of course, and cannot be overlooked. But understanding *what* the Church brings to the south, through evangelization and other dimensions of ministry, is *absolutely essential* to implementing our Catholic vision: a south—someday, perhaps not even in our lifetime—truly southern and truly Catholic.

NOTES

1. Sources in English include: Louis J. Gallagher, trans., *China in the Sixteenth Century: The Journals of Matthew Ricci* (Random House, 1953);

Jonathan D. Spence, *The Memory Palace of Matteo Ricci* (Viking, 1984); Vincent Cronin, *The Wise Man from the West* (Doubleday, 1957).

2. Pasquale M. D'Elia, S.J., *Fonti Ricciane* (Rome: La Libreria dello Stato, 1942), 3 vols.

3. See, for example, *Decree on the Church's Missionary Activity,* n. 22; *Pastoral Constitution on the Church in the Modern World,* n. 62.

4. The principles I intend to develop can be applied to any distinct cultural region, even though I will discuss them in the southern context. The term "south" here refers to the states of Alabama, Georgia, Mississippi, North Carolina, South Carolina, Tennessee and Virginia. See *Apostolic Regions of the United States* (Glenmary Research Center, 1978).

5. The population of the states of Alabama, Georgia, Mississippi, North Carolina, South Carolina, Tennessee and Virginia is 30,819,155 (U.S. Census 1980). Of these, 895,464 are Catholics; 19,360,271 are members of other Judaeo-Christian bodies; and 10,563,420 are unchurched (GRC statistics, 1980).

6. J.L. Witte, S.J., "Ecumenism and Evangelization," in *Documenta Missionalia 9* (Rome: Gregorian University, 1975), p. 205.

7. Vatican II, *Decree on Ecumenism,* n. 3.

8. See the remarks of Lukas Vischer, in "The Unity of the Church: A Report to the Central Committee [of the World Council of Churches]," *The Ecumenical Review* xxv:4 (October 1973), p. 488.

9. Vatican II, *Dogmatic Constitution on the Church,* n. 8.

10. Witte, *op. cit.,* pp. 209–218.

11. Paul VI, *Evangelii Nuntiandi,* n. 54.

12. "For the Church it is a question not only of preaching the Gospel in ever wider geographic areas or to ever greater numbers of people, but also of affecting and as it were upsetting, through the power of the Gospel, mankind's criteria of judgment, determining values, points of interest, lines of thought, sources of inspiration and models of life, which are in contrast with the Word of God and the plan of salvation" (Paul VI, *op. cit.,* n. 19).

13. In the southern states mentioned in footnote 4, Southern Baptists represent 19.6 percent of the total population. See *Churches and Church Membership in the United States 1980* (Glenmary Research Center, 1984).

14. This material is taken from Richard Tristano, *What Southern Catholics Need To Know About Evangelical Religion* (Glenmary Research Center, 1984).

15. As used here, the term "culture" refers to shared patterns of believing and acting generally expected of individuals and social systems. There is growing realization among church leaders of the nature and importance of culture itself. Inspired by discussions among missiologists in the early part of this century, which was reflected in the documents of Vatican II, a specialized lit-

erature on "inculturation" is now beginning to appear. See, for example, A.A. Roest-Crollius, "Inculturation and the Meaning of Culture," *Gregorianum* 61:2 (1980), pp. 253–273; Louis J. Luzbetak, *The Church and Cultures* (Divine Word Press, 1963).

16. Paul VI, *op. cit.*, n. 18.

17. *Dogmatic Constitution on the Church*, n. 13. In the same vein, the council's *Decree on Missionary Activity* says, "From the customs and traditions of their people, from their wisdom and their learning, from their arts and sciences, these churches borrow all those things which can contribute to the glory of their Creator, the revelation of the Savior's grace, or the proper arrangement of Christian life" (n. 22). And the *Pastoral Constitution on the Church in the Modern World* states, "The good news of Christ constantly renews the life and culture of fallen men. It combats and removes the errors and evils resulting from sinful allurements which are a perpetual threat. It never ceases to purify and elevate the morality of peoples. By riches coming from above, it makes fruitful, as it were from within, the spiritual qualities and gifts of every people and of every age. It strengthens, perfects, and restores them in Christ. Thus by the very fulfillment of her own mission the Church stimulates and advances human and civic culture" (n. 58). We cannot expect, therefore, that there will be no change as a region grows into the fullness of Christ; any change in values implies a cultural change. Ideally, however, the change will lead to an even fuller expression of the best qualities of the region's people.

18. See Vatican II, *Dogmatic Constitution on the Church*, n. 13 and Paul VI, *op. cit.*, nn. 61–65.

19. "A particular task of the Apostolic See consists exactly in serving this universal unity. Indeed, that is where its specific office lies, and, we may say, the charism of Peter and his successors": John Paul II, "One Church, Many Cultures," quoted in *Origins* 14:30 (January 10, 1985), p. 500.

20. The term "unchurched" refers to all persons who do not actively participate in any Judaeo-Christian religious body. The unchurched are not necessarily unbelievers; studies show that most unchurched have some relegious background and belief.

21. "Every effort must be made to ensure a full evangelization of culture, or more correctly of cultures. They have to be regenerated by an encounter with the Gospel. But this encounter will not take place if the Gospel is not proclaimed": Paul VI, *op. cit.*, n. 20.

22. See note 5.

DISCUSSION QUESTIONS

1. What are the values, beliefs and practices in the culture of the region that you live in that need to be affirmed, strengthened and celebrated?
2. What are the values, beliefs and practices that need a different stress than they now have?
3. What values, beliefs and practices are lacking and need to be supplied?
4. What values, beliefs and practices are evil and need to be condemned?

FOR FURTHER READING

Richard Tristano, *What Southern Catholics Need To Know About Evangelical Religion* (Atlanta: Glenmary Research Center, 1985). The origins of evangelical religion, the basic elements of faith and practice of Southern Baptists and United Methodists, and the role of evangelical religion in southern culture. Includes suggested readings.

Vincent Cronin, *Wise Man from the West* (New York: Doubleday, 1957). A popular life of Matthew Ricci, S.J.

Bernard Quinn, *Mission, Missions and the Creative Planning Process*. Theological basis for pastoral-missionary planning and action.

EVANGELIZATION: A GLOBAL PERSPECTIVE

Roman R. Vanasse, O. Praem.

The "global perspective" promised in the title will be sketched over the pages of the following five sections: (1) The Emergence of a "World Church," (2) The "Global Village" and the Church, (3) *Evangelii Nuntiandi* and the Universal Church, (4) The New Context of Evangelization, and (5) Conclusions.

THE EMERGENCE OF THE "WORLD CHURCH"

The focus for Jesus' ministry was the conversion of Israel, and it was only after his death and resurrection that the disciples were given the mission to be his "witnesses in Jerusalem, throughout Judea and Samaria, yes, even to the ends of the earth" (Acts 1:8). The first major struggle as the early Church sought to define its identity was between those who held that Gentile converts should be obliged to follow the whole law of Moses, and those, led by Paul, who believed that these elaborate dietary and other customs should not be imposed on the new converts.[1] This struggle between the "Judaizers" and their opponents was finally resolved by the Council of Jerusalem largely in favor of the apostle to the Gentiles, with the support of Peter and the other disciples.[2] It was this decision, fueled by the Spirit of Pentecost, which led to the veritable explosion of missionary activity resulting in the foundation of churches throughout the Roman empire by the time the last apostle died, and, thereafter, the gradual Christianizing of that empire until the conversion of Constantine.

The Church which developed eventually into "Christendom" when it included all of Europe grew through a subtle and complex interpenetration of faith and culture which today we call "inculturation."[3] The distinction between faith and culture is a modern one, however, and so played no conscious part in the missionary activity of the early Church. Until recently, in fact, Western culture was routinely exported along with the Gospel, despite the insights of some of the early missioners, such as Matteo Ricci.[4]

The pivotal event in the early history of the Church was the gradual realization of the disciples that they were more than a Jewish sect, but had received the mandate from Jesus to "go and teach all nations" (Mt 28:19). It was this realization which sparked the dramatic missionary thrust of the early Church.

Some nineteen hundred years later, in 1962, an event of similar magnitude happened during Vatican Council II when the Church gradually realized that it was no longer merely a European Church with headquarters in Rome and branches on every continent, but rather a world Church composed of local churches, each with its local customs, language and culture which together form the universal Church under the leadership of the Bishop of Rome.[5]

Many factors contributed to this realization, and for the purposes of this article we mention the following: (1) the initiation of serious dialogue with other world religions, along with a positive evaluation of their value; (2) the introduction of vernacular liturgy, one of the first acts of the council;[6] (3) the proclamation of the universal salvific will of God present effectively everywhere, even before the preaching of the Gospel.[7]

These, along with other factors such as the formation of national and regional conferences of bishops, have led to the situation in today's Church where it has become commonplace for Pope John Paul II (as well as his predecessor Paul VI) to travel frequently to all parts of the world and to speak often of the need to "inculturate" the Gospel, so that every member of the Church can be true both to his or her own culture and to the Gospel.[8]

Thus, the Church today is tending toward greater particularization, as local churches are becoming more aware of their own particular characteristics and problems. At the same time, the need for local churches to remain united with one another is also being felt more keenly.

THE "GLOBAL VILLAGE" AND THE CHURCH

As the Chinese curse would have it, we live in "interesting times." If we were to look in history for some parallel to our own century, it would not be the thirteenth century, the age of the "Summae," but rather the twelfth century, the age of the "quaestiones disputatae." There may be a St. Thomas out there ready to put it all together, but he or she hasn't emerged yet. Alvin Toffler, in his book *The Third Wave,* suggests that we have progressed from an agricultural to an industrial to a post-industrial society, while John Naisbitt, in his book *Megatrends,* describes the emerging world as one of "high-tech" and "high-touch" where the principal product is not consumer goods but rather information. Philosophers, economists and ecologists point out that we are living in an increasingly intricate and dense web of worldwide interdependencies.[9] The price of oil, the value of the dollar and its impact on American exports, and the huge debts owed by third world countries point to the reality of a world economy. Acid rain, the drought in sub-Saharan Africa, and the pollution of our oceans and rivers point to the effect that the wasteful habits of some nations have on the rest of the world. In April 1985, Helmut Schmidt, former head of the German government, gave a series of lectures on "The Reality of Interdependence and the Anachronism of National Strategies."[10]

A related phenomenon that is shrinking the world is the fact that through TV, satellites, radio and computers, all of us can become, at times, part of a world-consciousness or planetary awareness that is able to focus the attention of many millions of people from every part of the world simultaneously on one event such as the landing of the first man on the moon, a presidential inauguration, an earthquake, or starving children in Ethiopia. On Good Friday, April 5, 1985, at 10:50 A.M. EST, eight thousand radio stations around the planet played the song recorded by forty-six American rock stars called "We Are the World." Uncounted millions of people listened to the song and its message, since transistor radios are available in even the remotest regions.

For the Church as well, this shrinking of the world and the emergence of the "Global Village" provides a counterpoint and a force which helps to counteract the tendency for each country or region to become increasingly absorbed in its own affairs. Because of television, satellites and the electronic media, John Paul II has been seen and heard by more millions (probably even billions) of people than all of his predecessors combined. Because of his style and personality, he has probably had a greater impact on more people than any other Pope in history. He is able to speak out on questions of justice and peace which concern not only the audience which he is addressing, but the whole world—and be seen and heard instantly.

EVANGELII NUNTIANDI AND THE UNIVERSAL CHURCH

Most theologians would agree that the Apostolic Exhortation *Evangelii Nuntiandi* is one of the most important documents to be promulgated since Vatican II itself, both in terms of the impact it has had and the discussion it has stimulated. This papal document has its origins in the conciliar documents on the Church[11] and the 1974 Third General Assembly of the Synod of Bishops whose topic was evangelization.[12]

On the principle that the best commentary on a document is the document itself, I will quote briefly from six paragraphs and then merely add some reflections which I hope the reader will find helpful.

1. n. 15: ". . . the Christian community is never closed in upon itself . . . it is the whole Church that receives the mission to evangelize, and the work of each individual member is important for the whole."

2. n. 50: ". . . on the part of the evangelizers themselves, there has been the temptation to narrow down the field of their missionary activity. On the other hand, there has been the often humanly insurmountable resistance of the people being addressed by the evangelizer. . . . Despite such adversities the

Church constantly renews her deepest inspiration, that which comes to her directly from the Lord: To the whole world! To all creation! Right to the ends of the earth!''

3. n. 58: In his comments on ''small communities'' or *communutés de base*, Paul VI notes that they must ''remain firmly attached to the local church, and to the universal Church'' and ''show themselves to be universal in all things, and never sectarian.''

4. n. 61: ''This is how the Lord wanted his Church to be: universal . . . a flock which a single shepherd pastures. A universal Church without boundaries or frontiers . . .''

5. n. 62: ''. . . this universal Church is in practice incarnate in the individual churches made up of such or such an actual part of mankind, speaking such and such a language . . . a Church *toto orbe diffusa* would become an abstraction if she did not take body and life precisely through the individual churches.''

6. n. 64: ''. . . the individual churches should keep their profound openness towards the universal Church. . . .'' Otherwise, we have ''a Church deprived of this universality, a regionalist Church, with no horizon,'' in danger ''of a withering isolationism, and then, before long, of a crumbling away, with each of its cells breaking away from it just as it itself has broken away from the central nucleus. . . . The more an individual Church is attached to the universal Church . . . the more will it also be truly evangelizing, that is to say, capable of drawing upon the universal patrimony in order to enable its own people to profit from it, and capable too of communicating to the universal Church the experience and the life of this people, for the benefit of all.''

These and similar statements point out very clearly the danger of any particular church, whether on the level of a small group, a parish, a diocese or even a nation becoming so involved with its internal problems and projects that it loses sight of the larger reality of which it is but a part: the universal Church. Individual or local churches are somehow a microcosm and a mirror of the one universal Church. While responding to the needs of their own economies, cultures, history and languages, they must also remain profoundly open to the universal Church and to each other.

Since Vatican II, however, and even since the promulgation of *Evangelii Nuntiandi*, the world has undergone profound changes, and the reality of the internal composition of the universal Church has changed dramatically. The next section describes this new reality.

THE NEW CONTEXT OF EVANGELIZATION

The 1974 Synod was a turning point in this process of change, for it marked the first time that the bishops of the third church[13] not only outnumbered the others, but also constituted a dynamic and creative group which "managed" the meeting. The Western Church (i.e., Europe and North America), for better or for worse, is now a minority Church.

A look at some recent and current statistics, as well as some projections, will help us to realize the magnitude of the change which has taken place. At the opening of Vatican II, out of a grand total of twenty-five hundred bishops worldwide, only one hundred and fifty were Asian or African, and most dioceses in those lands were still ruled by European or American bishops. This reflected the fact that for centuries the Catholic Church had been neatly divided between "mission-sending" and "mission-receiving" countries. By contrast, in today's Church, out of the same total of twenty-five hundred bishops, fewer than one thousand are from Europe and North America, while the distinction between "mission-sending" and "mission-receiving" countries is becoming increasingly blurred. Some of the most important positions in the Vatican bureaucracy are now held by non-Europeans, and studies tell us that by the end of the century, seventy percent of all Catholics in the world will live in the developing countries.

There is already a significant mission-consciousness developing in "third world" countries, so that they are beginning to send missionaries to one another. For instance, Mexico and the Philippines are sending missionaries to Africa; some African countries are providing mission help to other African nations, where the need is greater; there is a growing missionary consciousness in South America, and the Korean Church is beginning to send missionaries to other countries, as is India. As these local churches grow toward greater maturity, they will increasingly turn to the evangelization of their own people, while at the same time sending missionaries abroad. Local churches will thus increasingly take responsibility for their own future, while simultaneously exercising their responsibility toward the universal Church under the leadership of the Bishop of Rome.[14]

It has become common today to refer to the whole college of bishops as having responsibility, under the leadership of the Pope, for the mission of the Church to the world.[15] All churches are summoned to generosity and mutual exchange, no church can retire within itself, and the loss of missionary dynamism is now described by many writers as a symptom of crisis or disease.[16]

Slowly, we are learning that we have as much to learn from other local churches as they have from us, and that we need their help as much as they need ours. All local churches are beginning to send and to receive from other local churches, not only funds, but personnel and other resources.[17]

At a time when we in the United States are being told that by the year 2000 fifty percent of the fifty thousand priests who are now active will have reached retirement age, the third world is seeing a tremendous increase in vocations. Many religious communities who have provinces in third world countries are now experiencing their greatest growth and large percentages of their new members coming from those lands.

CONCLUSIONS

What emerges from the above reflections is that all evangelization must look outward toward ever expanding horizons: from individual to family to group to parish to diocese to state to region to country and finally "to the ends of the earth."[18] Indeed, we need to look at all of our ministry and pastoral work from a global or world perspective, or at least include that dimension as an important consideration in all that we do. As Robert Muller says: "We learn so much about the past, and so little about world problems and interdependencies, its future and international institutions."[19] Nowhere is this truer than in most of our parish and diocesan programs, as well as in our seminaries, schools, universities and other local organizations.

Church leaders, pastoral workers, catechists and evangelizers of all kinds will soon face almost daily problems of a global interdependent nature: peace, food, quality of life, increasing numbers of old people, and a new kind of refugee: not political, but nutritional and ecological, as well as people increasingly hungry for human contact in a cold, technological world.

I believe there is an increasingly serious obligation on the part of all those who are in positions of leadership to make their people aware of their continuing obligation to share with the less fortunate of the world, and not just occasionally, when their attention is drawn to a particularly serious problem like starving children in Ethiopia, which happens to be brought to their attention by the mass media.

It is already difficult, and will soon become impossible to live in an international community without, in a social imitation of Christ, exercising some minimum of "kenosis" or self-emptying, of truly universal openness. If we are serious about being part of a Church which has made and maintains a "preferential option for the poor," this may soon demand concrete actions.[20] Even in India, life-expectancy is now at fifty years, up ten years in the last decade, and already we are facing a situation where starvation will be more common and the wealthier, more developed countries such as ours will have to make difficult choices about lowering their standard of living in order to help the poor.

The ultimate goal of all Catholic evangelization remains the same: "That all may be one, Father, even as you and I are one" (Jn 17:11). True evangelization means reinforcing whatever promotes unity while at the same time opposing all forces and tendencies which push us to any form of selfishness, or the exaltation of any person, class, culture or nation over any other. It is unacceptable to say that "we must take care of our own problems first" in this latter part of the twentieth century. While doing all we can to overcome the tendencies toward a too aggressive individualism in our society, which together with consumerism, indifference and relativism make the work of evangelization so difficult, we must at the same time draw upon the natural generosity and openness of the American people. There is a healthy shift in many fields today to what is called a "holistic," that is, an anti-fragmentary approach. I suggest that to be *truly* holistic, our awareness, our theology, our ministry and our efforts to evangelize others must include a truly universal dimension.

NOTES

1. See Donald Senior, C.P. and Carrol Stuhlmueller, C.P., *The Biblical Foundations for Mission* (Maryknoll, New York: Orbis Books, 1983), pp. 255–279.

2. Acts 16.

3. Much has been written about "inculturation." From May 12 to May 17, 1985, a seminar on "Integration of Faith and Culture: The Mission of the Church" was held at Duquesne University in Pittsburgh, sponsored by the Institute for World Concerns. During the seminar, the question of inculturation was studied from many perspectives: historical, anthropological, theological, cultural, etc. The papers from the seminar are due to be published in 1986.

4. See *The Memory Palace of Matteo Ricci,* by Jonathan D. Spence (New York: Viking Penguin Inc., 1984).

5. See Karl Rahner, "Toward a Fundamental Theological Interpretation of Vatican II," in *Theological Studies* 40 (December 1979), pp. 716–727.

6. Constitution on the Sacred Liturgy, *Sacrosanctum Concilium,* December 4, 1963.

7. See Dogmatic Constitution on the Church, *Lumen gentium,* Nov. 21, 1964; Decree on the Church's Missionary Activity, *Ad gentes divinitus,* Dec. 7, 1965; Pastoral Constitution on the Church in the Modern World, *Gaudium et spes,* Dec. 7, 1965.

8. Pope John Paul II, address to the Amerindians of Canada at the Shrine of St. Anne de Beaupre; also, the encyclical *Slavorum Apostoli* of July 2, 1985, nn. 21 and 22. The encyclical is especially significant for what it says about inculturation, and the great efforts made by Saints Cyril and Methodius not to impose the much more sophisticated and advanced Byzantine culture from which they came on the newly converted regions of northeastern Europe.

These early missioners are presented as being culturally sensitive, in the sense of respecting the culture of those to whom they preached, while also respecting traditional teachings.

9. See, for example, Robert Muller's *New Genesis* (Garden City, New York: Doubleday Image Books, 1984).

10. *New York Times,* April 6, 1985.

11. See note 7.

12. See Pope Paul VI, Apostolic Exhortation *Evangelii Nuntiandi,* December 8, 1975, n. 2. This was published in 1976 by the Publications Office of the United States Catholic Conference, Washington, D.C. 20005, with the English title "On Evangelization in the Modern World." This document will be referred to as EN in this essay.

13. The term "third church" has been popularized by Walbert Bühlmann, especially in his *The Coming of the Third Church* (Maryknoll, N.Y.: Orbis Books, 1978). It refers to the "young churches" or local churches in the less developed parts of the world, especially Africa and Asia.

14. See Omer Degrijse, C.I.C.M., *Going Forth: Missionary Consciousness in Third World Churches* (Maryknoll: Orbis Books, 1984).

15. All bishops "are consecrated not just for some one diocese, but for the salvation of the entire world." See *Ad Gentes,* n. 38; see also *Lumen Gentium,* n. 23 and *Christus Dominus,* nn. 4–7.

16. See previous section on *Evangelii Nuntiandi* and the universal church, especially EN, n. 64.

17. For instance, ten percent of all priests now actively working in Germany are from India, and several dioceses in the United States have asked for personnel from third world countries.

18. See Acts 1:8. "To the Ends of the Earth" is also the title of a pastoral statement on the missions by the bishops of the United States. The first draft is due to be published in 1986.

19. Robert Muller, *New Genesis* (see above, note 9).

20. See, for example, Second General Conference of Latin American Bishops: "The Church in the Present-Day Transformation of Latin America in the Light of the Council" (Medellín, 1968); Third General Conference of Latin American Bishops: "Evangelization at Present and in the Future of Latin America" (Puebla, 1979).

DISCUSSION QUESTIONS

The following study questions are meant to be reflective questions which will help the reader to tie the material in with his or her own experience. They are based on a method developed by Dr. Thomas Groome of Boston College.

A. *Before reading the article:*

1. When I hear phrases like "world Church" or "world mission," what are the ideas that surface in my mind? What is the current state of my knowledge and thought on this subject?

2. What are the sources of my current thinking? Have I done much reading in this field recently, or are these ideas which I have had for many years?

These questions can be pondered individually for a few minutes, and then discussed in a small group, if there is an opportunity to do this.

B. *After reading the article:*

1. What are the main differences between my ideas before reading the article, and the vision presented in this essay?

2. How has reading the article influenced my thinking? What ideas have I found most striking? Is there some practical action which I can take to implement any new understanding I might have reached?

Again, these questions are used most effectively if they are considered first individually for a few minutes, and then the answers are shared in a small group.

FOR FURTHER READING

Mission in Dialogue, edited by Mary Motte, F.M.M. and Joseph R. Lang, M.M. (Maryknoll, New York: Orbis Books, 1982), 688 pp. This book contains the proceedings of the SEDOS (Servizio Documentazione e Studi in Rome) research seminar on the future of mission, and covers many of the topics discussed in this essay. There are eight sections, covering the following topics on the local church: missionary dimensions, its mission in secular society, ecumenical relations, missionary institutes, other religious traditions, religious freedom, inculturation, liberation and justice. The papers were written by forty-two authors, and the book concludes with some reflections on the papers and on the seminar itself.

The Biblical Foundations of Mission by Donald Senior, C.P. and Carroll Stuhlmueller, C.P. (Maryknoll, New York: Orbis Books, 1983). These two Passionist Scripture scholars, both teaching at the Catholic Theological Union in Chicago, have given us a 371-page book which covers every aspect of Old Testament (Fr. Stuhlmueller) and New Testament (Fr. Senior) theology of mission. Both authors collaborated on the conclusion, which presents a synthesis of the more detailed study done in the earlier parts of the book.

CATHOLIC EVANGELIZATION IN THE UNITED STATES: AN AGENDA FOR THE FUTURE

Patrick J. Brennan

Any article claiming to offer an agenda or priorities for the future implies some things. Among those implications are: (1) the proposed agenda items are areas of present need not being given sufficient attention, or (2) they are being attended to but more attention will be demanded in the future, or (3) society has developed in such a way that new efforts or strategies are required for newly perceived needs. As I share these ideas about future directions, all three of these implications will rinse through the content: in some ways we are not working (qualitatively and quantitatively) in some areas that we should be; in others we have begun work, but much more is needed; and in still other areas, radically new attitudes and strategies need to be developed if we are to effectively evangelize some groups in the future. The items that follow are not listed in any ordered way. I leave it to you, the reader, with others, to prioritize or rank order these—or add others—as you reflect on your local church.

1. ADDING A TONE OF "FOUNDATIONAL EVANGELIZATION" TO ALL MINISTRIES

It is a mistake to presume baptized Christians have had primary conversion experiences, or have had the foundational experience of consciously choosing Jesus Christ as Truth for and Lord of life. Without such foundational evangelization and primary conversion, the rest of Catholic life such as sacraments and catechesis becomes increasingly irrelevant or non-intelligible. The proclamation of Jesus Christ as the Way, Truth, and Life, the essence of his alternate lifestyle called "the kingdom of God," and the good news of His life, death, and resurrection should be consciously added to each program and ministry. Opportunities ought to be provided for people to decide for Jesus, his values, vision and lifestyle—in a reflective, discerning sort of environment. To be real, the reflection, discernment, and decision process must involve both cognitive and affective dimensions of a person's

191

life. In this process people need help to look critically at the alternate visions, meaning systems, or spiritualities present in America, many of which are evangelically propagated through the media: materialism, consumerism, sexism, racism, militarism, agnosticism, atheism, and subtle forms of idolatry.

I am not suggesting that there is a "cookie cutter" or blueprint plan that parishes and ministers ought to implement to effect this foundational evangelization and primary conversion. Such is the approach of many fundamentalists and evangelical groups that have such narrow, mechanical, and hostile means of "saving" people. Rather, foundational evangelization needs to be retrieved as a *value*. The "how to do it" can be creatively discovered by ministers and parishioners as they prayerfully assess their own situations.

2. DISCOVERING THE POWER OF A CONVERGENCE APPROACH TO EVANGELIZATION

In paragraph 14 of *Evangelii Nuntiandi,* the late Paul VI speaks of evangelization as the basic feature—the central mission—of the Church as we approach the third millennium of Christianity.[1] Paul VI viewed evangelization not as the work of an elite few in a parish, diocese, or curia, but rather as the central work of the entire Church. The model of evangelization that the National Council for Catholic Evangelization has been advocating is a "convergence" model. This model places all ministries converging around the mission to evangelize. The most gratifying experiences I have had as a resource person or facilitator are the times when I work with diocesan agencies or various parish boards in developing a common vision and pastoral plan for a shared effort at evangelization. The convergence model of evangelization encourages people in ministry to discover and engage in a common mission in different ways, based on the gifts we have or the responsibilities that are ours. We are all about one and the same mission.

The absence of this convergence vision perpetuates a crippling, toxic phenomenon in the Church and parishes. It is, for want of a better term, "turfism." Rather than working in a spirit of unity and collaboration toward advancing the kingdom of God, we become stuck in a competitive rut of defending our own kingdoms.

3. THE NEED TO DEVELOP AN EVANGELIZING ATTITUDE

In a recent issue of his newsletter *Evangelization and Initiation,* Father Alvin Illig estimates that less than two percent of American Catholics have an evangelizing mentality.[2] His statistics reinforced an intuition I have had for some time. As American pragmatists, we are quick to run to the latest, most relevant program that "comes down the pike" with its promises of renewing the parish. Too often parishes and dioceses gallop through programs without an ecclesial conversion to the attitudes that those programs espouse. Before evangelization can become a program or strategy, it must first be experienced as an attitude. That attitude is best characterized by words like *invitation* and *mission*. The evangelizing attitude is one that strives to invite all the beneficiaries of evangelization listed in *Evangelii Nuntiandi* to kingdom living, ongoing conversion, and discipleship. The evangelizing attitude is missionary in nature. Rather than resting comfortably with the status quo of maintaining programs and sacramental practice, evangelizers realize that the essence of Church is mission. Not only are we God's chosen people; we are salt, light, and leaven for the world. Personal conversion is incomplete without a sensitivity also to the responsibility we have to address and transform the social order around us. Part of this missionary attitude includes care for those who are alienated from the Church or do not belong to a family of faith.

4. FROM ATTITUDES TO STRATEGIES

As Catholics break out of their personal salvation mind-set, as parishes stretch beyond maintenance, as we in fact convert to this evangelizing attitude, we then can begin to talk about strategies. I advocate "organic" growth models as the most effective strategies for evangelization. While we can learn from each other's successes and failures in evangelization efforts, I fear too often there is a malaise of creativity in Catholic parishes. In this malaise, we wait for one of the big publishing houses to finally produce the program that will answer all of our evangelical needs, or we import programs that have been used elsewhere. Tom Peters, in his recent book *A Passion for Excellence,* stresses that the businesses with the greatest potential for success in America are those where innovation is encouraged and supported.[3] Apply his principle to the Church in general, the diocese, or the parish. Do we as a Church encourage innovation? Specifically, are dioceses, campus ministry centers, and parishes encouraging innovation in efforts to evangelize? Imported programs that we can buy or bring in from elsewhere are terminal; they must end. Our mandate from Jesus to evangelize is not a terminal one; it is an ongoing responsibility which necessitates innovation and creativity with a view of a big picture and long-term growth. In short, communities catching the evangelization attitude will "organically grow" their own strategies and programs in an ongoing way. This organic, innovative approach presupposes things like learning from both success and failure, and shaping programs appropriately from year to year.

5. FROM HIERARCHIES TO NETWORKING: STRUCTURING FOR EVANGELIZATION

John Naisbitt, in his best-selling book *Megatrends,* notes that organizations and businesses in our country are shifting from hierarchical structuring to the more efficient and facilitating approach of networking.[4] A networking approach organizes people who are responsible for a given piece of work in collaborative sorts of relationships so that communication, decision making, and action can take place more quickly and efficiently. Hierarchies or bureaucracies often impede progress, frustrate creativity, and unnecessarily slow down prompt responses to immediate needs.

Are most dioceses properly networked or structured for the convergence approach to evangelization which I referred to earlier? Are most parishes so structured? Networking would mean that agencies of a curia are so structured that communication, decision making, and action for evangelization are facilitated. Networking would mean that parish boards of ministry, parish councils, and their equivalents are similarly structured in loose but collaborative ways. Questions that parishes and dioceses need to ponder are: Do our structures help or hinder? Are people being enabled, empowered, encouraged, and trained for ministry or are they being frustrated and patronized? Hierarchy will never completely go away in the Catholic Church, but it needs to be critiqued and tempered by *networking.*

6. A NEW SENSE OF MINISTRY

Discernment is a word used a lot these days. It is a phenomenon that I feel needs to be joined to ministry. These past twenty years, we have too often called people to perform tasks on the parish level. Often people are not equipped or gifted for those ministerial tasks and therefore become discouraged or burned out. In his insightful book, *Theology of Ministry,* Thomas O'Meara retrieves an ancient Christian approach to ministry: *the uses of one's charisms to realize the kingdom in a local community.*[5]

I find myself spending more time these days with parishioners helping them to do the listening, watching, waiting, and praying needed for discernment of their charisms. I help them to search out how God has gifted them with the Spirit. I still find myself doing "direct delivery" of ministry to people, but I also train parishioners how to use their own gifts effectively. The time has come for professionally trained ministers to train and enable others. Schools of ministry or training programs need to multiply—on the diocesan level, on regional levels within a diocese, or on a parish level provided the parish has sufficient resources for this. We need to move toward genuine ministering/evangelizing congregations who realize that the responsibility to minister flows from baptism. Perhaps the future meaning of the sacrament of holy orders will be to ordain people to bring order to the chaotic ministering congregations.

I do not want to give the impression, however, that the most important ministry is being done within the confines of the parish plant. Following up on the "mission" orientation referred to earlier, perhaps the most important ministry is bringing the meaning and healing of the Gospel to the marketplace. The neighborhood, work place, and family are the focus of ministry in this approach. This is the strategy of many evangelical churches that stress the necessity and importance of each member giving witness and evangelizing in the world. The training materials of many of the evangelical movements emphasize the importance of unlocking the evangelical potential of the entire community and mobilizing them for mission to the world.

It is alarming that George Gallup in recent research has found that the values and lifestyles of baptized Christians are not terribly different from those who have never been baptized.[6] Gallup's findings suggest that most Christians fail to live up to their ministerial responsibilities as baptized disciples.

Another dimension of ministerial renewal is facilitating the experience of people to put their crosses at the service of others. Father William Bausch, a priest in New Jersey, tries to network people in his parish who have had similar struggles or crosses. People who suffer from addictions, compulsions, emotional difficulties, or loss are put in contact with others who had similar problems but are "on the mend." These people who have already begun the healing process use the cross they have experienced as a gift for someone else who finds himself or herself in similar circumstances.

I conclude this section with a word of concern for American clergy. With the identity and role of priest becoming increasingly "fuzzy," and vocations to the priesthood not showing any significant signs of improvement, I fear for the morale, spirituality and happiness of American priests. The support, health and continuing formation of the clergy ought to be one of the top priorities of the bishops. At this point in history, priests can markedly improve or impede evangelical renewal.

7. PENETRATING THE "SCREENING" CONGREGATION

In his research Dr. John Savage, an expert in the ministry to inactive members, has found that the typical response of most congregations toward the inactive member is to "screen them out."[7] They leave, and we do little to reach out to them. The lack of reach-out becomes a source of even deeper alienation as inactive members become more deeply convinced that no one in the parish cares about them.

The "screening" congregation can be penetrated in a number of ways. I will mention two. First, each parish or Catholic institution would do well to develop a team of trained home visitation ministers who visit the homes of both active and inactive members. The success of these callers' ministries should not be measured by the number of people who return to church attendance, but rather by the establishment of a caring relationship between the person called upon and the caller-minister of care. Second, the congregation ought to be reminded of its responsibility (through personal reach-out and certainly through prayer) to be invested in the evangelization of inactive members and the unchurched.

8. THE DEVELOPMENT OF HEALING MINISTRIES

The Notre Dame study on the parish reported recently that a representative sample of American Catholics expressed a desire that the local parish become more and more a center for healing.[8] While the study specified that people would like more pastoral counseling available so that conflicts might be approached from a vantage point of faith, healing could also take the form of opening the doors of the parish or institution more and more to self-help programs and groups.

Jesus was not just a teacher or preacher. Most often he joined his words to gestures and activities of healing. The Christian community needs to become a healing and reconciling force in people's lives. In fact, it is often in a crisis struggle or period of transition that a person becomes ripe for evangelization and conversion. The healing moment or opportunity is a powerful time to evangelize and gently proclaim the good news of God's abiding love, the power of Jesus, and the influence of the Holy Spirit.

9. MINISTRY TO STAFFS

If parishes are to move toward the vision of foundational and convergence evangelization, activate their congregations, and develop organically grown strategies with their people, then parish staffs need resourcing, training, and formation. The "big bang" road shows of conventions on evangelization or other such national gatherings can serve the function of raising consciousness. But often people go home from these experiences with a lot of glowing ideas but little thought as to how to implement them. I am talking about quality adult education, visioning, goal setting, and time-lining with the leaders of the parish, helping the pastor and staff to, in effect, "get their act together."

Perhaps the National Council for Catholic Evangelization, operating on a regional basis as it does around the country, could begin to locate resource people and network them to provide this service to parishes or clusters of parishes.

10. DIOCESAN PLANNING

I mentioned earlier that because of the absence of the convergence approach, dioceses and parishes erode into "turfism." I want to reiterate the importance of beginning to address this problem. Many diocesan agencies and offices mirror to parishes compartmentalization—offices and directors each in their little space doing their thing. Parishes pick up on the mirroring and compartmentalize in their own ways. Dioceses are too often riderless horses, with no sense of vision, purpose, and direction. The local church becomes a reactive rather than proactive organism.

What parishes need to do as mentioned in section 9, dioceses also need to do. Dioceses, led by their bishops, and using available resources, need to generate visions, long term goals, and time-lines for evangelization. Again, evangelization is not something that we simply complete like a course or program as is sometimes suggested by a misuse of the materials of Renew's last semester. Rather, diocesan efforts at evangelization require ongoing, systematic, proactive, long and short term planning. Evangelization is a continuous process.

11. FULL-CYCLE YOUTH EVANGELIZATION

The youth ministry efforts which have been showing the most qualitative and quantitative success in recent years are non-denominational youth programs. These programs stress the importance of a full-cycle approach to youth. Such a full-cycle approach begins with social-relational ministries that include foundational evangelization. Those who exhibit growth beyond the primary level of fun-seeker are welcomed into a second stage of spiritual inquiry. Those who continue to deepen in faith are welcomed into a third stage of discipleship. Next, conversion is often celebrated through a ritual like baptism in the Holy Spirit. Finally, the completion of the cycle is the entrance of the converted young person into the ranks of workers or ministers for Christ.

I am not advocating the fundamentalist theology often undergirding some of these youth movements. It should be obvious to some of the readers, however, that full-cycle youth ministry follows the rhythm of the RCIA or the catechumenate. The rhythm of these youth efforts is congruent with our own theology and praxis for conversion ministry. The key to successful Catholic youth ministry in the future is not to be found in any one thing like moving confirmation to the high school years. Rather, it is to be found in well-funded, well-planned, well-ministered full-cycle youth evangelization that is catechumenal in nature, oriented toward conversion and commitment, inclusive of a sacramental dimension, and respects the freedom, discernment, and decision making of young people. Perhaps such efforts no longer should be thought of just in terms of parish. Perhaps parishes should begin thinking about models of full-cycle youth evangelization that are regional in nature, that is, with clusters of parishes financing and resourcing the effort. While much of what I have said has been directed toward ministry to adolescents, truly wholistic youth ministry targets not only the high school population but also the pre-adolescents of the junior high age group as well as the many sub-groups that make up the young adult population.

12. BETTER UNDERSTANDING OF THE RCIA AND THE APPLICATION OF ITS RHYTHM AND PRINCIPLES TO SACRAMENTAL PREPARATION

I find it amazing that eleven years after its publication, the Rite of Christian Initiation of Adults is experiencing such a spotty implementation around the country. Many parishes have not even attempted to implement it. Again I rely on the Paulist Evangelization Office for statistics. Father Illig suggests that only about twenty percent of American parishes use the rite.[9] I am convinced that the RCIA conveys values and principles that not only ought to be used with catechumens and inquirers but also should be applied to other parish ministries, especially sacramental preparation. A related concern is that some among the twenty percent using the rite do not use it well. In some instances all that is being offered are dressed up instruction classes with some RCIA jargon tagged on.

The RCIA implies the following:
(a) Conversion and evangelization must be intimately connected to the preparation for and celebration of sacraments.
(b) The community is the minister of conversion as the candidates gradually merge and grow into the community.
(c) Movement toward rituals ought to be a step-by-step process, with efforts made at discerning whether there is genuine conversion and growth taking place in preparing for sacraments.
(d) In addition to being signs, sacraments are rituals that celebrate vowing or radical life change toward Jesus and the kingdom.
(e) A variety of ministries—educational, liturgical, and guidance—are needed to adequately prepare for sacraments.

These five underlying principles of the RCIA ought not to be discarded for the sake of expediency. Conversion cannot happen in the same easy way that we make a cup of instant coffee—and American consumers seeking entrance into the Church ought to be reminded of that. Similarly, people approaching the parish for sacraments, for themselves or their children, ought to experience catechumenal-type journeys that include the values and strategies discussed above. When we separate sacraments from a conversion-oriented process, we run the risk of perpetuating the worst of cultural Catholicism, namely sacraments as holy things and vehicles of cheap grace.

13. MEDIA

The Church is failing terribly in the effective use of mass media for the proclamation of the Gospel. This dimension of evangelization cries out most loudly for innovation. Serious scrutiny needs to be given to where the Church invests funds in the future. Some of the millions of dollars being used to keep up unused buildings and real estate could be used more responsibly to bring the Gospel to places and people where it is not being heard.

On the diocesan and national levels talent ought to be surfaced with expertise on the many different formats that now are heard on radio stations. Public service religion programs ought to be developed that use the format of given stations: easy listening, rock, country, black, Hispanic, big band, news, and talk. While federal deregulation limits the amount of free time being given to the Church by local TV stations for religious programs, the explosion of cable TV, satellite dishes, and video recorders opens up even more creative areas for media evangelization. We need to learn from evangelicals, however, that "talking heads" engaged in "dry as dust" conversation is not what American people are hungering for. Creative Catholic programming should include drama, stories, and music which affect the imagination as well as the intellect. If diocesan leadership does not lead in this area, religious educators on the parish level ought to begin to take prophetic action.

14. RELIGIOUS EDUCATION: FROM SCHOOLING TO RELIGIOUS SOCIALIZATION

I fear that parochial schools and CCD programs so often present the Gospel as a subject to be known about rather than a vision and a life-giving personal force—Jesus. Schools and CCD are a product of a bygone era in the American Church. As John Westerhoff and others have written, the major shifts in American culture over the past twenty years have raised the need for a radically new approach to religious education.[10] While I am not advocating abolishing school and CCD programs, I believe that a major component of family involvement needs to be added to religious education. If this were the case, child-centered programs would cease to be the tail that wags the dog, the parish. The focus of the parish would become more the making of adult disciples and the formation of little domestic churches into which children are socialized. Not to move in such directions is to propagate and perpetuate what often amounts to religious baby-sitting services.

15. MAINLINING JUSTICE

Father Illig's statistic of a meager two percent of the typical parish being interested in evangelization might parallel the interest level regarding social justice. In the *Call to Conversion,* Jim Wallis challenges Christians to notice the spiritual *lukewarmness* and *political conformity* that most of us who call ourselves Christian fall into.[11] The call to justice in the Gospel is a radical call. The consciousness raising, moral discernment, and prophetic action that are needed for ministry toward justice are not just the work of the bishops or a few elite. Justice concerns are bottom-line Gospel concerns. Paul VI wrote in *Evangelii Nuntiandi* that "the Church . . . has the duty to proclaim the liberation of millions of human beings."[12]

In this mainlining of both justice concerns and activities, we as a Church need to exorcise a few of our own demons. Ecclesiastical pronouncements about social justice ring hollow when we are blind to the injustice present in our own systems and institutions. Until we value truth over tradition, equality and cooperation between the sexes over hierarchy and clericalism, good stewardship and creative investment of people's funds over questionable fiscal responsibility, the support and nurturance of each other in ministry over functional autonomy, our evangelizing toward justice remains contradictory and flawed. It is not enough to tackle safe justice issues. We need to confront some of our own intramural issues of justice.

CONCLUSION

As we face the future of Catholic evangelization, it will not be enough to run people through programs. We need to assure that basic evangelizing and re-evangelizing are happening in all of our ministries. Leaders need to facilitate a harnessing of ministers and ministries toward a common mission of evangelizing. There needs to be an ongoing fostering of an attitude of evangelization that leads to innovation in strategies. Careful scrutiny needs to be given to organizations and structures so that they help and not hinder the central mission. Ministry, especially to the marketplace, needs to be refocused on the use of charisms for the gradual coming of the kingdom. Evangelization needs to include a special sensitivity to the wounded and alienated. Staffs and diocesan offices need to engage in both short-term and long-term visioning and planning. Serious effort needs to be given to moving youth evangelization out of the dark ages. The richness of the RCIA needs to be applied to many areas of ministry and parish life. Media could be used to much greater advantage in bringing religious experience into people's homes. Models of religious education, really born for another age of American Catholics, need to give way to new models that are family based. Catholics need to be reminded over and over again of the need to continue the Lord's mission for justice. Part of this justice orientation necessitates a confrontation of the injustices that we as Church seem to have grown comfortable with.

These fifteen items are obviously not the only challenges awaiting the Church in America. But I do believe that these are at the heart of either potential growth and renewal or possible stagnation or decline. Let us who hope to be part of the Church's ongoing renewal efforts be attentive to and cooperative with the movement of the Holy Spirit as we experience a new Pentecost for Catholic evangelization.

NOTES

1. Pope Paul VI, *Evangelii Nuntiandi* (Publications Office; United States Catholic Conference, Washington, D.C. 1975).

2. Father Alvin Illig, "Why Fewer Converts?" *Evangelization and Initiation* (Washington: Paulist National Catholic Evangelization Association, July–August, 1985), p. 2.

3. Thomas Peters and Nancy Austin, *A Passion for Excellence* (New York: Random House, 1985).

4. John Naisbitt, *Megatrends* (New York: Warner Books, 1982).

5. Thomas Franklin O'Meara, *Theology of Ministry* (New York: Paulist Press, 1983).

6. George Gallup, Jr., *Forecast 2000* (New York: William Morrow and Company, Inc., 1984).

7. John Savage, *The Apathetic and Bored Church Member* (Pittsford, New York: Lead Consultants, 1976).

8. *Notre Dame Study of Catholic Parish Life: The U.S. Parish Twenty Years After Vatican II: An Introduction to the Study* (Notre Dame: Institute for Pastoral and Social Ministry, 1984), Report No. 1.

9. Illig, *op. cit.,* p. 2.

10. John Westerhoff, *Bringing Up Children in the Faith* (Minneapolis: Winston Press, 1980).

11. Jim Wallis, *The Call to Conversion* (San Francisco: Harper & Row, 1981).

12. Pope Paul VI, *op. cit.,* par. 30.

DISCUSSION QUESTIONS

1. What priorities for the future would you add to the fifteen contained in the article?

2. What are the biggest obstacles to effective evangelization in our Church today?

3. What assets or strengths do we have as a Church as we face the future?

4. What are creative ways that parishes could use to both "mainline justice" and use the media more effectively?

5. What are some practical ways to do foundational evangelization in parish programs and ministries?

FOR FURTHER READING

George Gallup, *Forecast 2000* (New York: William Morrow and Company, 1984). Gallup projects into a future world with which the Church must inter-face.

Andrew Greeley, *American Catholics Since the Council: An Unauthorized Report* (Chicago: Thomas More Association, 1985). Greeley's research should significantly direct our evangelizing efforts.

Thomas Groome, *Christian Religious Education* (San Francisco: Harper and Row, 1980). This is the most significant book in recent years on an evangelizing approach to catechesis.

Tad Guzie, *The Book of Sacramental Basics* (Ramsey, N.J.: Paulist Press, 1981). An easily readable book, offering a fresh look to sacraments.

Dean Hoge, *Converts, Drop Outs, and Returnees* (Washington, D.C.: USCC, 1981). Like Greeley's work, this book provides important sociological data for evangelization.

Urban Holmes, *Turning to Christ* (New York: Seabury Press, 1981). Holmes has on-target critiques of evangelicals and beautiful insights into evangelization as invitation.

Rev. Alvin Illig, "Why Fewer Converts?" *Evangelization and Initiation* (Washington: Paulist National Catholic Evangelization Association, July–August, 1985). Father Illig's association produces a helpful newsletter.

James Mackey, *Jesus: The Man and the Myth* (Ramsey, NJ: Paulist Press, 1979). Mackey is helpful in unpacking how Jesus understood the kingdom.

John Naisbitt, *Megatrends* (New York: Warner Books, 1982). Naisbitt captures well the mood of Americans.

Notre Dame Study of Catholic Parish Life: the U.S. Parish Twenty Years After Vatican II: An Introduction to the Study (Notre Dame: Institute for Pastoral and Social Ministry, 1984). This series synthesizes a great deal of material on the status of the Church today.

Thomas O'Meara, *Theology of Ministry* (Ramsey, N.J.: Paulist Press, 1983). O'Meara blends history and theology into a significant overview of ministry.

Thomas Peters and Nancy Austin, *A Passion for Excellence* (New York: Random House, 1985). Though written for business, the books contains helpful insights into working with people in general.

Pope Paul VI, *Evangelii Nuntiandi* (Washington, D.C.: United States Catholic Conference, 1975). This encyclical begins to raise consciousness about Catholic evangelization.

John Savage, *The Apathetic and Bored Church Member* (Pittsford: LEAD Consultants, 1976). Savage gets behind presenting symptoms to the human pain present in many inactive church members.

United States Catholic Conference, *The Rite of Christian Initiation of Adults* (New York: Pueblo Publishing Company, 1976), pp. 3–287. The Rite holds the best potential for renewing the Church.

Jim Wallis, *A Call To Conversion* (San Francisco: Harper & Row, 1981). Wallis' book is both beautifully written and challenging.

John Westerhoff, *Bringing Up our Children in the Faith* (Minneapolis: Winston Press, 1980). Westerhoff advocates a socialization model of religious education.

NOTES ON THE CONTRIBUTORS

MS. PATRICIA BARBERNITZ

Ms. Barbernitz has worked professionally in religious education for seventeen years. Her ministry in parishes has included developing evangelization and adult formation opportunities. Specializing in the RCIA, Ms. Barbernitz has not only prepared ministers to implement this rite in the parish, but also has written the books *RCIA: What It is, How It Works* (Liguori Publications, 1983), and *RCIA Team Manual* (Paulist Press, 1986) and a number of articles on evangelization and Christian initiation.

REV. MSGR. DAVID BOHR

Msgr. Bohr was ordained a priest of the Diocese of Scranton in 1971. He received an S.T.L. in dogmatic theology from the Gregorian University and an S.T.D. in moral theology from the Accademia Alfonsiana in Rome. His doctoral dissertation entitled *Evangelization in America* was published by Paulist Press in 1977. Msgr. Bohr was one of the founders of the National Council for Catholic Evangelization and served as this organization's first chairperson. He is currently the director of the Diocesan Religious Education Institute and the director of the Offices for Evangelization and Continuing Education of Priests in Scranton, Pennsylvania.

REV. KENNETH BOYACK, C.S.P.

Fr. Boyack, a Paulist, serves as Associate Director of the Paulist National Catholic Evangelization Association in Washington, D.C. He earned an M.A. in theology and a Doctor of Ministry from the Catholic University of America. Fr. Boyack was the Conference Coordinator in 1985 for the National Council for Catholic Evangelization's Conference, *"Evangelii Nuntiandi* Ten Years Later: An American Meditation.'' He is Chairperson of the Paulist Fathers' Board of Evangelization. Fr. Boyack's publications include *A Parish Guide to Adult Initiation* (Paulist Press, 1980) and (with Robert D. Duggan and Paul Huesing) *The Catholic Faith Inventory* (Paulist Press, 1986).

REV. PATRICK J. BRENNAN

Fr. Brennan was ordained a priest for the Archdiocese of Chicago in 1973 and in 1980 was appointed Director of Evangelization for that Archdiocese. He holds a Master of Divinity, a licentiate in sacred theology, and a Doctor of Ministry degree from St. Mary of the Lake Seminary in Mundelein. He was elected the first president of the National Council for Catholic Evangelization in June 1984. Fr. Brennan is the author of *Spirituality for an Anxious Age* (Thomas More, 1985), *Penance and Reconciliation: Guidelines for Contemporary Catholics* (Thomas More, 1986), *The Evangelizing Parish* (Tabor, 1986), and the ongoing series *Parish Spirituality* (Office for Chicago Catholic Evangelization).

REV. LAURENCE BRETT

Fr. Brett, a priest of the Diocese of Bridgeport, Connecticut, is the author of *Share the Word,* the nation's largest Catholic Bible study/sharing program. He also serves as the principal teacher of the Scriptures on *Share the Word* television. Fr. Brett is active in the preaching ministry, particularly through presenting liturgical and preaching workshops for the three branches of the military. The author of a number of articles, Fr. Brett's most recent book is *Redeemed Creation: Sacramentals Today* published by Michael Glazier, Inc.

REV. CYPRIAN DAVIS, O.S.B.

A Benedictine monk of St. Meinrad Archabbey, Indiana, Fr. Cyprian received his licentiate and doctoral degrees in historical sciences from the University of Louvain and currently serves as professor of Church history in the St. Meinrad School of Theology. Actively committed to civil rights, Fr. Cyprian became one of the founding members of the Black Catholic Clergy Caucus in 1968. He has contributed articles to the *New Catholic Encyclopedia* and other publications. Fr. Cyprian served on the bishops' subcommittee that helped to prepare the draft for the bishops' pastoral letter on racism, "Brothers and Sisters to Us" (1979). He also collaborated in the preliminary drafts of the black bishops' pastoral letter on evangelization, "What We Have Seen and Heard" (1984).

REV. REGIS A. DUFFY, O.F.M.

Fr. Duffy is professor of theology at The Washington Theological Union, Silver Spring, Maryland, and has been visiting professor at Princeton Theological Seminary and the University of Notre Dame. In addition to publications in scholarly journals and editing, he has published three books: *Real Presence: Worship, Sacraments and Commitment* (1982), *A Roman Catholic Theology of Pastoral Care* (1983), and *On Becoming a Catholic: The Challenge of Christian Initiation* (1984). His talks, *The Way Christians Walk Together,* are distributed in video-cassettes by Tabor Publishers (1984).

REV. ROBERT D. DUGGAN

Fr. Duggan is a priest of the Archdiocese of Washington, D.C. Holding a doctorate in theology from the Catholic University of America, he is presently Director of the Office of Worship of the Archdiocese of Washington, D.C. Fr. Duggan has served in parishes throughout the Archdiocese of Washington, D.C., as well as on the faculty of the North American College in Rome. He has taught on a part-time basis at the Washington Theological Union and at the Catholic University of America. Fr. Duggan's publications include an edited book of essays entitled *Conversion and the Catechumenate* (Paulist Press, 1984), and (with Kenneth Boyack and Paul Huesing) *The Catholic Faith Inventory* (Paulist Press, 1986).

REV. JAMES B. DUNNING

Fr. Dunning is the President of the North American Forum on the Catechumenate and a consultant for parish renewal. He previously held the positions of President and Executive Director of the National Organization for Continuing Education of Priests and of Coordinator of Adult Education for the Archdiocese of Seattle. Fr. Dunning earned a Ph.D. in religion and religious education from the Catholic University of America. The author of numerous articles, his books include *New Wine, New Wineskins: Exploring the Rite of Christian Initiation of Adults* and *Ministries: Sharing God's Gifts.*

DR. THOMAS H. GROOME

Dr. Groome is associate professor of theology and religious education at Boston College. His educational background includes a Master of Divinity degree from St. Patrick's Seminary in Carlow, Ireland, an M.A. in religious education from Fordham University, and a doctorate in religion and education from the Union Theological Seminary and Columbia University Teachers College, New York City. Dr. Groome's publications include *Christian Religious Education: Sharing Our Story and Vision* (San Francisco: Harper and Row, 1980), and more than twenty published articles that appeared in scholarly collections and journals of religious education, pastoral ministry and theology. Dr. Groome is the senior author of *The God With Us* religion series (K–8) from W.H. Sadlier and has lectured widely throughout the United States, England, Canada, Australia, and Ireland.

DR. DEAN R. HOGE

Dr. Hoge is professor of sociology at the Catholic University of America. He is a graduate of Harvard Divinity School (B.D.) and Harvard Graduate School (Ph.D., Sociology). In 1981 he authored *Converts, Dropouts, Returnees: A Study of Religious Change Among Catholics,* and in 1984 he co-authored (with Raymond Potvin and Kathleen Ferry) *Research on Men's Vocations to the Priesthood and the Religious Life.* At present he is researching the vocation shortage.

REV. ALVIN A. ILLIG, C.S.P.

Fr. Illig is the founder and director of the Paulist National Catholic Evangelization Association, the publisher of the nation's largest Catholic Bible study/sharing program, *Share the Word* magazine, and the coordinator of the new *Share the Word* television program. He held the position of Executive Director of the National Conference of Catholic Bishops' Committee on Evangelization for five years. Prior to working for two years as a primary evangelizer in Mississippi, Fr. Illig spent twenty years in New York with the Paulist Press. The focus of Fr. Illig's work today is on the 90,000,000 unchurched Americans, of whom 15,000,000 are inactive Catholics.

REV. EUGENE LAVERDIERE, S.S.S.

Fr. LaVerdiere, a member of the Congregation of the Blessed Sacrament, is the editor of *Emmanuel* magazine and an associate editor of *The Bible Today*. He is also an adjunct professor of New Testament studies at Catholic Theological Union in Chicago. He holds a licentiate in theology from the University of Fribourg and a licentiate in Sacred Scripture from the Pontifical Biblical Institute. His doctorate in New Testament and early Christian literature is from the University of Chicago. He is the author of many books, articles, audio-cassettes and video-cassettes. His most recent books include *Luke,* vol. 5 in the *New Testament Message* (Wilmington: Michael Glazier, 1980), *The New Testament in the Life of the Church* (Notre Dame: Ave Maria Press, 1980) and *When We Pray* (Notre Dame: Ave Maria Press, 1983).

REV. LOUIS J. LUZBETAK, S.V.D.

Fr. Luzbetak's special interest is the application of anthropology to Church mission. He studied at the Gregorian University, Rome (S.T.L. and J.C.B.) and received his Ph.D. in anthropology, linguistics, and missiology at Fribourg, Switzerland. Fr. Luzbetak did his anthropological and missiological fieldwork in New Guinea. The former President of the American Society of Missiology, Fr. Luzbetak has authored numerous articles and several books, including *The Church and Cultures,* the prize-winner of Fordham University's Pierre Charles Award for most significant work of the year (1963) on mission. The book was translated into five languages. The holder of a number of honors, Fr. Luzbetak is currently finishing a Maryknoll Walsh-Price Fellowship.

MR. ADAN MEDRANO

Mr. Medrano is President of HTN, Inc., a non-profit corporation which produces "Nuestra Familia," a national weekly Catholic half-hour television program in Spanish. His fifteen-year career in communications has included being publisher of *El Visitante Dominical,* the national Catholic Spanish-language newspaper. As early as 1975 he served on the executive committee of the board of directors of UNDA-USA, the national Catholic association of broadcasters and allied communicators. In July 1985 he was elected President of the Association of Catholic Television and Radio Syndicators.

MS. GERTRUDE MORRIS

Ms. Morris, former Director of Evangelization for the National Office for Black Catholics, was born and educated in New York City. She has conducted "One-to-One In Christ," the NOBC Evangelization Program, in some twenty cities across the country. She was one of the founding members of the National Council for Catholic Evangelization and represented Episcopal Region #4 on the NCCE Board of Directors. Ms. Morris is a permanent member of The Grail, an international movement of laywomen dedicated to working for social justice and world peace.

SR. CATHERINE PINKERTON, C.S.J.

Sr. Catherine, a member of the Sisters of St. Joseph of Cleveland, is presently a lobbyist at NETWORK: A Catholic Social Justice Lobby in Washington, D.C. Her past ministries have included secondary education and administration, formation work within her religious congregation and pastoral planning within the Diocese of Cleveland. She has served as President of the Sisters of St. Joseph, Cleveland, and of the Leadership Conference of Women Religious.

REV. BERNARD QUINN

Father Quinn, a native of Kansas City, Missouri, was ordained for the Glenmary Home Missioners in 1953 and has served mission pastorates in West Virginia and Georgia. He holds a doctorate in missiology from the Gregorian University in Rome. The author of a number of articles and books including *Mission, Missions and the Creative Planning Process,* Fr. Quinn has been associated since 1966 with the Glenmary Research Center now located in Atlanta, Georgia.

MR. AND MRS. TOM AND LYN SCHEURING

Throughout their eighteen years of married life, Tom and Lyn Scheuring have been actively involved in ministry in the Church and are blessed with three children. They were the recipients of the 1984 National Award for Catholic Lay Evangelization presented by the Paulist Fathers. Tom and Lyn have authored two books: *Two for Joy: On Married Spirituality,* and *God Longs For Family,* a book on family evangelization. In 1981 they founded an evangelistic lay ministry with the poor called LAMP Ministries which serves in the New York, Brooklyn, and Newark Dioceses.

REV. ROMAN R. VANASSE, O. PRAEM.

Father Vanasse, a Canon Regular of Premontre, earned his S.T.D. in theology at the Gregorian University in Rome under the direction of Bernard J.F. Lonergan, S.J. He has been novice-master, director of development, and community planner at St. Norbert Abbey in Wisconsin, and professor of systematic theology at the Catholic Theological Union in Chicago. Fr. Vanasse has had extensive experience in conducting seminars and workshops on a broad range of topics in theology. At present, he serves as National Secretary for Education at the National Office of the Society for the Propagation of the Faith in New York City.

MS. MARSHA WHELAN

Ms. Whelan has been involved in evangelization ministry since 1979. She currently serves as the Director of the Office of Evangelization for the Archdiocese of Miami and as the President of the National Council for Catholic Evangelization. Co-author of "Good News/*Buena Noticia* I: A Training Program for One-to-One Catholic Evangelization," Ms. Whelan holds a Master's degree in religious education from the Catholic University of America and a Master's degree in public administration from Nova University. She is currently President of the Association for Retarded Citizens of Dade County, Florida.